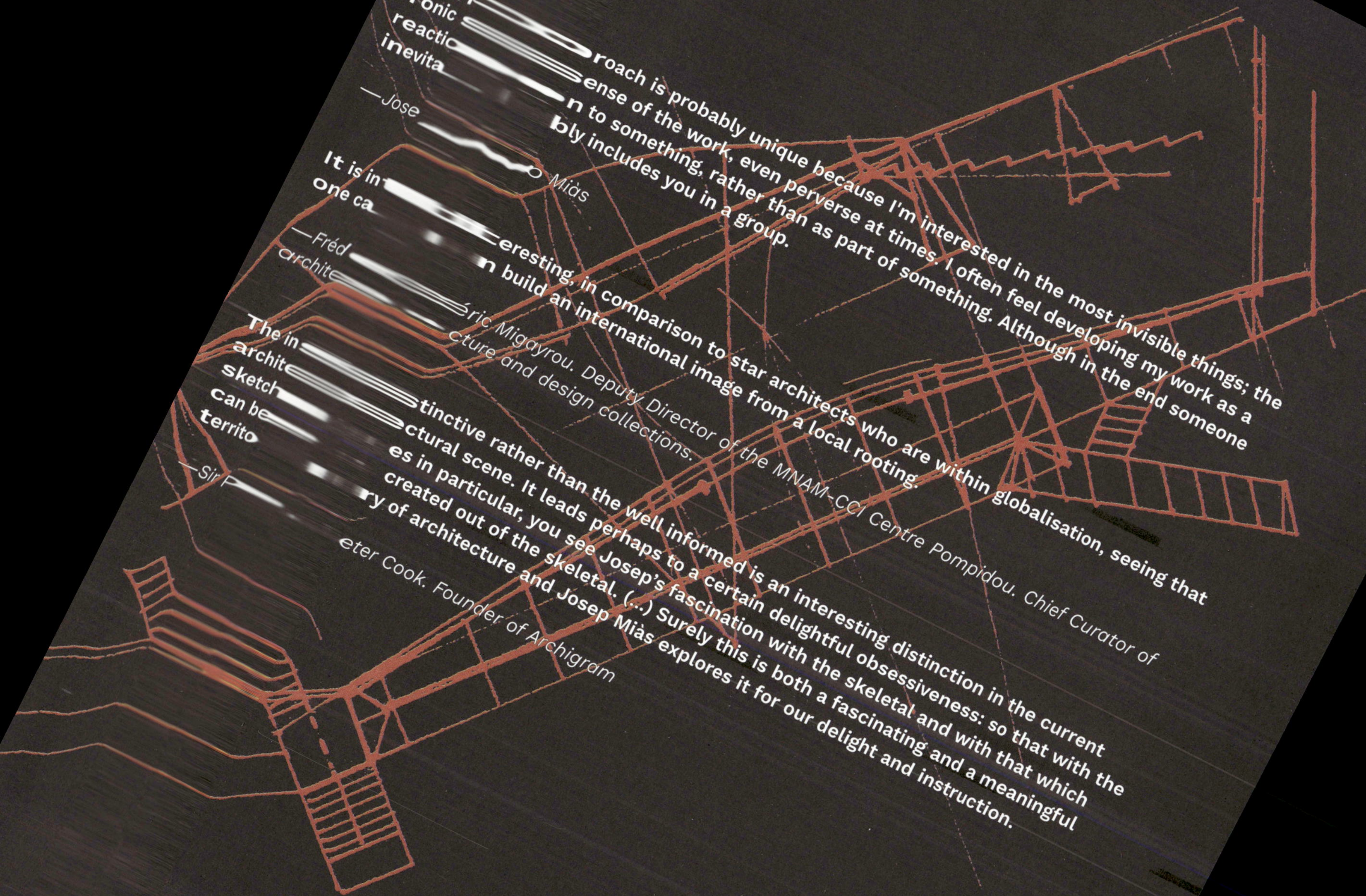

My approach is probably unique because I'm interested in the most invisible things; the ironic sense of the work, even perverse at times. I often feel developing my work as a reaction to something, rather than as part of something. Although in the end someone inevitably includes you in a group.

—Josep Miàs

It is interesting, in comparison to star architects who are within globalisation, seeing that one can build an international image from a local rooting.

—Frédéric Migayrou. Deputy Director of the MNAM-CCI Centre Pompidou. Chief Curator of architecture and design collections.

The instinctive rather than the well informed is an interesting distinction in the current architectural scene. It leads perhaps to a certain delightful obsessiveness: so that with the sketches in particular, you see Josep's fascination with the skeletal and with that which can be created out of the skeletal. (...) Surely this is both a fascinating and a meaningful territory of architecture and Josep Miàs explores it for our delight and instruction.

—Sir Peter Cook. Founder of Archigram

The Governmer and the Barcel recognized the career of MIAS

the first monog at the Museum and Architectur dedicated to a working firm.

of Catalonia
a City Council
ternational
chitects with
phic exhibition
Design
of Barcelona,
rrently

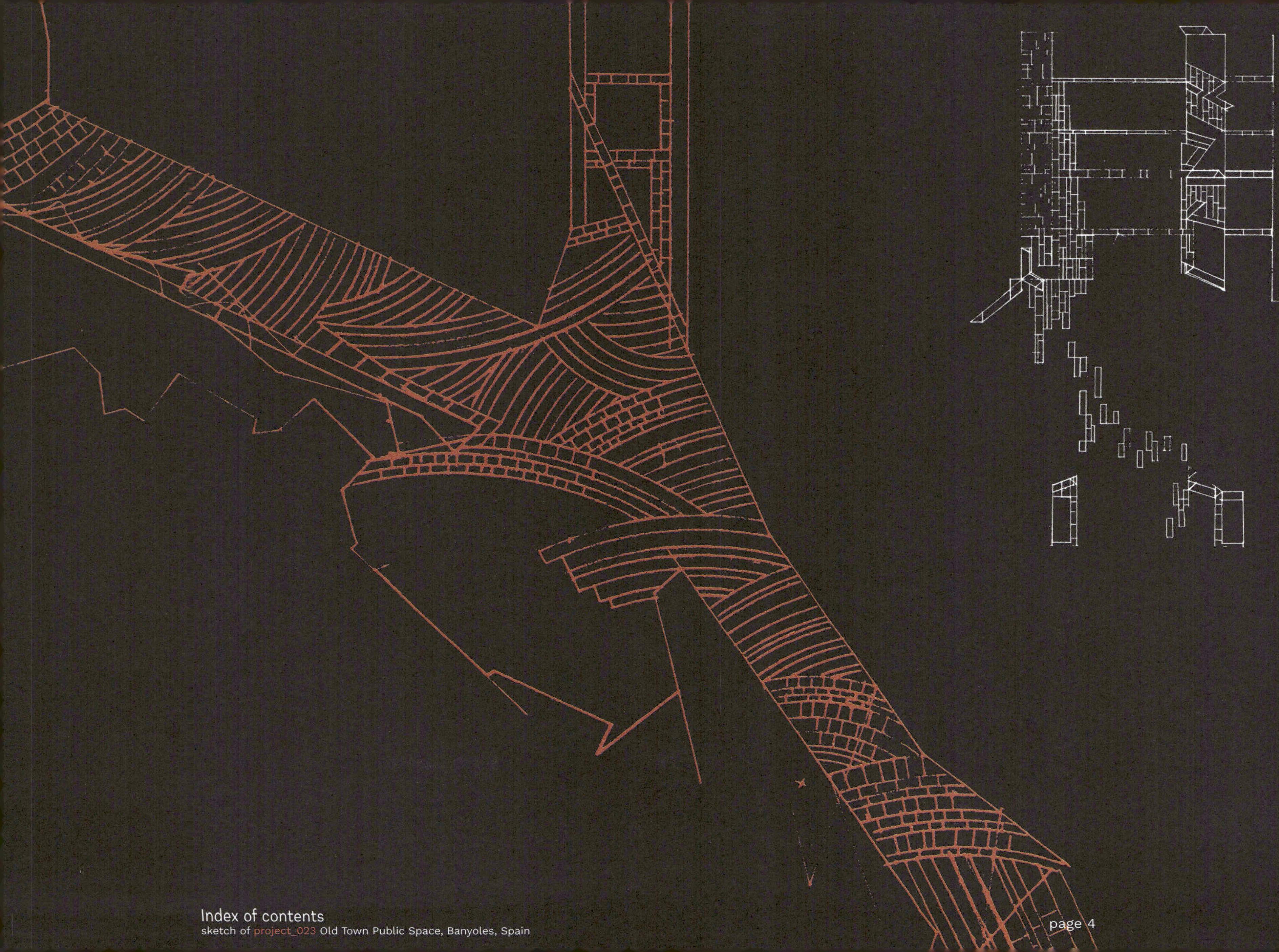

Index of contents
sketch of project_023 Old Town Public Space, Banyoles, Spain

SUMMARY

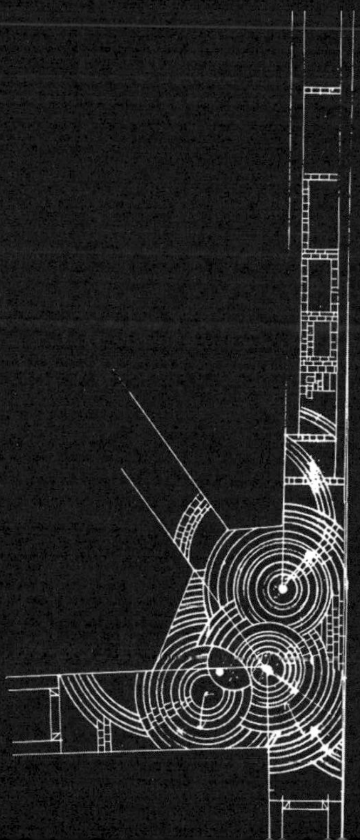

Index of contents
sketch of project_023 Old Town Public Space, Banyoles, Spain

INDEX OF CONTENTS

Index of contents

DHUB Barcelona Design Museum

'MIAS The *Making* of Making (Architecture)'

1995

project_001 / models_01 - 05

Banys Vells Swimming Club and Bar, Banyoles, Spain
42°07'16"N 02°45'29"E
pages 8, 12, 40, 92, 208-211, 320-321

project_001
model_01
Banys Vells Swimming Club and Bar, Banyoles, Spain
Paper
19x13x4 cm

project_001
model_02
Banys Vells Swimming Club and Bar, Banyoles, Spain
Plaster
28x14x4 cm

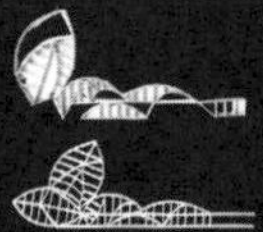

project_001
model_03
Banys Vells Swimming Club and Bar, Banyoles, Spain
Paper, Wood
25x10x1 cm

project_001
model_04
Banys Vells Swimming Club and Bar, Banyoles, Spain
Paper, Wood
38x27x12 cm

project_001
model_05_DHUB
Banys Vells Swimming Club and Bar, Banyoles, Spain
scale_1:150
Zinc Plated Welded Wire
35x12x4cm

2001 - 2007

project_003 / models_01 - 47

Barceloneta Market and Public Space, Barcelona, Spain
41°22'49.3"N 2°11'21.1"E
pages 8-9, 12-13, 39-40, 68-81, 208-211, 228-231, 234-235, 322-329, 382-383

project_003
model_01
Barceloneta Market and Public Space, Barcelona, Spain
Enamelled Welded Wire
32x4x9 cm

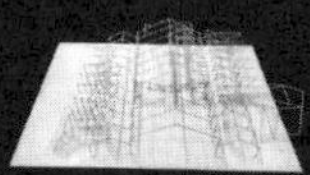

project_003
model_02
Barceloneta Market and Public Space, Barcelona, Spain
Enamelled Welded Wire
46x29x9 cm

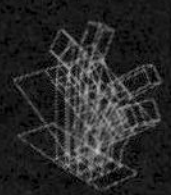

project_003
model_03
Barceloneta Market and Public Space, Barcelona, Spain
Enamelled Welded Wire
32x20x27 cm

project_003
model_04
Barceloneta Market and Public Space, Barcelona, Spain
Enamelled Welded Wire
6x(27x20x1) cm

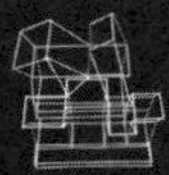

project_003
model_05
Barceloneta Market and Public Space, Barcelona, Spain
Enamelled Welded Wire
13x11x9 cm

project_003
model_06
Barceloneta Market and Public Space, Barcelona, Spain
Enamelled Welded Wire
14,5x10x6 cm

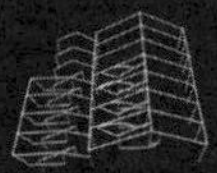

project_003
model_07
Barceloneta Market and Public Space, Barcelona, Spain
Enamelled Steel
21x19x9 cm

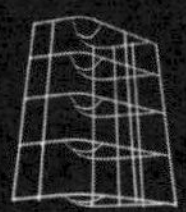

project_003
model_08
Barceloneta Market and Public Space, Barcelona, Spain
Enamelled Welded Wire
14x18x4 cm

project_003
model_09
Barceloneta Market and Public Space, Barcelona, Spain
Enamelled Welded Wire
24x39x4 cm

project_003
model_10
Barceloneta Market and Public Space, Barcelona, Spain
Enamelled Welded Wire
59x16x1 cm

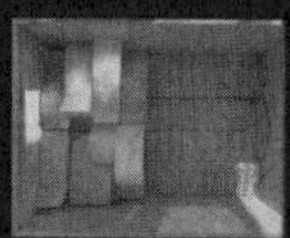

project_003
model_11
Barceloneta Market and Public Space, Barcelona, Spain
Welded Wire
32x46x20 cm

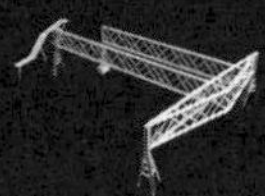

project_003
model_12
Barceloneta Market and Public Space, Barcelona, Spain
Wood
70x53x30 cm

project_003
model_13
Barceloneta Market and Public Space, Barcelona, Spain
Wood
46x26x10 cm

project_003
model_14
Barceloneta Market and Public Space, Barcelona, Spain
Wood, Pape
32x42x10 cm

project_003
model_15
Barceloneta Market and Public Space, Barcelona, Spain
Wood
73x12x21 cm

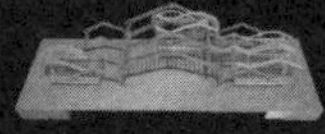

project_003
model_16
Barceloneta Market and Public Space, Barcelona, Spain
Wood
104x34x31 cm

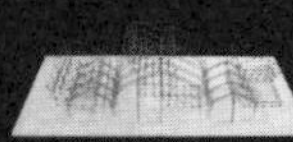

project_003
model_17
Barceloneta Market and Public Space, Barcelona, Spain
Welded Wire
42x78x20 cm

project_003
model_18
Barceloneta Market and Public Space, Barcelona, Spain
Enamelled Steel, Paper Wood
185x61x25 cm

project_003
model_19
Barceloneta Market and Public Space, Barcelona, Spain
Wood
164x63,5x19 cm

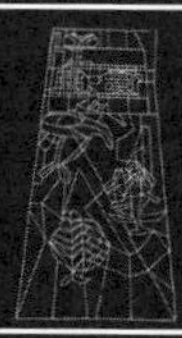

project_003
model_20
Barceloneta Market and Public Space, Barcelona, Spain
Enamelled Welded Wire
88x29x6 cm

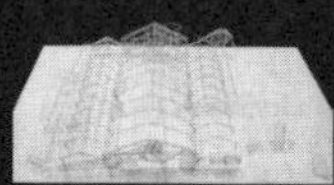

project_003
model_21
Barceloneta Market and Public Space, Barcelona, Spain
Enamelled Welded Wire, Wood
64x115x18 cm

project_003
model_22
Barceloneta Market and Public Space, Barcelona, Spain
Enamelled Welded Wire
24x21x17 cm

project_003
model_23
Barceloneta Market and Public Space, Barcelona, Spain
White Cardboard
39x27x2 cm

project_003
model_24
Barceloneta Market and Public Space, Barcelona, Spain
Enamelled Welded Wire
54,5x80x12 cm

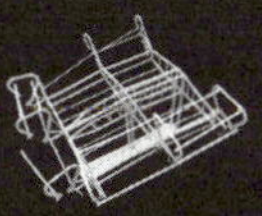
project_003
model_25
Barceloneta Market and Public Space, Barcelona, Spain
White Cardboard
34x33x25 cm

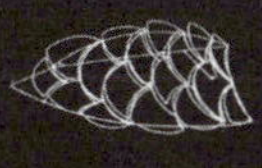
project_003
model_26
Barceloneta Market and Public Space, Barcelona, Spain
Enamelled Welded Wire
22,5x11,5x4 cm

project_03
model_27
Barceloneta Market and Public Space, Barcelona, Spain
Enamelled Welded Wire
34x14x8 cm

project_003
model_28
Barceloneta Market and Public Space, Barcelona, Spain
Enamelled Welded Wire
13x8x6 cm

project_003
model_29
Barceloneta Market and Public Space, Barcelona, Spain
Wood
67x19x22,5 cm

project_003
model_30
Barceloneta Market and Public Space, Barcelona, Spain
Cardboard

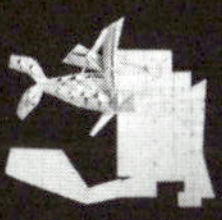
project_003
model_31
Barceloneta Market and Public Space, Barcelona, Spain
Wood

project_003
model_32
Barceloneta Market and Public Space, Barcelona, Spain
Cardboard

project_003
model_33
Barceloneta Market and Public Space, Barcelona, Spain
Enamelled Welded Wire

project_003
model_34
Barceloneta Market and Public Space, Barcelona, Spain
Cardboard

project_003
model_35
Barceloneta Market and Public Space, Barcelona, Spain
Enamelled Welded Wire

project_003
model_36
Barceloneta Market and Public Space, Barcelona, Spain
Enamelled Welded Wire

project_003
model_37
Barceloneta Market and Public Space, Barcelona, Spain
Enamelled Welded Wire

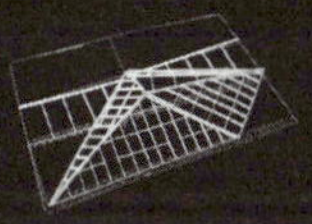
project_003
model_38
Barceloneta Market and Public Space, Barcelona, Spain
Enamelled Welded Wire

project_003
model_39
Barceloneta Market and Public Space, Barcelona, Spain
Enamelled Welded Wire
20x20x6,5 cm

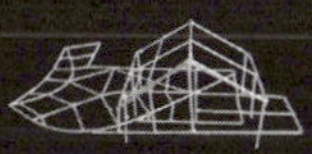
project_003
model_40
Barceloneta Market and Public Space, Barcelona, Spain
Enamelled Welded Wire
15x12x5,5 cm

project_003
model_41
Barceloneta Market and Public Space, Barcelona, Spain
EC2020-2-AR85
Centre Pompidou
Permanent Collection
Enamelled Welded Wire
9,5x30x55 cm

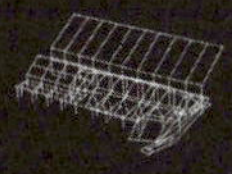
project_003
model_42
Barceloneta Market and Public Space, Barcelona, Spain
EC2020-2-AR84
Centre Pompidou
Permanent Collection
Enamelled Welded Wire
9,5x30x55 cm

project_003
model_43
Barceloneta Market and Public Space, Barcelona, Spain
EC2020-2-AR46
Centre Pompidou
Permanent Collection
Enamelled Welded Wire
12,5x30x22 cm

project_003
model_44
Barceloneta Market and Public Space, Barcelona, Spain
EC2020-2-AR48
Centre Pompidou
Permanent Collection
Zinc Plated Welded Wire, Wood
185x59x26 cm

project_003
model_45
Barceloneta Market and Public Space, Barcelona, Spain
EC2020-2-AR47
Centre Pompidou
Permanent Collection
Enamelled Welded Wire
9,5x30x55 cm

project_003
model_46_DHUB
Barceloneta Market and Public Space, Barcelona, Spain
scale_1:250
Zinc Plated Welded Wire
33x22x7cm

project_003
model_47_DHUB
Barceloneta Market and Public Space, Barcelona, Spain
Wood
116x175x35 cm

2004 - 2010

project_004 / models_01 - 18

Municipal Market and Public Space, Rubí, Spain
41°29'21"N 02°02'06"E
pages 9, 13-14, 222, 246-249

project_004
model_01
Municipal Market and Public Space, Rubí, Spain
Wood
48x59x65 cm

project_004
model_02
Municipal Market and Public Space, Rubí, Spain
Plexiglass And Steel
100x57x17 cm

project_004
model_03
Municipal Market and Public Space, Rubí, Spain
Enamelled Welded Wire
33x5x6 cm

project_004
model_04
Municipal Market and Public Space, Rubí, Spain
Enamelled Welded Wire
80x15x14 cm

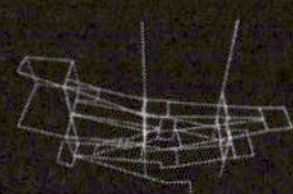
project_004
model_05
Municipal Market and Public Space, Rubí, Spain
Enamelled Welded Wire
52x20x28 cm

project_004
model_06
Municipal Market and Public Space, Rubí, Spain
White Matte Paper 77x62x46 cm

project_004
model_07
Municipal Market and Public Space, Rubí, Spain
White Matte Paper 28x18x12 cm

project_004
model_08
Municipal Market and Public Space, Rubí, Spain
White Matte Paper 25x19x5 cm

project_004
model_09
Municipal Market and Public Space, Rubí, Spain
White Matte Paper 90x47x22 cm

project_004
model_10
Municipal Market and Public Space, Rubí, Spain
Enamelled Welded Wire 35x176x25 cm

project_004
model_11
Municipal Market and Public Space, Rubí, Spain
Enamelled Welded Wire, Paper, Wood 81x81x26 cm

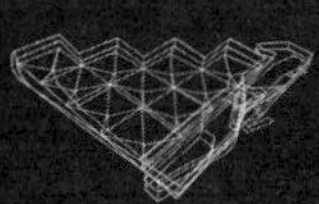

project_004
model_12
Municipal Market and Public Space, Rubí, Spain
Enamelled Welded Wire 52x36x8 cm

project_004
model_13
Municipal Market and Public Space, Rubí, Spain
Cardboard, Enamelled Welded Wire 41x39x17 cm

project_04
model_14
Municipal Market and Public Space, Rubí, Spain
Enamelled Welded Wire, Cardboard unknown cm

project_004
model_15
Municipal Market and Public Space, Rubí, Spain
Enamelled Welded Wire, Cardboard

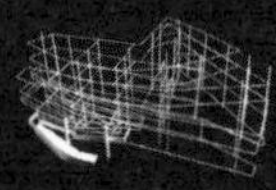

project_004
model_16
Municipal Market and Public Space, Rubí, Spain
Enamelled Welded Wire

project_004
model_17
Municipal Market and Public Space, Rubí, Spain
Enamelled Welded Wire

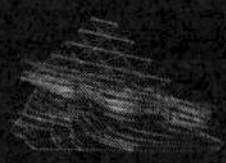

project_004
model_18_DHUB
Municipal Market and Public Space, Rubí, Spain
scale_1:250 Zinc Plated Welded Wire 31x34x5 cm

2011 - 2012

project_005 / models_01 - 10

Topographic House, Llavaneres, Spain
41°34'32"N 02°28'59"E
pages 9, 14, 40-41, 95, 101-103, 105, 208, 226-227, 298-303, 382, 407

project_005
model_01
Topographic House, Llavaneres, Spain
White Matte Paper 40x23x8 cm

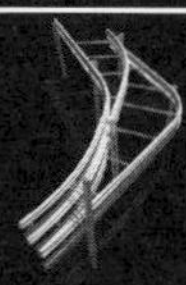

project_005
model_03
Topographic House, Llavaneres, Spain
White Paper, Enamelled Welded Wire 98x46x14 cm

project_005
model_04
Topographic House, Llavaneres, Spain
White Paper, Enamelled Welded Wire 85x82x18 cm

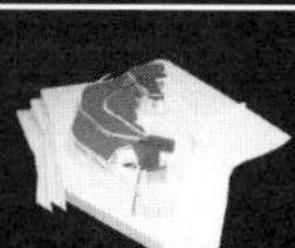

project_005
model_05
Topographic House, Llavaneres, Spain
Cardboard 92x120x30 cm

project_005
model_06
Topographic House, Llavaneres, Spain
Cardboard

project_005
model_07
Topographic House, Llavaneres, Spain
Cardboard

project_05
model_08
Topographic House, Llavaneres, Spain
Cardboard

project_005
model_09
Topographic House, Llavaneres, Spain
EC2020-2-AR58
Centre Pompidou Permanent Collection
Nickel Plated Welded Wire 6,5x15x35 cm

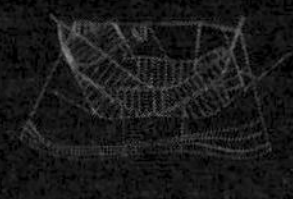

project_005
model_10_DHUB
Topographic House, Llavaneres, Spain
scale_1:100 Zinc Plated Welded Wire 38x20x9cm

2000 - 2004

project_006 / models_01 - 19

Golf Clubhouse and Sports Centre, Fontanals de Cerdanya, Spain
42°23'48"N 01°52'37"E
pages 8, 9, 14-15, 82-93, 208-211, 312-319, 382

project_006
model_01
Golf Clubhouse and Sports Centre, Fontanals de Cerdanya, Spain
Wood, White Cardboard 30x26x4 cm

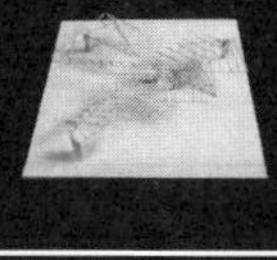

project_006
model_02
Golf Clubhouse and Sports Centre, Fontanals de Cerdanya, Spain
Wood 30x30x6 cm

project_006
model_03
Golf Clubhouse and Sports Centre, Fontanals de Cerdanya, Spain
Wood, White Cardboard 30x30x5 cm

project_006
model_04
Golf Clubhouse and Sports Centre, Fontanals de Cerdanya, Spain
Wood, White Cardboard 26x30x5 cm

project_006
model_05
Golf Clubhouse and Sports Centre, Fontanals de Cerdanya, Spain
Wood, White Cardboard 30x31x4 cm

project_006
model_06
Golf Clubhouse and Sports Centre, Fontanals de Cerdanya, Spain
White Matte Paper 33x31x5 cm

project_06
model_07
Golf Clubhouse and Sports Centre, Fontanals de Cerdanya, Spain
Wood
25x30x5 cm

project_006
model_08
Golf Clubhouse and Sports Centre, Fontanals de Cerdanya, Spain
Wood
31x30x5 cm

project_006
model_09
Golf Clubhouse and Sports Centre, Fontanals de Cerdanya, Spain
Wood
32x30x5 cm

project_006
model_10
Golf Clubhouse and Sports Centre, Fontanals de Cerdanya, Spain
Wood
35x31x5 cm

project_006
model_11
Golf Clubhouse and Sports Centre, Fontanals de Cerdanya, Spain
Wood
14x28x20 cm

project_006
model_12
Golf Clubhouse and Sports Centre, Fontanals de Cerdanya, Spain
Wood
22x36x24 cm

project_006
model_13
Golf Clubhouse and Sports Centre, Fontanals de Cerdanya, Spain
Cardboard
29x20x10 cm

project_006
model_14
Golf Clubhouse and Sports Centre, Fontanals de Cerdanya, Spain
Enamelled Welded Wire
16x12x7 cm

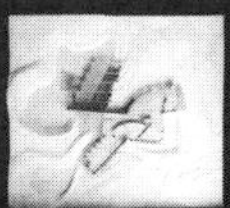

project_006
model_15
Golf Clubhouse and Sports Centre, Fontanals de Cerdanya, Spain
EC2020-2-AR85
Centre Pompidou
Permanent Collection
Wood

project_006
model_16
Golf Clubhouse and Sports Centre, Fontanals de Cerdanya, Spain
Wood

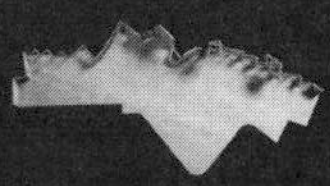

project_006
model_17
Golf Clubhouse and Sports Centre, Fontanals de Cerdanya, Spain
Wood

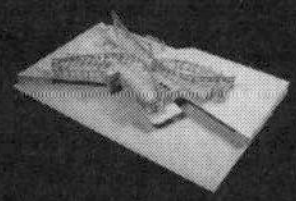

project_006
model_18
Golf Clubhouse and Sports Centre, Fontanals de Cerdanya, Spain
Wood

project_006
model_19_DHUB
Golf Clubhouse and Sports Centre, Fontanals de Cerdanya, Spain
scale_1:250
Zinc Plated Welded Wire
37x27x14 cm

2007 - 2012

project_007 / models_01 - 19

Pedestrian Bridge, Palafolls, Spain
41°39'50"N 02°44'50"E
pages 1, 8, 15-16, 41, 106-111, 208-211, 234-235, 294-297, 382-383

project_007
model_01
Pedestrian Bridge, Palafolls, Spain
Wood
37x17x36 cm

project_007
model_02
Pedestrian Bridge, Palafolls, Spain
Wood
40x45x20 cm

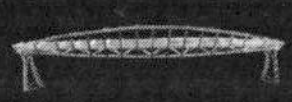

project_007
model_03
Pedestrian Bridge, Palafolls, Spain
Wood
42x158x32 cm

project_007
model_04
Pedestrian Bridge, Palafolls, Spain
Wood
34x13x20 cm

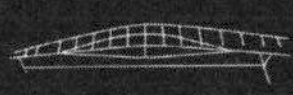

project_007
model_05
Pedestrian Bridge, Palafolls, Spain
Enamelled Welded Wire
42x5x8 cm

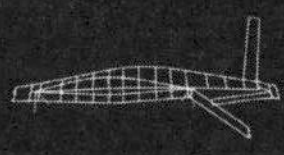

project_007
model_06
Pedestrian Bridge, Palafolls, Spain
Enamelled Welded Wire
46x28x8 cm

project_007
model_07
Pedestrian Bridge, Palafolls, Spain
Enamelled Welded Wire
80x16x4 cm

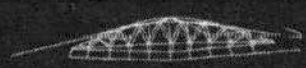

project_007
model_08
Pedestrian Bridge, Palafolls, Spain
Enamelled Welded Wire
53x10x9 cm

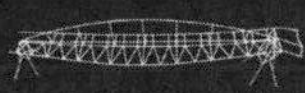

project_007
model_09
Pedestrian Bridge, Palafolls, Spain
Enamelled Welded Wire
81x13x22 cm

project_007
model_10
Pedestrian Bridge i, Palafolls, Spain
Enamelled Welded Wire
127x17x12,5 cm

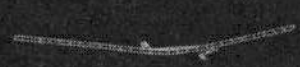

project_007
model_11
Pedestrian Bridge, Palafolls, Spain
Enamelled Welded Wire
100x9x3 cm

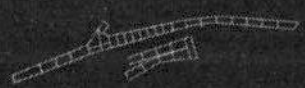

project_007
model_12
Pedestrian Bridge, Palafolls, Spain
Enamelled Welded Wire
97x14x5 cm

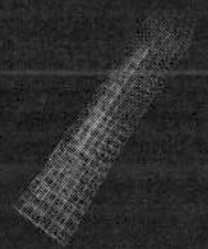

project_007
model_13
Pedestrian Bridge, Palafolls, Spain
Enamelled Welded Wire
152x26x35 cm

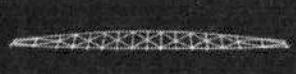

project_007
model_14
Pedestrian Bridge, Palafolls, Spain
Enamelled Welded Wire
29,5x3x0,1 cm

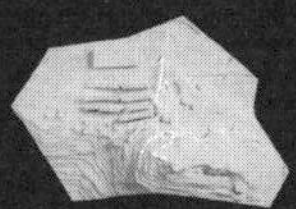

project_007
model_16
Pedestrian Bridge, Palafolls, Spain
Wood

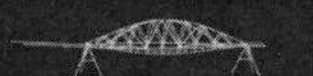

project_007
model_17
Pedestrian Bridge, Palafolls, Spain
EC2020-2-AR-40
Centre Pompidou
Permanent Collection
Enamelled Welded Wire
9x5x40 cm

project_007
model_18
Pedestrian Bridge, Palafolls, Spain
EC2020-2-AR-41
Centre Pompidou
Permanent Collection
Enamelled Welded Wire
10x83x10 cm

project_007
model_19_DHUB
Pedestrian Bridge, Palafolls, Spain
scale_1:100
Zinc Plated Welded Wire
72x11x10cm

2005 - 2006

project_008 / models_01 - 19

Butterfly House, Besalú, Spain
42°12'00"N 02°41'43"E
pages 9, 16, 40, 94, 98-100, 104, 208-211, 306-309, 374, 383

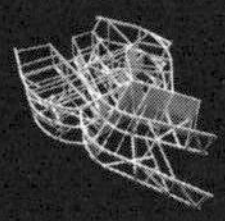

project_008
model_01
Butterfly House, Besalú, Spain
Cardboard
47x33,5x13 cm

project_008
model_02
Butterfly House, Besalú, Spain
Wood
15x22x11 cm

project_008
model_03
Butterfly House, Besalú, Spain
Enamelled Welded Wire
40x30x5 cm

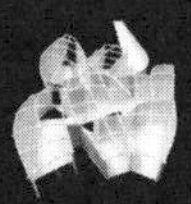

project_008
model_04
Butterfly House, Besalú, Spain
Enamelled Welded Wire, Cardboard
30x17x9 cm

project_008
model_05
Butterfly House, Besalú, Spain
Enamelled Welded Wire, Cardboard
15x36x5 cm

project_008
model_06
Butterfly House, Besalú, Spain
Wood
34x20x4 cm

project_008
model_07
Butterfly House, Besalú, Spain
Welded Wire
47x80x21 cm

project_008
model_08
Butterfly House, Besalú, Spain
Welded Wire, Cardboard
58x37x13 cm

project_008
model_09
Butterfly House, Besalú, Spain
Cardboard
29x15x8 cm

project_008
model_10
Butterfly House, Besalú, Spain
Welded Wire, Cardboard , Paper
93x63x21 cm

project_008
model_11
Butterfly House, Besalú, Spain
Welded Wire, Cardboard , Paper
62x38x21 cm

project_008
model_12
Butterfly House, Besalú, Spain
Welded Wire, Cardboard , Paper
57x30x15 cm

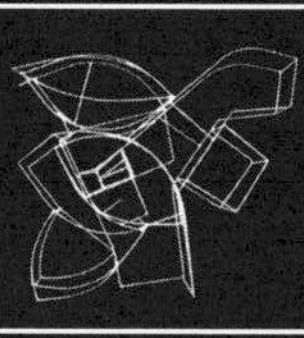

project_008
model_13
Butterfly House, Besalú, Spain
Welded Wire
20x19x6,5 cm

project_008
model_14
Butterfly House, Besalú, Spain
Cardboard
41x24x5,5 cm

project_008
model_15
Butterfly House, Besalú, Spain
Wood
unknown cm

project_008
model_16
Butterfly House, Besalú, Spain
Enamelled Welded Wire
unknown cm

project_008
model_17
Butterfly House, Besalú, Spain
Enamelled Welded Wire
unknown cm

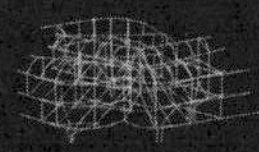

project_008
model_18
Butterfly House, Besalú, Spain
EC2020-2-AR60
Centre Pompidou
Permanent Collection
Enamelled Welded Wire
9 x 25 x 16 cm

project_008
model_19_DHUB
Butterfly House, Besalú, Spain
scale_1:100
Zinc Plated Welded Wire
25x15x11cm

2007 - 2008

project_009 / models_01 - 19

Lower Funicular Station at Tibidabo Amusement Park, Barcelona, Spain
41°24'59"N 02°07'51"E
pages 8, 16-17, 67, 208-211, 330-332, 383

project_009
model_01
Lower Funicular Station at Tibidabo Amusement Park, Barcelona, Spain
Welded Wire, Cardboard
50x48x20 cm

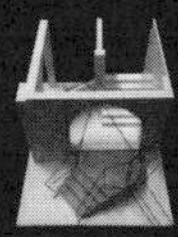

project_009
model_02
Lower Funicular Station at Tibidabo Amusement Park, Barcelona, Spain
Wood, Welded Wire, Cardboard
34x45x24 cm

project_009
model_03
Lower Funicular Station at Tibidabo Amusement Park, Barcelona, Spain
Enamelled Welded Wire
16,5x11,5x15 cm

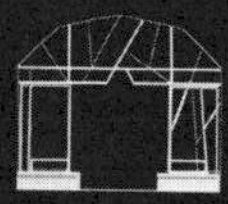

project_009
model_94
Lower Funicular Station at Tibidabo Amusement Park, Barcelona, Spain
Cardboard
35x5x30 cm

project_009
model_05
Lower Funicular Station at Tibidabo Amusement Park, Barcelona, Spain
Wood, Cardboard
15x11x16 cm

project_009
model_06
Lower Funicular Station at Tibidabo Amusement Park, Barcelona, Spain
Wood, Welded Wire
66x52x27 cm

project_009
model_07
Lower Funicular Station at Tibidabo Amusement Park, Barcelona, Spain
Paper, Cardboard
91x43x27 cm

	project_009 model_08 Lower Funicular Station at Tibidabo Amusement Park, Barcelona, Spain	Enamelled Welded Wire, Cardboard 43x42x26 cm
	project_009 model_09 Lower Funicular Station at Tibidabo Amusement Park, Barcelona, Spain	Wood, Enamelled Welded Wire 71x70x48 cm
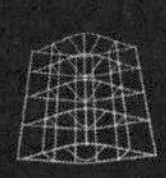	project_009 model_10 Lower Funicular Station at Tibidabo Amusement Park, Barcelona, Spain	Enamelled Welded Wire 19x17x5 cm
	project_009 model_11 Lower Funicular Station at Tibidabo Amusement Park, Barcelona, Spain	Wood 26x17x21 cm
	project_009 model_12 Lower Funicular Station at Tibidabo Amusement Park, Barcelona, Spain	Wood 43x33x3 cm
	project_009 model_13 Lower Funicular Station at Tibidabo Amusement Park, Barcelona, Spain	Enamelled Welded Wire
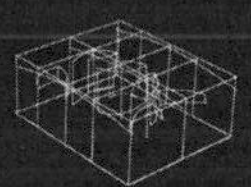	project_009 model_14 Lower Funicular Station at Tibidabo Amusement Park, Barcelona, Spain	Enamelled Welded Wire
	project_009 model_15 Lower Funicular Station at Tibidabo Amusement Park, Barcelona, Spain	Wood
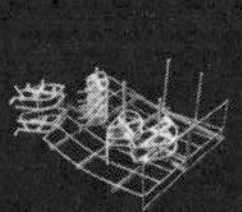	project_009 model_16 Lower Funicular Station at Tibidabo Amusement Park, Barcelona, Spain	Wood
	project_009 model_17 Lower Funicular Station at Tibidabo Amusement Park, Barcelona, Spain	Cardboard
	project_009 model_18 Lower Funicular Station at Tibidabo Amusement Park, Barcelona, Spain EC2020-2-AR49 Centre Pompidou Permanent Collection	Enamelled Welded Wire 10x20x20 cm
	project_009 model_19_DHUB Lower Funicular Station at Tibidabo Amusement Park, Barcelona, Spain	scale_1:50 Zinc Plated Welded Wire 25x22x10 cm

2008

project_011 / models_01 - 02

Can Sisó House, Banyoles, Spain
42°07'10"N 02°45'59"E
pages 17

	project_011 model_01 Can Sisó House, Banyoles, Spain	Wood, Paper 68x34x17 cm
	project_011 model_02 Can Sisó House, Banyoles, Spain	Wood, Paper 26x64x20 cm

2008 - 2009

project_012 / models_01 - 18

Historical Building Refurbishment at Tibidabo Amusement Park, Barcelona, Spain
41°25'17"N 02°07'08"E
pages 9, 17-18, 66, 333-334

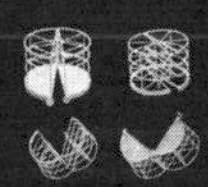	project_012 model_01 Historical Building Refurbishment at Tibidabo Amusement Park, Barcelona, Spain	Enamelled Welded Wire, Cardboard 85x50x25 cm
	project_012 model_02 Historical Building Refurbishment at Tibidabo Amusement Park, Barcelona, Spain	Enamelled Welded Wire 85x52x27,5 cm
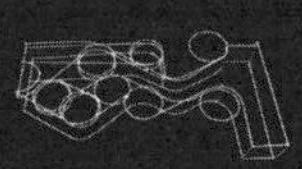	project_012 model_03 Historical Building Refurbishment at Tibidabo Amusement Park, Barcelona, Spain	Enamelled Welded Wire 26x14x3,5 cm
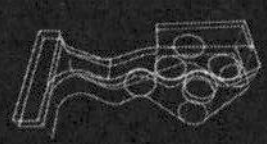	project_012 model_04 Historical Building Refurbishment at Tibidabo Amusement Park, Barcelona, Spain	Enamelled Welded Wire 24x13x6 cm
	project_012 model_05 Historical Building Refurbishment at Tibidabo Amusement Park, Barcelona, Spain	Enamelled Welded Wire 50x26x8,5 cm
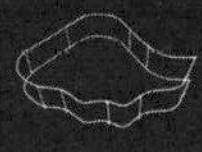	project_012 model_06 Historical Building Refurbishment at Tibidabo Amusement Park, Barcelona, Spain	Enamelled Welded Wire 14x12,5x4 cm
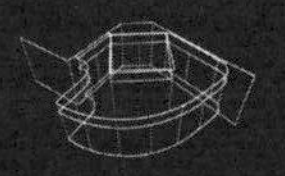	project_012 model_07 Historical Building Refurbishment at Tibidabo Amusement Park, Barcelona, Spain	Enamelled Welded Wire 24x14x6 cm
	project_012 model_08 Historical Building Refurbishment at Tibidabo Amusement Park, Barcelona, Spain	Enamelled Welded Wire, Cardboard 100x46x13 cm
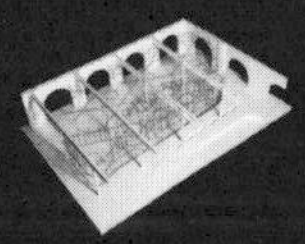	project_012 model_09 Historical Building Refurbishment at Tibidabo Amusement Park, Barcelona, Spain	Enamelled Welded Wire, Cardboard 56x97x13 cm
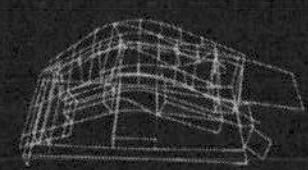	project_012 model_10 Historical Building Refurbishment at Tibidabo Amusement Park, Barcelona, Spain	Enamelled Welded Wire 33x14x10,5 cm
	project_012 model_11 Historical Building Refurbishment at Tibidabo Amusement Park, Barcelona, Spain	Enamelled Welded Wire 32x20x7 cm
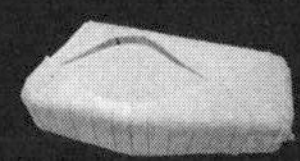	project_012 model_12 Historical Building Refurbishment at Tibidabo Amusement Park, Barcelona, Spain	Welded Wire, Paper 79x111x15 cm
	project_012 model_13 Historical Building Refurbishment at Tibidabo Amusement Park, Barcelona, Spain	Enamelled Welded Wire 18x14x14 cm
	project_012 model_14 Historical Building Refurbishment at Tibidabo Amusement Park, Barcelona, Spain	Enamelled Welded Wire 23x20x12 cm

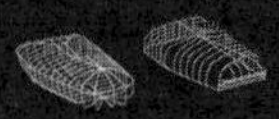

project_012
model_15
Historical Building Refurbishment at Tibidabo Amusement Park, Barcelona, Spain

Wood

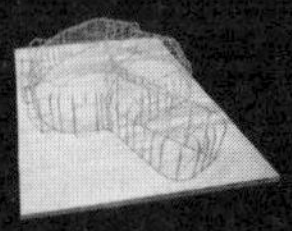

project_012
model_16
Historical Building Refurbishment at Tibidabo Amusement Park, Barcelona, Spain

Wood, Enamelled Welded Wire

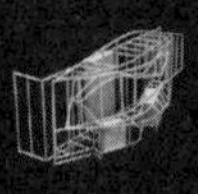

project_012
model_17
Historical Building Refurbishment at Tibidabo Amusement Park, Barcelona, Spain

Wood

project_012
model_18_DHUB
Historical Building Refurbishment at Tibidabo Amusement Park, Barcelona, Spain

scale_1:150
Zinc Plated Welded Wire
34x23x12 cm

2013

project_013 / models_01 - 07

Bus Stop, Palafolls, Spain
41°40'13"N 02°44'57"E
pages 8, 18, 64-66, 208, 336

project_013
model_01
Bus Stop, Palafolls, Spain

Wood
72x48x49 cm

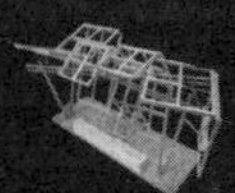

project_013
model_02
Bus Stop, Palafolls, Spain

Wood
32x55x35 cm

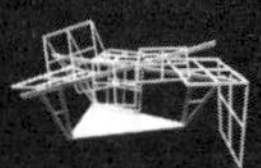

project_013
model_03
Bus Stop, Palafolls, Spain

Wood
18x30x18 cm

project_013
model_04
Bus Stop, Palafolls, Spain

Wood
27x29x17 cm

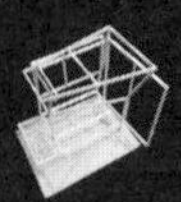

project_013
model_05
Bus Stop, Palafolls, Spain

Wood
30x26x31 cm

project_013
model_06
Bus Stop, Palafolls, Spain

Enamelled Welded Wire

project_013
model_07_DHUB
Bus Stop, Palafolls, Spain

scale_1:20
Zinc Plated Welded Wire
24x11x14cm

2017 - 2019

project_014 / models_01 - 02

Therapeutic Community Centre, Calella, Spain
41°36'57"N 02°39'50"E
pages 9, 18, 62-63, 342-343

project_014
model_01
Therapeutic Community Centre, Calella, Spain

Wood
22x22,5x42 cm

project_014
model_02
Therapeutic Community Centre, Calella, Spain

Wood
26x14x9 cm

2007 - 2013

project_015 / models_01 - 24

Can Zariquiey Therapeutic Centre, Arenys de Munt, Spain
41°35'57"N 02°32'38"E
pages 9, 18-19, 54-61, 344-347, 408

project_015
model_01
Can Zariquiey Therapeutic Centre, Arenys de Munt, Spain

Wood
22x20x11,5 cm

project_015
model_02
Can Zariquiey Therapeutic Centre, Arenys de Munt, Spain

Wood
68x35x19,5 cm

project_015
model_03
Can Zariquiey Therapeutic Centre, Arenys de Munt, Spain

Wood
50x28x29 cm

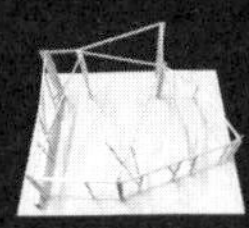

project_015
model_04
Can Zariquiey Therapeutic Centre, Arenys de Munt, Spain

Wood
41x32x15 cm

project_015
model_05
Can Zariquiey Therapeutic Centre, Arenys de Munt, Spain

Wood, Cardboard
49x36,5x13 cm

project_015
model_06
Can Zariquiey Therapeutic Centre, Arenys de Munt, Spain

Wood, Welded Wire, Cardboard
56x53x12 cm

project_015
model_07
Can Zariquiey Therapeutic Centre, Arenys de Munt, Spain

Wood, Cardboard
119x118x37,5 cm

project_015
model_08
Can Zariquiey Therapeutic Centre, Arenys de Munt, Spain

Wood, Cardboard
25,5x22x9 cm

project_015
model_09
Can Zariquiey Therapeutic Centre, Arenys de Munt, Spain

Wood
46x30x24 cm

project_015
model_10
Can Zariquiey Therapeutic Centre, Arenys de Munt, Spain

Wood
20x17,5x24 cm

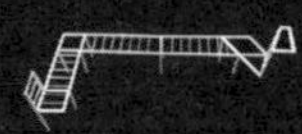

project_015
model_11
Can Zariquiey Therapeutic Centre, Arenys de Munt, Spain

Wood
60x26x20 cm

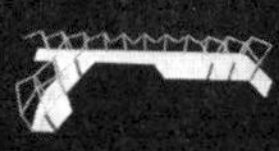

project_015
model_12
Can Zariquiey Therapeutic Centre, Arenys de Munt, Spain

Wood
63x25x10 cm

project_015
model_13
Can Zariquiey Therapeutic Centre, Arenys de Munt, Spain

Wood
99x80x38 cm

project_015
model_14
Can Zariquiey Therapeutic Centre, Arenys de Munt, Spain

Wood, Cardboard
47x39x12 cm

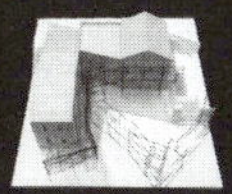
project_015
model_15
Can Zariquiey Therapeutic Centre, Arenys de Munt, Spain
Welded Wire, Wood, Cardboard
41x43x16 cm

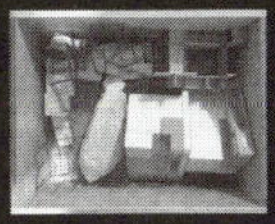
project_015
model_16
Can Zariquiey Therapeutic Centre, Arenys de Munt, Spain
Wood, Welded Wire, Cardboard
42x32x17 cm

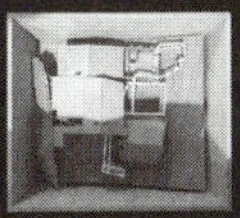
project_015
model_17
Can Zariquiey Therapeutic Centre, Arenys de Munt, Spain
White Matte Paper, Grey Cardboard
39x32x15 cm

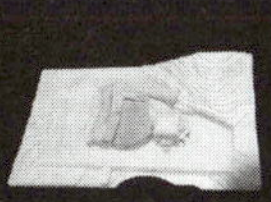
project_015
model_18
Can Zariquiey Therapeutic Centre, Arenys de Munt, Spain
Wood
54x31x10 cm

project_015
model_19
Can Zariquiey Therapeutic Centre, Arenys de Munt, Spain
Enamelled Welded Wire
27x17x6 cm

project_015
model_20
Can Zariquiey Therapeutic Centre, Arenys de Munt, Spain
Wood, Cardboad
94x42x15 cm

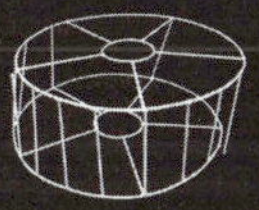
project_015
model_21
Can Zariquiey Therapeutic Centre, Arenys de Munt, Spain
Enamelled Welded Wire
14x14,5x5,5 cm

project_015
model_22
Can Zariquiey Therapeutic Centre, Arenys de Munt, Spain
Enamelled Welded Wire

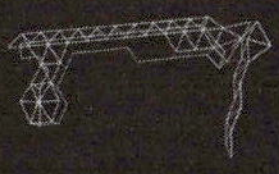
project_015
model_23
Can Zariquiey Therapeutic Centre, Arenys de Munt, Spain
Enamelled Welded Wire

project_015
model_24_DHUB
Can Zariquiey Therapeutic Centre, Arenys de Munt, Spain
scale_1:150
Zinc Plated Welded Wire
30x24x7cm

2005 - 2009

project_016 / model_01

San Bernardo Apartments, Madrid, Spain
40°25'34"N 03°42'25"W
pages 8, 19, 338-339

project_016
model_01
San Bernardo Apartments, Madrid, Spain
Wood

in progress

project_018 / models_01 - 03

City Centre Housing, Barcelona, Spain
41°22'46"N 02°10'02"E
pages 19, 52-53

project_018
model_01
City Centre Housing, Barcelona, Spain
Cardboard
82x16x38 cm

project_018
model_02
City Centre Housing, Barcelona, Spain
Wood
82x16x38 cm

project_018
model_03
City Centre Housing, Barcelona, Spain
Wood
20x24x30 cm

2018 - 2019

project_019 / model_01

Alfasoni Musical Centre, Barcelona, Spain
41°24'28"N 02°11'44"E
pages 9, 19, 270-271

project_019
model_01
Alfasoni Musical Centre, Barcelona, Spain
Wood, Grey Cardboard
30x42x13 cm

2002 - 2005

project_021 / models_01 - 11

Promenade House, Caselles d'Avall, Spain
42°08'37"N 02°44'17"E
pages 9, 19, 305

project_021
model_01
Promenade House, Caselles d'Avall, Spain
Wood
54x37x40 cm

project_021
model_02
Promenade House, Caselles d'Avall, Spain
Wood
33x55x9 cm

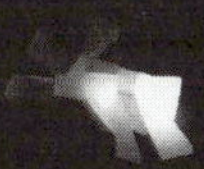
project_021
model_03
Promenade House, Caselles d'Avall, Spain
Cardboard

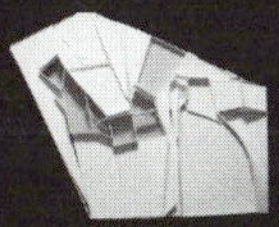
project_021
model_05
Promenade House, Caselles d'Avall, Spain
Cardboard

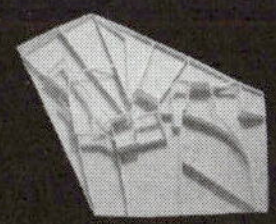
project_021
model_07
Promenade House, Caselles d'Avall, Spain
Cardboard

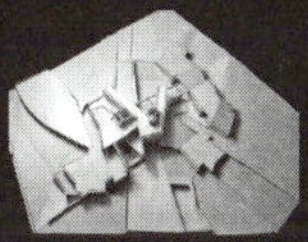
project_021
model_09
Promenade House, Caselles d'Avall, Spain
Wood

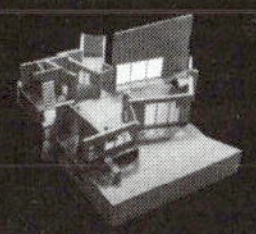
project_021
model_11
Promenade House, Caselles d'Avall, Spain
Wood

2000 - 2004

project_022 / models_01 - 10

Landscape House, Mollet de Peralada, Spain
42°21'36"N 3°00'02"E
pages 9, 19-20, 304

project_022
model_01
Landscape House, Mollet de Peralada, Spain
Wood, Welded Wire, Paper
57x35x11 cm

project_022
model_02
Landscape House, Mollet de Peralada, Spain
Wood
28x38x7 cm

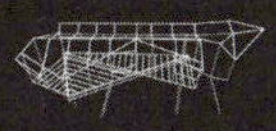
project_022
model_03
Landscape House, Mollet de Peralada, Spain
Enamelled Welded Wire
43x13x23 cm

project_022
model_04
Landscape House, Mollet de Peralada, Spain
Wood, Aluminum
54x39x16 cm

project_022
model_06
Landscape House, Mollet de Peralada, Spain
Wood

project_022
model_07
Landscape House, Mollet de Peralada, Spain
Cardboard

project_022
model_08
Landscape House, Mollet de Peralada, Spain
Wood

project_022
model_09
Landscape House, Mollet de Peralada, Spain
Enamelled Welded Wire

project_022
model_10
Landscape House, Mollet de Peralada, Spain
Enamelled Welded Wire
46x36x14 cm

1999 - 2006

project_023 / models_01 - 11

Old Town Public Space, Banyoles, Spain
42°07'05"N 02°45'53"E
pages 2-3, 8, 20, 40, 42-49, 348-357

project_023
model_02
Old Town Public Space, Banyoles, Spain
Wood
29x22x12 cm

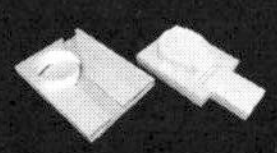

project_023
model_03
Old Town Public Space, Banyoles, Spain
Wood, Paper
26x20x5 cm

project_023
model_04
Old Town Public Space, Banyoles, Spain
Wood
25x20x16 cm

project_023
model_05
Old Town Public Space, Banyoles, Spain
Wood
15x10x16 cm

project_023
model_06
Old Town Public Space, Banyoles, Spain
Wood
76x41x6 cm

project_023
model_07
Old Town Public Space, Banyoles, Spain
Cardboard
15x10x4,5 cm

project_023
model_08
Old Town Public Space, Banyoles, Spain
Wood , Cardboard

project_023
model_09
Old Town Public Space, Banyoles, Spain
Cardboard
15x7x3 cm

project_023
model_10
Old Town Public Space, Banyoles, Spain
Cardboard

project_023
model_11
Old Town Public Space, Banyoles, Spain
Wood

2007 - 2010

project_024 / models_01 - 13

Annexa Joan Puigbert School, Girona, Spain
41°58'42"N 02°49'38"E
pages 9, 20, 280-283

project_024
model_02
Annexa Joan Puigbert School, Girona, Spain
Cardboard, Paper
59x32x32 cm

project_024
model_03
Annexa Joan Puigbert School, Girona, Spain
Wood, Cardboard
58x80x36 cm

project_024
model_04
Annexa Joan Puigbert School, Girona, Spain
Wood, Cardboard
65x74x36 cm

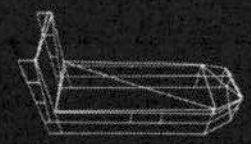

project_024
model_05
Annexa Joan Puigbert School, Girona, Spain
Enamelled Welded Wire
29x10x17 cm

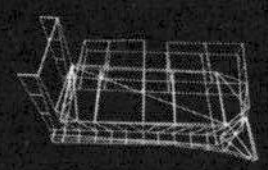

project_024
model_06
Annexa Joan Puigbert School, Girona, Spain
Enamelled Welded Wire
32x22x15 cm

project_024
model_07
Annexa Joan Puigbert School, Girona, Spain
Enamelled Welded Wire, Paper
29x17x13 cm

project_024
model_08
Annexa Joan Puigbert School, Girona, Spain
White Matte Paper, Wood
85x134x26 cm

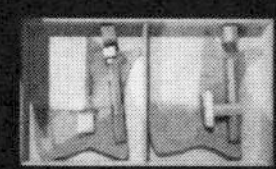

project_024
model_09
Annexa Joan Puigbert School, Girona, Spain
Wood, Grey Cardboard
67x37x7 cm

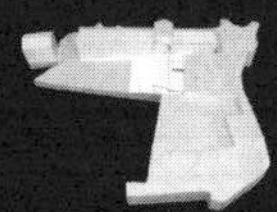

project_024
model_10
Annexa Joan Puigbert School, Girona, Spain
Wood, Paper
63x75x15 cm

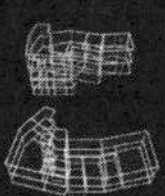

project_024
model_11
Annexa Joan Puigbert School, Girona, Spain
Enamelled Welded Wire
17x15x8 cm

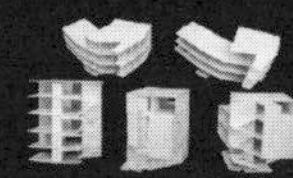

project_024
model_12
Annexa Joan Puigbert School, Girona, Spain
White Cardboard
29x52x13 cm

project_024
model_13_DHUB
Annexa Joan Puigbert School, Girona, Spain
scale_1:250
Zinc Plated Welded Wire
34x15x6cm

2006 - 2011

project_025 / models_01 - 17

Plug-in Building at 22@, Barcelona, Spain
41°23'44"N 02°11'31"E
pages 8, 21, 41, 122-128, 223-225, 272-279, 383

project_025 model_01 Plug-in Building at 22@, Barcelona, Spain — Wood 82x53x9 cm

project_025 model_02 Plug-in Building at 22@, Barcelona, Spain — Wood 82x55x10 cm

project_025 model_03 Plug-in Building at 22@, Barcelona, Spain — Enamelled Welded Wire 38x38x20 cm

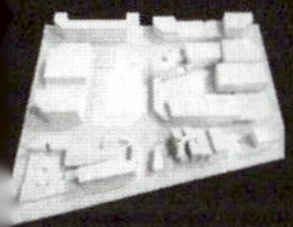

project_025 model_04 Plug-in Building at 22@, Barcelona, Spain — Wood 60x55x7 cm

project_025 model_05 Plug-in Building at 22@, Barcelona, Spain — Cardboard 124x70x80 cm

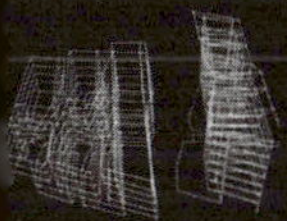

project_025 model_06 Plug-in Building at 22@, Barcelona, Spain — Welded Wire 27x27x32 cm

project_025 model_07 Plug-in Building at 22@, Barcelona, Spain — Paper, Cardboard 80x58x22 cm

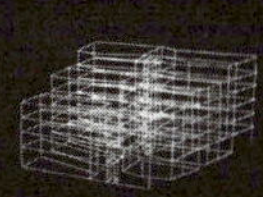

project_025 model_08 Plug-in Building at 22@, Barcelona, Spain — Wood, Welded Wire, White Matte Paper 57x100x42 cm

project_025 model_09 Plug-in Building at 22@, Barcelona, Spain — Enamelled Steel 80x80x51 cm

project_025 model_10 Plug-in Building at 22@, Barcelona, Spain — Wood 43x23x10 cm

project_025 model_11 Plug-in Building at 22@, Barcelona, Spain — Wood 34x19x10 cm

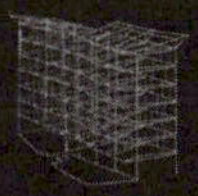

project_025 model_12 Plug-in Building at 22@, Barcelona, Spain — Enamelled Welded Steel 20x19x8 cm

project_025 model_14 Plug-in Building at 22@, Barcelona, Spain — Enamelled Welded Steel 40x12x6 cm

project_025 model_15 Plug-in Building at 22@, Barcelona, Spain — Enamelled Welded Steel

project_025 model_16 Plug-in Building at 22@, Barcelona, Spain EC2020-2-AR83 Centre Pompidou Permanent Collection — Nickel Plated Welded Steel

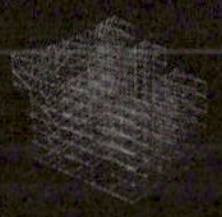

project_025 model_17_DHUB Plug-in Building at 22@, Barcelona, Spain — scale_1:150 Zinc Plated Welded Wire 26x25x15cm

in progress

project_026 / models_01 - 05

Marina del Prat Vermell Social Housing, Barcelona, Spain
41°21'6N 02°08'34"E
pages 9, 21, 256-259

project_026 model_01 Marina del Prat Vermell Social Housing, Barcelona, Spain — White Matte Paper 51x33x10 cm

project_026 model_02 Marina del Prat Vermell Social Housing, Barcelona, Spain — White Matte Paper 70x50x13 cm

project_026 model_03 Marina del Prat Vermell Social Housing, Barcelona, Spain — White Matte Paper 28,5x40x7 cm

project_026 model_04 Marina del Prat Vermell Social Housing, Barcelona, Spain — Wood 81x29x40 cm

project_026 model_05_DHUB Marina del Prat Vermell Social Housing, Barcelona, Spain — scale_1:250 Zinc Plated Welded Wire 36x13x11cm

2009 - 2012

project_027 / models_01 - 11

Torrebaró Social Housing, Barcelona, Spain
41°27'36"N 02°10'50"E
pages 9, 21-22, 40-41, 138-144, 208, 254-255, 377

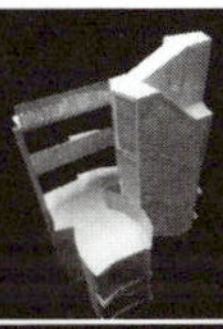

project_027 model_01 Torrebaró Social Housing, Barcelona, Spain — Wood 54x35x61,5 cm

project_027 model_02 Torrebaró Social Housing, Barcelona, Spain — Wood 65x54x87 cm

project_027 model_03 Torrebaró Social Housing, Barcelona, Spain — Plaster 40x40x36 cm

project_027 model_04 Torrebaró Social Housing, Barcelona, Spain — Enamelled Welded Wire, Paper 28x26x42 cm

project_027 model_05 Torrebaró Social Housing, Barcelona, Spain — White Matte Paper 26x19x20 cm

project_027 model_06 Torrebaró Social Housing, Barcelona, Spain — Enamelled Welded Wire, Paper 30x30x46 cm

project_027
model_07
Torrebaró Social Housing, Barcelona, Spain
Wood, Welded Wire, Paper 36x34x25 cm

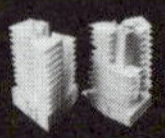
project_027
model_08
Torrebaró Social Housing, Barcelona, Spain
White Matte Paper 14x14x21 cm

project_027
model_09
Torrebaró Social Housing, Barcelona, Spain
White Matte Paper 32x42x48 cm

project_027
model_10_DHUB
Torrebaró Social Housing, Barcelona, Spain
scale_1:150 Zinc Plated Welded Wire 15x18x27cm

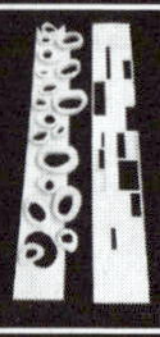
project_027
model_11
Torrebaró Social Housing, Barcelona, Spain
Wood 15x68x4 cm

project_027
model_12
Torrebaró Social Housing, Barcelona, Spain
Wood, Paper

in progress

project_028 / models_01 - 09

Cocobolo Centre, Panama City, Panama
09°00'00"N 79°30'00"W
pages 9, 22, 145-149, 160, 208

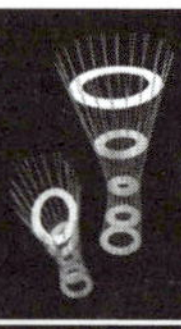
project_028
model_01
Cocobolo Centre, Panama City, Panama
Wood, White Matte Paper 30x20x64 cm

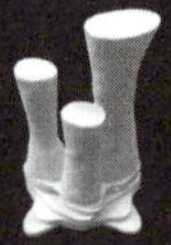
project_028
model_02
Cocobolo Centre, Panama City, Panama
Wood 12x7x18 cm

project_028
model_04
Cocobolo Centre, Panama City, Panama
Wood

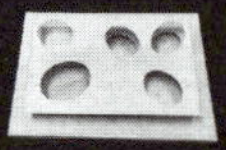
project_028
model_05
Cocobolo Centre, Panama City, Panama
Wood

project_028
model_06
Cocobolo Centre, Panama City, Panama
Wood 21x21x61 cm

project_028
model_07
Cocobolo Centre, Panama City, Panama
Wood 32x15x19 cm

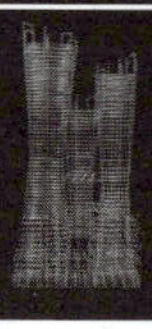
project_028
model_09_DHUB
Cocobolo Centre, Panama City, Panama
scale_1:400 Zinc Plated Welded Wire 25x16x50cm

2007 - 2011

project_029 / models_01 - 87

iGuzzini Lighting Iberian Headquarters, Sant Cugat del Vallès, Spain
41°29'28"N 02°03'27"E
pages 8, 22-25, 41, 178-203, 208, 212-213, 216-221, 236-243, 382-383

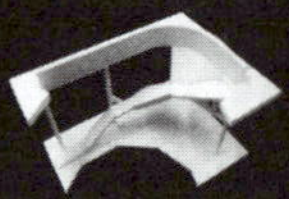
project_029
model_01
iGuzzini Lighting Iberian Headquarters, Sant Cugat del Vallès, Spain
Wood 41,2x30x26 cm

project_029
model_02
iGuzzini Lighting Iberian Headquarters, Sant Cugat del Vallès, Spain
Enamelled Welded Wire 20x23x24 cm

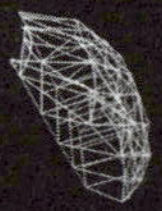
project_029
model_03
iGuzzini Lighting Iberian Headquarters, Sant Cugat del Vallès, Spain
Enamelled Welded Wire, 36,5x28x16 cm

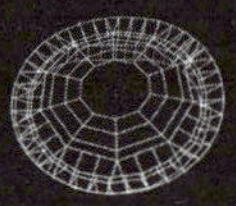
project_029
model_04
iGuzzini Lighting Iberian Headquarters, Sant Cugat del Vallès, Spain
Enamelled Welded Wire 43x42,5x6,5 cm

project_029
model_05
iGuzzini Lighting Iberian Headquarters, Sant Cugat del Vallès, Spain
Enamelled Welded Wire 40x34x20 cm

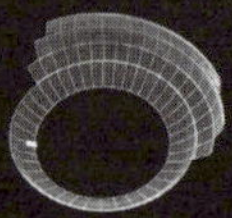
project_029
model_06
iGuzzini Lighting Iberian Headquarters, Sant Cugat del Vallès, Spain
Enamelled Welded Wire 50x49x21 cm

project_029
model_07
iGuzzini Lighting Iberian Headquarters, Sant Cugat del Vallès, Spain
Wood 51x64x63 cm

project_029
model_08
iGuzzini Lighting Iberian Headquarters, Sant Cugat del Vallès, Spain
Wood 92x42x50 cm

project_029
model_09
iGuzzini Lighting Iberian Headquarters, Sant Cugat del Vallès, Spain
Plexiglass And Copper 55x55x50 cm

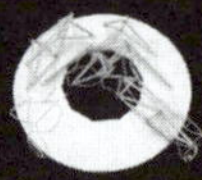
project_029
model_10
iGuzzini Lighting Iberian Headquarters, Sant Cugat del Vallès, Spain
Wood, Cardboard 34x34x6 cm

project_029
model_11
iGuzzini Lighting Iberian Headquarters, Sant Cugat del Vallès, Spain
Wood 42x14x17 cm

project_029
model_12
iGuzzini Lighting Iberian Headquarters, Sant Cugat del Vallès, Spain
Wood 40x40x12 cm

project_029
model_13
iGuzzini Lighting Iberian Headquarters, Sant Cugat del Vallès, Spain
Welded Wire , White Cardboard 95x71x42 cm

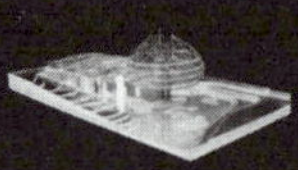
project_029
model_14
iGuzzini Lighting Iberian Headquarters, Sant Cugat del Vallès, Spain
Plexiglass, Welded Wire 71x40x20 cm

project_029
model_15
iGuzzini Lighting Iberian Headquarters, Sant Cugat del Vallès, Spain
Welded Wire, White Cardboard 56x56x7 cm

project_029
model_16
iGuzzini Lighting
Iberian Headquarters,
Sant Cugat del Vallès,
Spain

Steel, Wood
60x47,5x10
cm

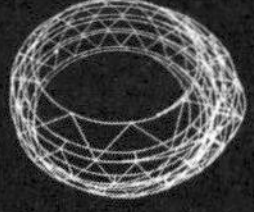

project_029
model_17
iGuzzini Lighting
Iberian Headquarters,
Sant Cugat del Vallès,
Spain

Enamelled
Welded
Wire
43x40x15
cm

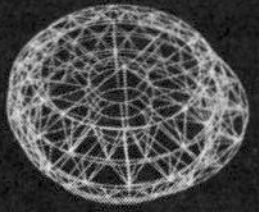

project_029
model_18
iGuzzini Lighting
Iberian Headquarters,
Sant Cugat del Vallès,
Spain

Enamelled
Welded
Wire
42x38x21
cm

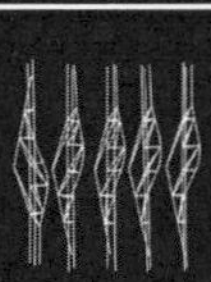

project_029
model_19
iGuzzini Lighting
Iberian Headquarters,
Sant Cugat del Vallès,
Spain

Enamelled
Welded
Wire
9x9x36 cm

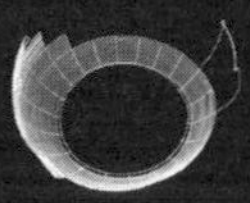

project_029
model_20
iGuzzini Lighting
Iberian Headquarters,
Sant Cugat del Vallès,
Spain

Enamelled
Welded
Wire
50,5x46x23
cm

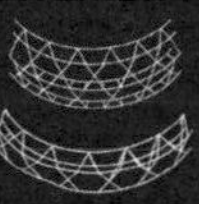

project_029
model_21
iGuzzini Lighting
Iberian Headquarters,
Sant Cugat del Vallès,
Spain

Enamelled
Welded
Wire
33x10x10 cm
each

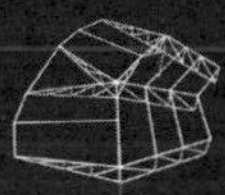

project_029
model_22
iGuzzini Lighting
Iberian Headquarters,
Sant Cugat del Vallès,
Spain

Enamelled
Welded
Wire
30x28x8 cm

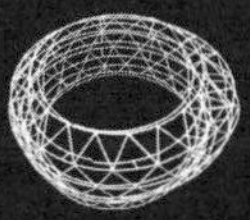

project_029
model_23
iGuzzini Lighting
Iberian Headquarters,
Sant Cugat del Vallès,
Spain

Enamelled
Welded
Wire
22x20x10
cm

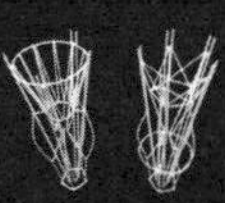

project_029
model_24
iGuzzini Lighting
Iberian Headquarters,
Sant Cugat del Vallès,
Spain

Enamelled
Welded
Wire
15x7x17 cm

project_029
model_25
iGuzzini Lighting
Iberian Headquarters,
Sant Cugat del Vallès,
Spain

Enamelled
Welded
Wire
65x34x20
cm

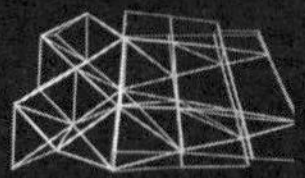

project_029
model_26
iGuzzini Lighting
Iberian Headquarters,
Sant Cugat del Vallès,
Spain

Wood
94x62x15
cm

project_029
model_27
iGuzzini Lighting
Iberian Headquarters,
Sant Cugat del Vallès,
Spain

Welded Wire,
Paper
35x35x25 cm

project_029
model_28
iGuzzini Lighting
Iberian Headquarters,
Sant Cugat del Vallès,
Spain

Wood
99x68x60
cm

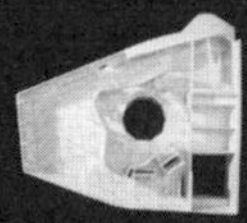

project_029
model_29
iGuzzini Lighting
Iberian Headquarters,
Sant Cugat del Vallès,
Spain

Cardboard
87x81x18 cm

project_029
model_30
iGuzzini Lighting
Iberian Headquarters,
Sant Cugat del Vallès,
Spain

Wood
87x50x31
cm

project_029
model_31
iGuzzini Lighting
Iberian Headquarters,
Sant Cugat del Vallès,
Spain

Wood
10x10x35 cm

project_029
model_32
iGuzzini Lighting
Iberian Headquarters,
Sant Cugat del Vallès,
Spain

Enamelled
Welded
Wire
42x26x8 cm

project_029
model_33
iGuzzini Lighting
Iberian Headquarters,
Sant Cugat del Vallès,
Spain

Wood
18x18x14 cm

project_029
model_34
iGuzzini Lighting
Iberian Headquarters,
Sant Cugat del Vallès,
Spain

White Matte
Paper
49x20x15
cm

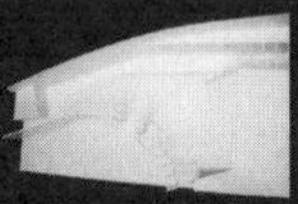

project_029
model_35
iGuzzini Lighting
Iberian Headquarters,
Sant Cugat del Vallès,
Spain

White Matte
Paper
103x82x20
cm

project_029
model_36
iGuzzini Lighting
Iberian Headquarters,
Sant Cugat del Vallès,
Spain

Paper
42x56x6 cm

project_029
model_37
iGuzzini Lighting
Iberian Headquarters,
Sant Cugat del Vallès,
Spain

Wood
85x115x27
cm

project_029
model_38
iGuzzini Lighting
Iberian Headquarters,
Sant Cugat del Vallès,
Spain

Paper
60x34x49
cm

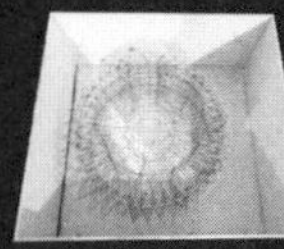

project_029
model_39
iGuzzini Lighting
Iberian Headquarters,
Sant Cugat del Vallès,
Spain

Welded Wire
102x92x42
cm

project_029
model_40
iGuzzini Lighting
Iberian Headquarters,
Sant Cugat del Vallès,
Spain

Welded
Wire, White
Cardboad
90x90x38
cm

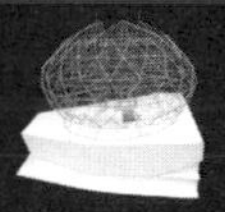

project_029
model_41
iGuzzini Lighting
Iberian Headquarters,
Sant Cugat del Vallès,
Spain

Welded
Wire, White
Cardboad
58x68x52
cm

project_029
model_42
iGuzzini Lighting
Iberian Headquarters,
Sant Cugat del Vallès,
Spain

Wood
45x82x51
cm

project_029
model_43
iGuzzini Lighting
Iberian Headquarters,
Sant Cugat del Vallès,
Spain

Wood
46x26x7 cm

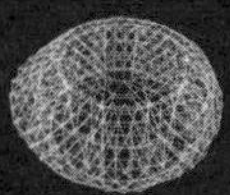

project_029
model_44
iGuzzini Lighting
Iberian Headquarters,
Sant Cugat del Vallès,
Spain

Enamelled
Welded
Wire
81x76x41 cm

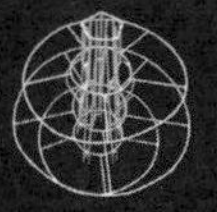

project_029
model_45
iGuzzini Lighting
Iberian Headquarters,
Sant Cugat del Vallès,
Spain

Enamelled
Welded
Wire
20x20x20
cm

project_029
model_46
iGuzzini Lighting
Iberian Headquarters,
Sant Cugat del Vallès,
Spain

Enamelled
Welded Wire
16x14x1 cm

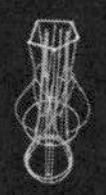

project_029
model_47
iGuzzini Lighting
Iberian Headquarters,
Sant Cugat del Vallès,
Spain

Enamelled
Welded Wire
7x7x18 cm

project_029
model_48
iGuzzini Lighting
Iberian Headquarters,
Sant Cugat del Vallès,
Spain

Enamelled
Welded Wire
12x12x16 cm

project_029
model_49
iGuzzini Lighting
Iberian Headquarters,
Sant Cugat del Vallès,
Spain

Wood
50x50x152
cm

project_0029
model_50
iGuzzini Lighting
Iberian Headquarters,
Sant Cugat del Vallès,
Spain

White
Cardboard
80x60x23
cm

project_029
model_51
iGuzzini Lighting
Iberian Headquarters,
Sant Cugat del Vallès,
Spain

Wood
81x42x11 cm

project_029
model_52
iGuzzini Lighting
Iberian Headquarters,
Sant Cugat del Vallès,
Spain

White Paper,
Wire
50x51x9 cm

project_029
model_53
iGuzzini Lighting
Iberian Headquarters,
Sant Cugat del Vallès,
Spain

Wood
55x30x119
cm

project_029
model_54
iGuzzini Lighting
Iberian Headquarters,
Sant Cugat del Vallès,
Spain

Wood
60x12x1 cm

project_029
model_55
iGuzzini Lighting
Iberian Headquarters,
Sant Cugat del Vallès,
Spain

Textile,
Wood
54x34x2,5
cm

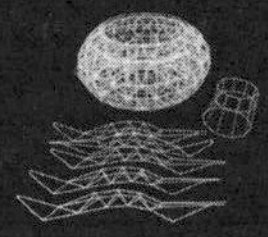

project_029
model_56
iGuzzini Lighting
Iberian Headquarters,
Sant Cugat del Vallès,
Spain

Enamelled
Welded Wire
57x54x28
cm

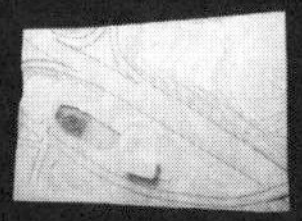

project_029
model_60
iGuzzini Lighting
Iberian Headquarters,
Sant Cugat del Vallès,
Spain

Wood,
Welded Wire
164x107x10
cm

project_029
model_63_DHUB
iGuzzini Lighting
Iberian Headquarters,
Sant Cugat del Vallès,
Spain

Wood
180x180x90
cm

project_029
model_64
iGuzzini Lighting
Iberian Headquarters,
Sant Cugat del Vallès,
Spain

Wood

project_029
model_65
iGuzzini Lighting
Iberian Headquarters,
Sant Cugat del Vallès,
Spain
EC2020-2-AR24
Centre Pompidou
Permanent Collection

Zinc Plated
Welded
Wire, Wood
69x80x51
cm

project_029
model_67
iGuzzini Lighting
Iberian Headquarters,
Sant Cugat del Vallès,
Spain

Wood

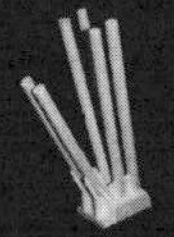

project_029
model_68
iGuzzini Lighting
Iberian Headquarters,
Sant Cugat del Vallès,
Spain

Wood

project_029
model_69
iGuzzini Lighting
Iberian Headquarters,
Sant Cugat del Vallès,
Spain
EC2020-2-AR80
Centre Pompidou
Permanent Collection

Enamelled
Welded Wire
39 x 120 x
56 cm

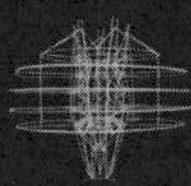

project_029
model_70
iGuzzini Lighting
Iberian Headquarters,
Sant Cugat del Vallès,
Spain
EC2020-2-AR12
Centre Pompidou
Permanent Collection

Enamelled
Welded Wire
33 x 40 x
40 cm

project_029
model_71
iGuzzini Lighting
Iberian Headquarters,
Sant Cugat del Vallès,
Spain
EC2020-2-AR13
Centre Pompidou
Permanent Collection

Enamelled
Welded Wire
10 x 42 x
30 cm

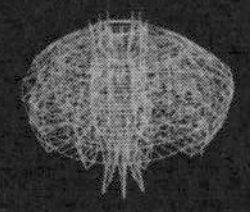

project_029
model_72
iGuzzini Lighting
Iberian Headquarters,
Sant Cugat del Vallès,
Spain
EC2020-2-AR14
Centre Pompidou
Permanent Collection

Enamelled
Welded Wire
60 x 55 x
50 cm

project_029
model_73
iGuzzini Lighting
Iberian Headquarters,
Sant Cugat del Vallès,
Spain
EC2020-2-AR15
Centre Pompidou
Permanent Collection

Enamelled
Welded Wire
20 x 30 x
25 cm

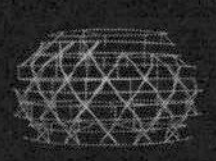

project_029
model_74
iGuzzini Lighting
Iberian Headquarters,
Sant Cugat del Vallès,
Spain
EC2020-2-AR16
Centre Pompidou
Permanent Collection

Enamelled
Welded Wire
18 x 30 x
17 cm

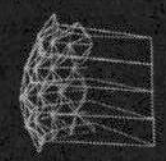

project_029
model_75
iGuzzini Lighting
Iberian Headquarters,
Sant Cugat del Vallès,
Spain
EC2020-2-AR17
Centre Pompidou
Permanent Collection

Enamelled
Welded Wire
16 x 20 x
20 cm

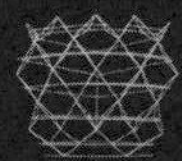

project_029
model_76
iGuzzini Lighting
Iberian Headquarters,
Sant Cugat del Vallès,
Spain
EC2020-2-AR18
Centre Pompidou
Permanent Collection

Enamelled
Welded Wire
20 x 20 x
20 cm

project_029
model_77
iGuzzini Lighting
Iberian Headquarters,
Sant Cugat del Vallès,
Spain
EC2020-2-AR20
Centre Pompidou
Permanent Collection

Enamelled
Welded Wire
33 x 14 x
14 cm

project_029
model_78
iGuzzini Lighting
Iberian Headquarters,
Sant Cugat del Vallès,
Spain
EC2020-2-AR21
Centre Pompidou
Permanent Collection

Enamelled
Welded Wire
33 x 13 x
13 cm

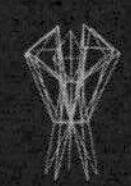

project_029
model_79
iGuzzini Lighting
Iberian Headquarters,
Sant Cugat del Vallès,
Spain
EC2020-2-AR22
Centre Pompidou
Permanent Collection

Enamelled
Welded Wire
22 x 15 x
15 cm

project_029
model_80
iGuzzini Lighting
Iberian Headquarters,
Sant Cugat del Vallès,
Spain
EC2020-2-AR45
Centre Pompidou
Permanent Collection

Enamelled
Welded Wire
25 x 50 x
55 cm

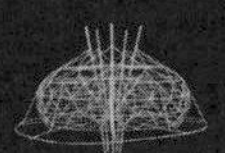

project_029
model_81
iGuzzini Lighting
Iberian Headquarters,
Sant Cugat del Vallès,
Spain
EC2020-2-AR27
Centre Pompidou
Permanent Collection

Enamelled
Welded Wire
20 x 35 x
25 cm

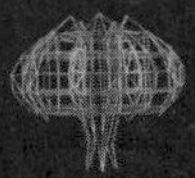

project_029
model_82
iGuzzini Lighting
Iberian Headquarters,
Sant Cugat del Vallès,
Spain
EC2020-2-AR23
Centre Pompidou
Permanent Collection

Nickel Plated Welded Wire
19 x 21 x 21 cm

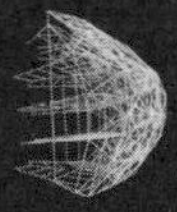

project_029
model_83
iGuzzini Lighting
Iberian Headquarters,
Sant Cugat del Vallès,
Spain
EC2020-2-AR79
Centre Pompidou
Permanent Collection

Enamelled Welded Wire
45x40x60 cm

project_029
model_84
iGuzzini Lighting
Iberian Headquarters,
Sant Cugat del Vallès,
Spain
EC2020-2-AR26
Centre Pompidou
Permanent Collection

Resine Plated Steel
167 x 63 x 63 cm

project_029
model_85
iGuzzini Lighting
Iberian Headquarters,
Sant Cugat del Vallès,
Spain
EC2020-2-AR25
Centre Pompidou
Permanent Collection

Zinc Plated Welded Wire, Wood
75x72x105 cm

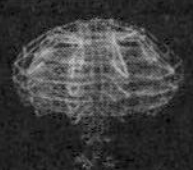

project_029
model_86_DHUB
iGuzzini Lighting
Iberian Headquarters,
Sant Cugat del Vallès,
Spain

scale_1:150
Zinc Plated Welded Wire
25x26x24 cm

progress

roject_030 / models_01 - 28

e Cloud Andorra Telecom Headquarters,
dorra La Vella, Andorra
°30'29"N 01°31'57"E
ges 8, 25-26, 162-171, 208, 382-383

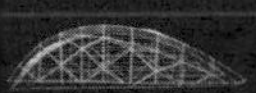

project_030
model_01
The Cloud
Andorra Telecom
Headquarters,
Andorra La Vella,
Andorra

Wood
95x45x32 cm

project_030
model_02
The Cloud
Andorra Telecom
Headquarters,
Andorra La Vella,
Andorra

Wood
29x54x61,5 cm

project_030
model_03
The Cloud
Andorra Telecom
Headquarters,
Andorra La Vella,
Andorra

Wood

project_030
model_04
The Cloud
Andorra Telecom
Headquarters,
Andorra La Vella,
Andorra

Enamelled Welded Wire
40x31x5 cm

project_030
model_05
The Cloud
Andorra Telecom
Headquarters,
Andorra La Vella,
Andorra

Wood, Cardboard
51x15x34 cm

project_030
model_06
The Cloud
Andorra Telecom
Headquarters,
Andorra La Vella,
Andorra

Wood
27x15x56 cm

project_030
model_07
The Cloud
Andorra Telecom
Headquarters,
Andorra La Vella,
Andorra

Wood
79x111x15 cm

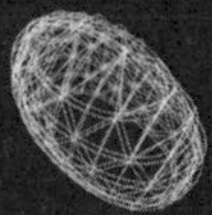

project_030
model_08
The Cloud
Andorra Telecom
Headquarters,
Andorra La Vella,
Andorra

Enamelled Welded Wire
52x28x34 cm

project_030
model_09
The Cloud
Andorra Telecom
Headquarters,
Andorra La Vella,
Andorra

Wood
19x30x25 cm

project_030
model_10
The Cloud
Andorra Telecom
Headquarters,
Andorra La Vella,
Andorra

Canvas
1x16x12 cm

project_030
model_11
The Cloud
Andorra Telecom
Headquarters,
Andorra La Vella,
Andorra

Canvas
5x2x12 cm

project_030
model_12
The Cloud
Andorra Telecom
Headquarters,
Andorra La Vella,
Andorra

White Cardboard
55x32x14.5 cm

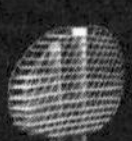

project_030
model_13
The Cloud
Andorra Telecom
Headquarters,
Andorra La Vella,
Andorra

White Cardboard, Welded Wire
45x11,5x36 cm

project_030
model_14
The Cloud
Andorra Telecom
Headquarters,
Andorra La Vella,
Andorra

White Cardboard, Welded Wire
76x58x20 cm

project_030
model_15
The Cloud
Andorra Telecom
Headquarters,
Andorra La Vella,
Andorra

Wood, White Cardboard
18x80x1,5 cm

project_030
model_16
The Cloud
Andorra Telecom
Headquarters,
Andorra La Vella,
Andorra

Paper, Cardboard
42.5x30x7.5 cm

project_030
model_17
The Cloud
Andorra Telecom
Headquarters,
Andorra La Vella,
Andorra

Cardboard
48x28x31.5 cm

project_030
model_18
The Cloud
Andorra Telecom
Headquarters,
Andorra La Vella,
Andorra

White Cardboard
21.5x28x8.5 cm

project_030
model_19
The Cloud
Andorra Telecom
Headquarters,
Andorra La Vella,
Andorra

Wood
15x12.5x2.5 cm

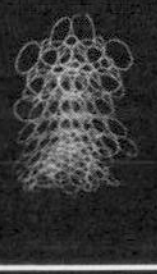

project_030
model_20
The Cloud
Andorra Telecom
Headquarters,
Andorra La Vella,
Andorra

Enamelled Welded Wire
28x20x48 cm

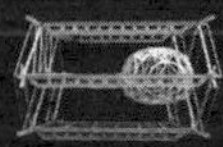

project_030
model_21
The Cloud
Andorra Telecom
Headquarters,
Andorra La Vella,
Andorra

Welded Wire
95x80x58 cm

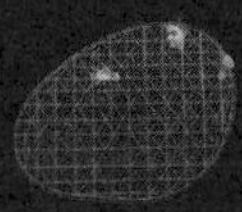

project_030
model_22_DHUB
The Cloud
Andorra Telecom
Headquarters,
Andorra La Vella,
Andorra

Enamelled Welded Wire
165x 135x50 cm

project_030
model_23
The Cloud
Andorra Telecom
Headquarters,
Andorra La Vella,
Andorra
EC2020-2-AR54
Pompidou Collection

Zinc Plated Welded Wire
61x77x32 cm

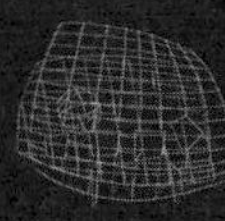

project_030
model_24
The Cloud
Andorra Telecom
Headquarters,
Andorra La Vella,
Andorra
EC2020-2-AR52
Pompidou Collection

Enamelled Welded Wire
33x38x11 cm

project_030
model_25
The Cloud
Andorra Telecom Headquarters, Andorra La Vella, Andorra
EC2020-2-AR53
Pompidou Collection

Zinc Plated Welded Wire
61 x 77 x 20 cm

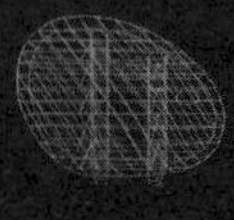

project_030
model_26
The Cloud
Andorra Telecom Headquarters, Andorra La Vella, Andorra
EC2020-2-AR55
Pompidou Collection

Nickel Plated Welded Wire
25 x 31,5 x 10 cm

project_030
model_27
The Cloud
Andorra Telecom Headquarters, Andorra La Vella, Andorra
EC2020-2-AR55
Pompidou Collection

Wood
170x180x50 cm

project_030
model_28_DHUB
The Cloud
Andorra Telecom Headquarters, Andorra La Vella, Andorra

scale_1:250
Zinc Plated Welded Wire
31x9x23cm

2017

project_031 / models_01 - 04

Nebula Caixa Forum, Valencia, Spain
39°27'14"N 00°20'59"W
pages 9, 26, 41, 159-161

project_031
model_01
Nebula Caixa Forum, Valencia, Spain

Plexiglas

project_031
model_02
Nebula Caixa Forum, Valencia, Spain

Plexiglas, Wood

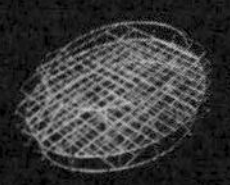

project_031
model_03
Nebula Caixa Forum, Valencia, Spain

Zinc Plated Welded Wire

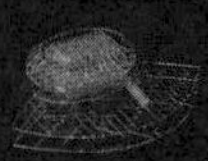

project_031
model_04_DHUB
Nebula Caixa Forum, Valencia, Spain

scale_1:300
Zinc Plated Welded Wire
31x17x13cm

2015

project_032 / models_01 - 02

Palau Sant Jordi VIP Lounge, Barcelona, Spain
41°21'45"N 02°09'09"E
pages 9, 26, 284-285

project_032
model_01
Palau Sant Jordi VIP Lounge, Barcelona, Spain

Cardboard, Wood

project_032
model_02
Palau Sant Jordi VIP Lounge, Barcelona, Spain

Cardboard, Wood
9x12x16,5 cm

2017 - 2019

project_033 / models_01 - 08

Embruixabruixes Attraction at Tibidabo Amusement Park, Barcelona, Spain
41°25'16"N 02°07'11"E
pages 9, 26, 335

project_033
model_01
Embruixabruixes Attraction at Tibidabo Amusement Park, Barcelona, Spain

Enamelled Welded Wire
80x4x12,5 cm

project_033
model_02
Embruixabruixes Attraction at Tibidabo Amusement Park, Barcelona, Spain

Enamelled Welded Wire
83x24x14 cm

project_033
model_03
Embruixabruixes Attraction at Tibidabo Amusement Park, Barcelona, Spain

Enamelled Welded Wire
19x14x12 cm

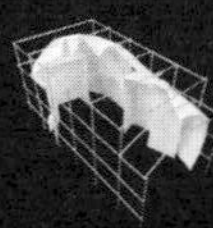

project_033
model_04
Embruixabruixes Attraction at Tibidabo Amusement Park, Barcelona, Spain

Enamelled Welded Wire, Cardboard

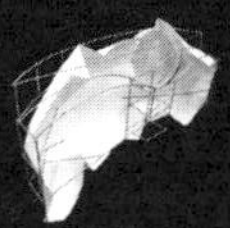

project_033
model_05
Embruixabruixes Attraction at Tibidabo Amusement Park, Barcelona, Spain

Enamelled Welded Wire, Cardboard

project_033
model_06
Embruixabruixes Attraction at Tibidabo Amusement Park, Barcelona, Spain

Enamelled Welded Wire, Cardboard

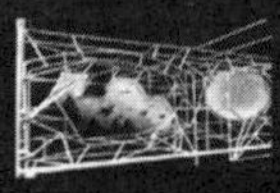

project_033
model_07
Embruixabruixes Attraction at Tibidabo Amusement Park, Barcelona, Spain

Enamelled Welded Wire, Cardboard

project_033
model_08
Embruixabruixes Attraction at Tibidabo Amusement Park, Barcelona, Spain

Enamelled Welded Wire, Cardboard

2013

project_034 / models_01 - 07

Brazilian Antarctic Station, South Sethland Islands, Antarctica
62°05'06"S 58°23'28"W
pages 8, 26, 41, 159, 208, 403

project_034
model_01
Brazilian Antarctic Station, South Sethland Islands, Antarctica

Wood
70,5x29x24 cm

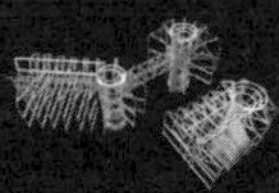

project_034
model_02
Brazilian Antarctic Station, South Sethland Islands, Antarctica

Wood, Pape
69x47x28 cm

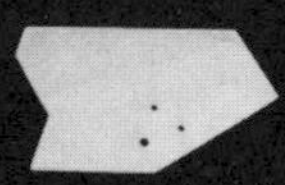

project_034
model_03
Brazilian Antarctic Station, South Sethland Islands, Antarctica

Textile, Wood
55x34x9 cm

project_034
model_04
Brazilian Antarctic Station, South Sethland Islands, Antarctica

Wood
45x24x21 cm

project_034
model_05
Brazilian Antarctic Station, South Sethland Islands, Antarctica

Wood, Paper
21x20x20
18x20x20 cm

project_034
model_07_DHUB
Brazilian Antarctic Station, South Sethland Islands, Antarctica

scale_1:200
Zinc Plated Welded Wir
34x22x9cm

2017 - 2021
project_035 / models_01 - 02
Cucadellum Funicular to Tibidabo Amusement Park, Barcelona, Spain
41°24'59"N 02°07'51"E
pages 8, 27, 40, 112-121, 286-293

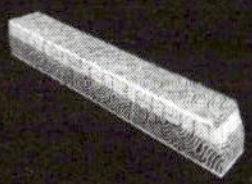
project_035
model_01
Cucadellum Funicular to Tibidabo Amusement Park, Barcelona, Spain
Printed Paper
27x5x5 cm

project_035
model_02_DHUB
Cucadellum Funicular to Tibidabo Amusement Park, Barcelona, Spain
scale_1:25
Zinc Plated Welded Wire

2017 - 2019
project_036 / models_01 - 04
Welcome Square and Headquarters at Tibidabo Amusement Park, Barcelona, Spain
41°25'19"N 02°07'09"E
pages 9, 27, 252-253

project_036
model_01
Welcome Square and Headquarters at Tibidabo Amusement Park, Barcelona, Spain
Wood
39x28x19,5 cm

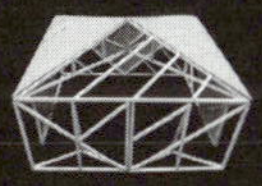
project_036
model_02
Welcome Square and Headquarters at Tibidabo Amusement Park, Barcelona, Spain
Wood, Cardboard
24x20,5x18 cm

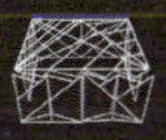
project_036
model_03
Welcome Square and Headquarters at Tibidabo Amusement Park, Barcelona, Spain
Enamelled Welded Wire
12,5x10,5x9 cm

project_036
model_04
Welcome Square and Headquarters at Tibidabo Amusement Park, Barcelona, Spain
Enamelled Welded Wire
17x22x10 cm

2014
project_037 / models_01 - 08
Passenger Terminal and Service Centre, Kinmen, Taiwan
24°25'3"N 118°17'36"E
pages 8, 27, 41, 171-177, 208-211, 383

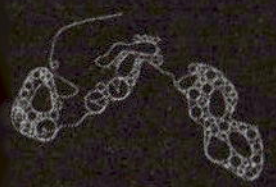
project_037
model_01
Passenger Terminal and Service Centre, Kinmen, Taiwan
Enamelled Welded Wire
56x30x4 cm

project_037
model_02
Passenger Terminal and Service Centre, Kinmen, Taiwan
Enamelled Welded Wire
(42x42x42) cm

project_037
model_03
Passenger Terminal and Service Centre, Kinmen, Taiwan
Wood
170x170x20 cm

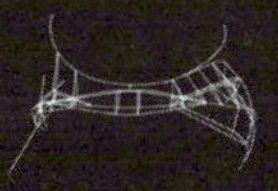
project_037
model_04
Passenger Terminal and Service Centre, Kinmen, Taiwan
Enamelled Welded Wire
43x26x12 cm

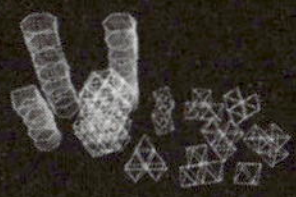
project_037
model_05
Passenger Terminal and Service Centre, Kinmen, Taiwan
Enamelled Welded Wire
63x30x30 cm

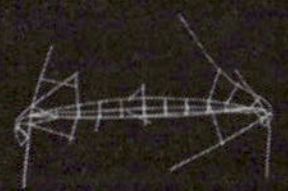
project_037
model_06
Passenger Terminal and Service Centre, Kinmen, Taiwan
Enamelled Welded Wire
50x28x17 cm

project_037
model_08
Passenger Terminal and Service Centre, Kinmen, Taiwan
EC2020-2-AR78 Centre Pompidou Permanent Collection
Enamelled Welded Wire
25x40x40 cm

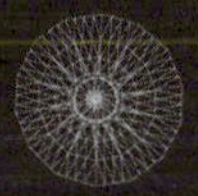
project_037
model_09
Passenger Terminal and Service Centre, Kinmen, Taiwan
EC2020-2-AR78 Centre Pompidou Permanent Collection
Enamelled Welded Wire
25x40x40 cm

project_037
model_10_DHUB
Passenger Terminal and Service Centre, Kinmen, Taiwan
scale_1:300
Zinc Plated Welded Wire
24x24x10 cm

2017 - 2022
project_038 / models_01 - 12
Can Vidalet Market, Esplugues de Llobregat, Spain
41°22'26"N 02°06'02"E
pages 8, 27, 130, 132-133, 136, 232-233, 262-265, 383

project_038
model_01
Can Vidalet Market, Esplugues de Llobregat, Spain
Wood
43x43x3 cm

project_038
model_03
Can Vidalet Market, Esplugues de Llobregat, Spain
Wood
35x35x28 cm

project_038
model_04
Can Vidalet Market, Esplugues de Llobregat, Spain
Wood
24x24x5 cm

project_038
model_05
Can Vidalet Market, Esplugues de Llobregat, Spain
Wood
132x95x28 cm

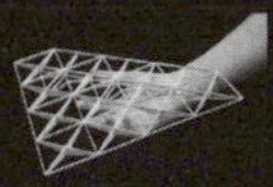
project_038
model_06
Can Vidalet Market, Esplugues de Llobregat, Spain
Wood
26,5x26,5x2 cm

project_038
model_07
Can Vidalet Market, Esplugues de Llobregat, Spain
Wood
74x117x5 (h=20cm with pilars) cm

project_038
model_08
Can Vidalet Market, Esplugues de Llobregat, Spain
Plaster
81x29x42 cm

project_038
model_09
Can Vidalet Market, Esplugues de Llobregat, Spain
Wood
60x24x15 cm

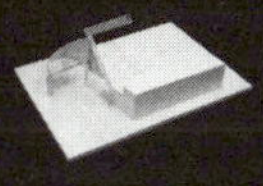
project_038
model_10
Can Vidalet Market, Esplugues de Llobregat, Spain
Wood
42x30x23 cm

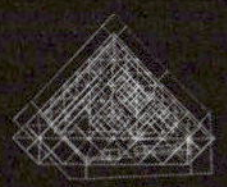
project_038
model_11
Can Vidalet Market, Esplugues de Llobregat, Spain
EC2020-2-AR57 Centre Pompidou Permanent Collection
Nickel Plated Welded Wire
9x28x33 cm

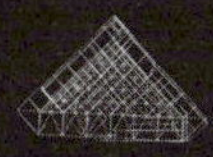
project_038
model_12_DHUB
Can Vidalet Market, Esplugues de Llobregat, Spain
scale_1:300
Zinc Plated Welded Wire
30x19x5cm

2017 - 2022

project_039 / models_01 - 04

La Plana Market, Esplugues de Llobregat, Spain
41°22'22"N 02°05'03"E
pages 8, 28, 131, 134-136, 208-211, 266-267, 383

project_039
model_01
La Plana Market, Esplugues de Llobregat, Spain
Wood
87x112x33 cm

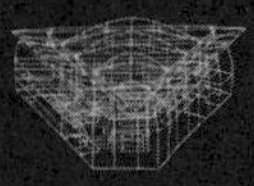

project_039
model_02
La Plana Market, Esplugues de Llobregat, Spain
EC2020-2-AR64 Centre Pompidou Permanent Collection
Nickel Plated Welded Wire
11,5x25x35 cm

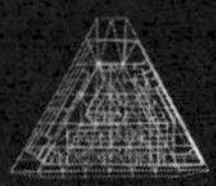

project_039
model_03_DHUB
La Plana Market, Esplugues de Llobregat, Spain
scale_1:250
Zinc Plated Welded Wire
21x26x6cm

project_039
model_04
La Plana Market, Esplugues de Llobregat, Spain
Wood

2015 - 2016

project_040 / models_01 - 07

New Camp Nou FC Barcelona Stadium, Barcelona, Spain
41°22'51"N 02°07'22"E
pages 9, 28, 41, 150-158, 382

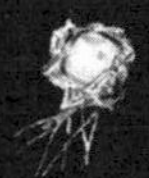

project_040
model_01
New Camp Nou FC Barcelona Stadium, Barcelona, Spain
Cardboard, Paper
65x50,5x4 cm

project_040
model_02
New Camp Nou FC Barcelona Stadium, Barcelona, Spain
Enamelled Welded Wire

project_040
model_03
New Camp Nou FC Barcelona Stadium, Barcelona, Spain
EC2020-2-AR51 Centre Pompidou Permanent Collection
Enamelled Welded Wire
10x27x24 cm

project_040
model_04_DHUB
New Camp Nou FC Barcelona Stadium, Barcelona, Spain
scale_ 1:1000
Zinc Plated Welded Wire
48x31x8 cm

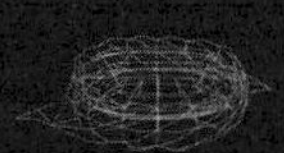

project_040
model_05
New Camp Nou FC Barcelona Stadium, Barcelona, Spain
EC2020-2-AR51 Centre Pompidou Permanent Collection
Enamelled Welded Wire

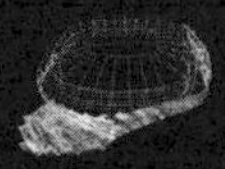

project_040
model_06
New Camp Nou FC Barcelona Stadium, Barcelona, Spain
Enamelled Welded Wire

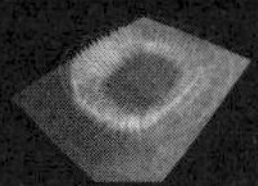

project_040
model_07
New Camp Nou FC Barcelona Stadium, Barcelona, Spain
Plexiglass Paper, Styrofoam
68x92x22 cm

2013

project_041 / models_01 - 02

Andersen House of Fairytales Museum, Odense, Denmark
55°23'53"N 10°23'25"E
pages 28, 40

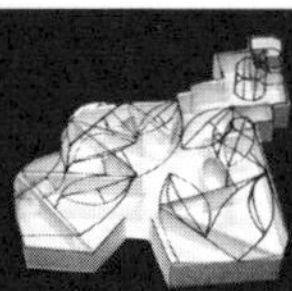

project_041
model_01
Andersen House of Fairytales Museum, Odense, Denmark
Cardboard, Enamelled Welded Wire
22x20x6 cm

project_041
model_02_DHUB
Andersen House of Fairytales Museum, Odense, Denmark
scale_1:500
Zinc Plated Welded Wire
19x21x4cm

2014

project_042 / model_01

Intra Pavilion at Marmomac Fair, Verona, Italy
45°26'19"N 10°59'34"E
pages 28

project_042
model_01
Intra Pavilion at Marmomac Fair, Verona, Italy
Wood
95x51x29,5 cm

2010

project_043 / models_01 - 03

Main Square and Public Space, Colombes, France
48°54'55"N 02°13'43"E
pages 28, 40

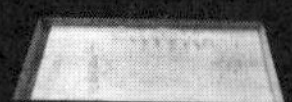

project_043
model_01
Main Square and Public Space, Colombes, France
Enamelled Welded Wire
78x32x10 cm

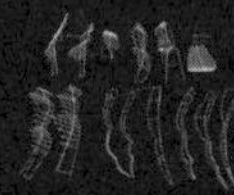

project_043
model_02
Main Square and Public Space, Colombes, France
Enamelled Welded Wire

project_043
model_03
Main Square and Public Space, Colombes, France
Enamelled Welded Wire

2009

project_044 / models_01 - 09

Auditorium, Elx, Spain
38°16'14"N 00°42'28"W
pages 28-29, 137

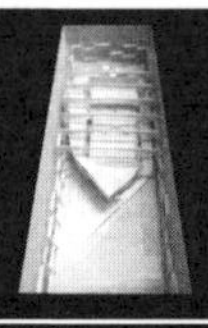

project_044
model_01
Auditorium, Elx, Spain
Wood
130x50x27 cm

project_044
model_02
Auditorium, Elx, Spain
Welded Wire, Cardboard
63x21x16 cm

project_044
model_03
Auditorium, Elx, Spain
Welded Wire, Cardboard
40x13x8 cm

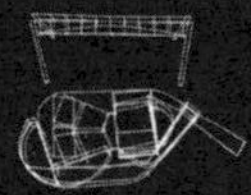

project_044
model_04
Auditorium, Elx, Spain
Enamelled Welded Wire
25x20x12 cm

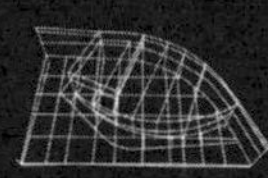

project_044
model_05
Auditorium, Elx, Spain
Enamelled Welded Wire
29x17x7 cm

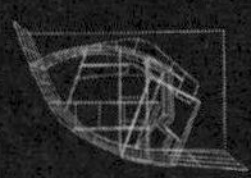

project_044
model_06
Auditorium, Elx, Spain
Enamelled Welded Wire
33x17x8 cm

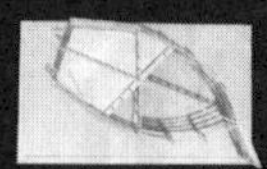

project_044
model_07
Auditorium, Elx, Spain
Wood
24x41x9 cm

project_044
model_08
Auditorium, Elx, Spain
Wood
36x31x11 cm

project_044
model_09_DHUB
Auditorium, Elx, Spain
scale_1:300
Zinc Plated Welded Wire
29x14x7cm

2011
project_045 / models_01 - 02
AZIZ Production and Recording Centre, Dakar, Senegal
14°43'02"N 17°28'04"W
pages 29

project_045
model_01
AZIZ Production and Recording Centre, Dakar, Senegal
Wood
52x92x8 cm

project_045
model_02
AZIZ Production and Recording Centre, Dakar, Senegal
Wood, Enamelled Welded Wire
100x53x20 cm

2009
project_046 / models_01 - 03
Isabella I Square, Girona, Spain
41°58'43"N 02°49'36"E
pages 29

project_046
model_01
Isabella I Square, Girona, Spain
Wood
50x55x13 cm each

project_046
model_02
Isabella I Square, Girona, Spain
Wood, Cardboard
88x68x14 cm

project_046
model_03
Isabella I Square, Girona, Spain
Wood, Cardboard
100x70x22 cm

2010
project_047 / models_01 - 02
Port Pavilion, Bilbao, Spain
43°15'46"N 02°56'06"W
pages 29

project_047
model_01
Port Pavilion, Bilbao, Spain
Wood
51x22x7,5 cm

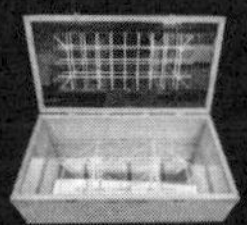

project_047
model_02
Port Pavilion, Bilbao, Spain
Wood, Cardboard
63x32x33 cm

2011
project_048 / models_01 - 03
Research Centre and Public Space at CERN, Geneva, Switzerland
46°13'59"N 06°03'20"E
pages 8, 29

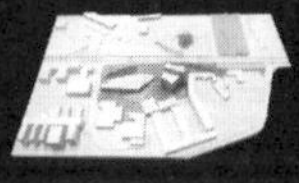

project_048
model_01
Research Centre and Public Space at CERN, Geneva, Switzerland
Wood
57x38x6,5 cm

project_048
model_02
Research Centre and Public Space at CERN, Geneva, Switzerland
Wood
50x79x19 cm

project_048
model_03
Research Centre and Public Space at CERN, Geneva, Switzerland
Enamelled Welded Wire
65x12x4 cm

2010
project_049 / model_01
Nou Barris Civic Centre, Barcelona, Spain
41°27'13"N 02°11'15"E
pages 29

project_049
model_01
Nou Barris Civic Centre, Barcelona, Spain
Wood, Cardboard, Paper
65x40x15 cm

2018
project_050 / models_01 - 03
Les Rotes Public Space, Banyoles, Spain
42°07'17"N 2°45'39"E
pages 29

project_050
model_01
Les Rotes Public Space, Banyoles, Spain
Wood
23x60x11,5 cm

project_050
model_02
Les Rotes Public Space, Banyoles, Spain
Wood, Enamelled Welded Wire
13X8X7,5 cm

project_050
model_03
Les Rotes Public Space, Banyoles, Spain
Enamelled Welded Wire
25,5x8x16,5 cm

2008
project_051 / models_01 - 03
Lycée Français School, Madrid, Spain
40°31'45"N 03°37'42"W
pages 29

project_051
model_01
Lycée Français School, Madrid, Spain
Cardboard, Paper
95x72x27 cm

project_051
model_02
Lycée Français School, Madrid, Spain
Wood, Welded Wire
30x44x20 cm

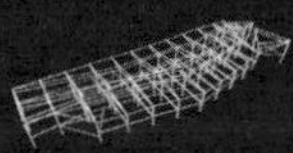

project_051
model_03
Lycée Français School, Madrid, Spain
Enamelled Welded Wire
90x31x12 cm

2015
project_052 / model_01
Fire Station, Vilafranca Del Penedès, Spain
41°20'48"N 01°41'48"E
pages 29

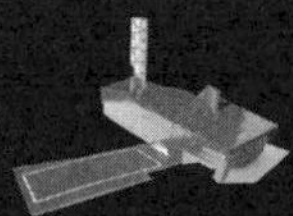

project_052
model_01
Fire Station, Vilafranca Del Penedès, Spain
Cardboard
38x82x15 cm

2018

project_053 / model_01

City Centre Housing, Mataró, Spain
41°32'25"N 02°26'39"E
pages 30

project_053
model_01
City Centre Housing, Mataró, Spain

Wood, Grey Cardboard, Paper
34x46x10 cm

2003

project_054 / models_01 - 04

Nam June Paik Art Centre, Seoul Capital Area, South Korea
37°16'09"N 127°06'37"E
pages 30, 41

project_054
model_01
Nam June Paik Art Centre, Seoul Capital Area, South Korea

Wood , Paper
34x46x10 cm

project_054
model_02
Nam June Paik Art Centre, Seoul Capital Area, South Korea

Wood , Paper
34x46x10 cm

project_054
model_03
Nam June Paik Art Centre, Seoul Capital Area, South Korea

Wood, Welded Wire
42x67x18 cm

project_054
model_04
Nam June Paik Art Centre, Seoul Capital Area, South Korea

Enamelled Welded Wire
20x9x8,5 cm

2011

project_055 / models_01 - 02

Bridge Pavilion Museum at Expo 2008, Zaragoza, Spain
41°40'01"N 00°54'18"W
pages 30

project_055
model_01
Bridge Pavilion Museum at Expo 2008, Zaragoza, Spain

Welded Wire
34x46x10 cm

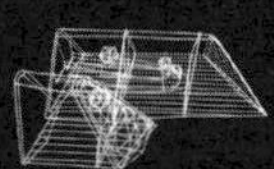

project_055
model_02
Bridge Pavilion Museum at Expo 2008, Zaragoza, Spain

Enamelled Welded Wire
66x41x24 cm

2008

project_056 / models_01 - 03

University Building, Günzburg, Germany
48°27'12"N 10°16'39"E
pages 30

project_056
model_01
University Building, Günzburg, Germany

Welded Wire, Cardboard
61x75x23 cm

project_056
model_02
University Building, Günzburg, Germany

Welded Wire, Cardboard
82.5x59x16 cm

project_056
model_03
University Building, Günzburg, Germany

Enamelled Welded Wire
26x14x9 cm

2002

project_057 / models_01 - 10

Thalassotherapy Centre, Gijón, Spain
43°31'46"N 05°40'38"W
pages 30

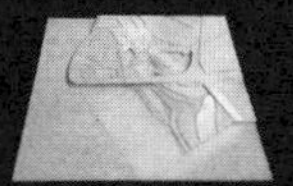

project_057
model_01
Thalassotherapy Centre,, Gijón, Spain

Plexiglass, Wood
58x52x4 cm

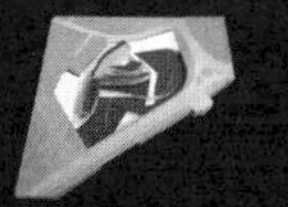

project_057
model_02
Thalassotherapy Centre, Gijón, Spain

Wood, Paper
51x51x8 cm

project_057
model_03
Thalassotherapy Centre, Gijón, Spain

White Matte Paper
24x10x8 cm

project_057
model_04
Thalassotherapy Centre, Gijón, Spain

Enamelled Welded Wire, Cardboard
33x41.5x15 cm

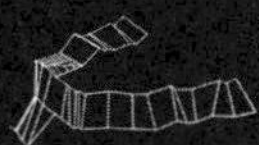

project_057
model_05
Thalassotherapy Centre, Gijón, Spain

Enamelled Welded Wire
25x18x5 cm

project_057
model_06
Thalassotherapy Centre, Gijón, Spain

Enamelled Welded Wire
22x11x4 cm

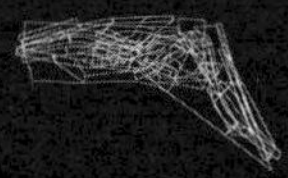

project_057
model_07
Thalassotherapy Centre, Gijón, Spain

Enamelled Welded Wire
38x27x5 cm

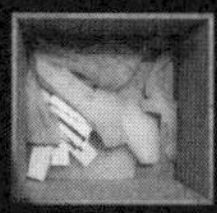

project_057
model_08
Thalassotherapy Centre, Gijón, Spain

Translucent Glass
37.5x34x13 cm

project_057
model_09
Thalassotherapy Centre, Gijón, Spain

Enamelled Welded Wire
36x29x7 cm

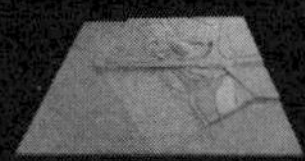

project_057
model_10
Thalassotherapy Centre, Gijón, Spain

Wood
58x52x6 cm

2016

project_058 / models_01 - 02

Sport Centre, Figueres, Spain
42°16'00"N 02°57'00"E
pages 30

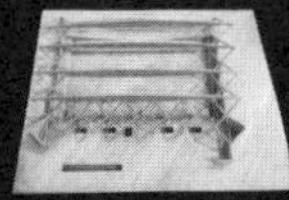

project_058
model_01
Sport Centre, Figueres, Spain

Wood
31x39x5 cm

project_058
model_02
Sport Centre, Figueres, Spain

Wood
32x64x46 cm

2008

project_059 / models_01 - 02

La Nau Disco, Girona, Spain
41°59'00"N 02°49'00"E
pages 30-31

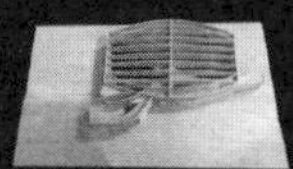

project_059
model_01
La Nau Disco, Girona, Spain

Wood
18x28x6 cm

project_059
model_02
La Nau Disco, Girona, Spain
Wood
49x35x7 cm

2008

project_060 / models_01 - 02

Sports Hall, Porqueres, Spain
42°07'19"N 02°44'53"E
pages 31

project_060
model_01
Sports Hall, Porqueres, Spain
Wood
32x35x5 cm

project_060
model_02
Sports Hall, Porqueres, Spain
Paper, Cardboard
35x32x6 cm

2007

project_061 / models_01 - 08

Llull Travel Lodge Hotel at 22@, Barcelona, Spain
41°23'00" N 02°11'00" E
pages 31, 129

project_061
model_01
Llull Travel Lodge Hotel at 22@, Barcelona, Spain
Wood
22x12x6 cm

project_061
model_02
Llull Travel Lodge Hotel at 22@, Barcelona, Spain
Wood
45,5x25x12 cm

project_061
model_03
Llull Travel Lodge Hotel at 22@, Barcelona, Spain
Enamelled Welded Wire
43x23x13 cm

project_061
model_04
Llull Travel Lodge Hotel at 22@, Barcelona, Spain
Wood
14x23x20 cm

project_061
model_05
Llull Travel Lodge Hotel at 22@, Barcelona, Spain
Enamelled Welded Wire
46x48x16 cm

project_061
model_07
Llull Travel Lodge Hotel at 22@, Barcelona, Spain
Plaster
29x52x13 cm

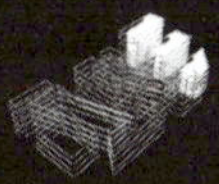

project_061
model_08
Llull Travel Lodge Hotel at 22@, Barcelona, Spain
Wood
22x11x4,5 cm

2008

project_062 / models_01 - 05

Llagostera Library, Girona, Spain
41°59'00"N 02°49'00"E
pages 31

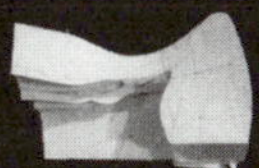

project_062
model_01
Llagostera Library, Girona, Spain
Paper
30x17x12 cm

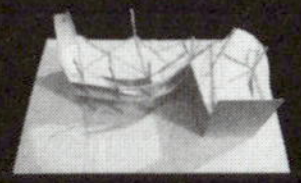

project_062
model_02
Llagostera Library, Girona, Spain
Wood , Paper
31x24x13 cm

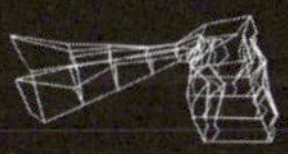

project_062
model_03
Llagostera Library, Girona, Spain
Enamelled Welded Wire
32x18x8 cm

project_062
model_04
Llagostera Library, Girona, Spain
White Cardboard
34x19x13 cm

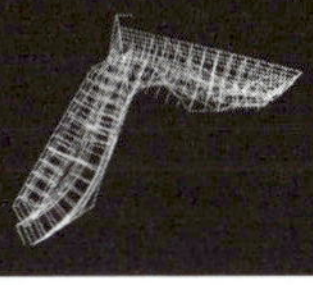

project_062
model_05
Llagostera Library, Girona, Spain
Enamelled Welded Wire
98x53x29 cm

2008

project_063 / models_01 - 02

Folding House, Banyoles, Spain
41°24'48"N 02°12'06"E
pages 31

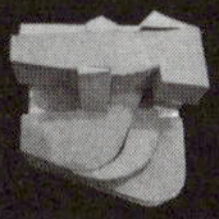

project_063
model_01
Folding House, Banyoles, Spain
Paper
15x16x7 cm

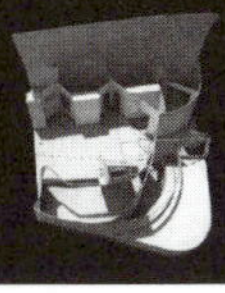

project_063
model_02
Folding House, Banyoles, Spain
Cardboard
26x33,5x18 cm

2013

project_064 / models_01 - 10

Baltic Sea Park, Pärnu, Estonia
58°23'17"N 24°29'54"E
pages 31-32, 111

project_064
model_01
Baltic Sea Park, Pärnu, Estonia
White Matte Paper
15x11x14 cm

project_064
model_02
Baltic Sea Park, Pärnu, Estonia
Enamelled Welded Wire
31x20x7,5 cm

project_064
model_03
Baltic Sea Park, Pärnu, Estonia
Enamelled Welded Wire
31,5x20x5 cm

project_064
model_04
Baltic Sea Park, Pärnu, Estonia
Enamelled Welded Wire
14x8x5 cm

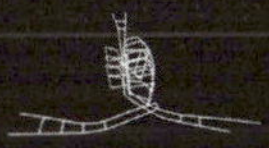

project_064
model_05
Baltic Sea Park, Pärnu, Estonia
Enamelled Welded Wire
21,5x16x4 cm

project_064
model_06
Baltic Sea Park, Pärnu, Estonia
Enamelled Welded Wire
8,5x8,5x5 cm

project_064
model_07
Baltic Sea Park, Pärnu, Estonia
Enamelled Welded Wire
10x8,5x14 cm

project_064
model_08
Baltic Sea Park, Pärnu, Estonia
Enamelled Welded Wire
24x13x9 cm

project_064
model_09
Baltic Sea Park,
Pärnu, Estonia

Enamelled
Welded
Wire
10x6x3 cm

project_064
model_10_DHUB
Baltic Sea Park,
Pärnu, Estonia

scale_1:400
Zinc Plated
Welded
Wire
37x16x9cm

2010

project_065 / model_01

Can Ricart Centre, Barcelona, Spain
41°23'00" N 02°11'00" E
pages 32

project_065
model_01
Can Ricart Centre,
Barcelona, Spain

Wood
107x66x26
cm

2008

project_066 / models_01 - 03

Sport Centre, Blanes, Spain
41°40'332N 2°47'24"E
pages 32

project_066
model_01
Sport Centre, Blanes,
Spain

Wood,
Welded
Wire
60x37x16
cm

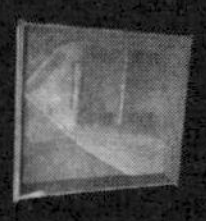

project_066
model_02
Sport Centre, Blanes,
Spain

Wood,
Welded
Wire
82x95x16
cm

project_066
model_03
Sport Centre, Blanes,
Spain

Wood
193x53x19
cm

2019 - 2022

project_067 / model_01

El Forn Museum, Sant Cugat de Sesgarrigues, Spain
41°28'00"N 02°05'00"E
pages 32

project_067
model_01
El Forn Museum,
Sant Cugat de
Sesgarrigues, Spain

Wood
55x24x18
cm

2019 - 2022

project_068 / models_01 - 02

Multiple Sclerosis Foundation Headquarters, Barcelona, Spain
41°22'43"N 2°09'39"E
pages 9, 32, 337

project_068
model_01
Multiple Sclerosis
Foundation
Headquarters,
Barcelona, Spain

Wood,
Printed
Paper
40x53x5,5
cm

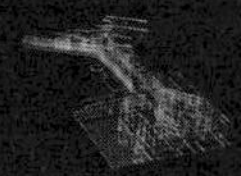

project_068
model_02
Multiple Sclerosis
Foundation
Headquarters,
Barcelona, Spain

scale_1:100
Zinc Plated
Welded
Wire
51x27x7,5
cm

2019 - 2022

project_069 / model_01

Cal Xerta Paper Centre, Sant Pere De Riudebitlles, Spain
41°27'15"N 1°42'13"E
pages 9, 32, 268-269

project_069
model_01
Cal Xerta Paper
Centre,
Sant Pere De
Riudebitlles, Spain

White
Matte
Paper
54x54x43
cm

2008

project_070 / models_01 - 02

Floating House, India
28°36'50"N 77°12'30"E
pages 32

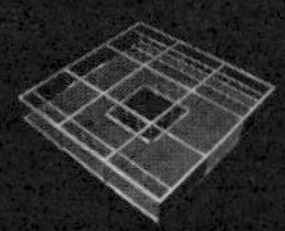

project_070
model_01
Floating House, India

Wood,
Enamelled
Steel,
Paper
110x55x26
cm

project_070
model_02
Floating House, India

Wood,
Cardboard,
Paper
105x137x7
cm

2010

project_071 / model_01

Yablonsky Musical Centre, Puigcerdà, Spain
42°25'54"N 01°55'42"E
pages 32

project_071
model_01
Yablonsky Musical
Centre, Puigcerdà,
Spain

Welded
Wire,
Cardboard
84x45x17,5
cm

2008

project_072 / model_01

Mas Jordà Social Housing, Palafolls, Spain
41°40'09"N 02°45'02"E
pages 32

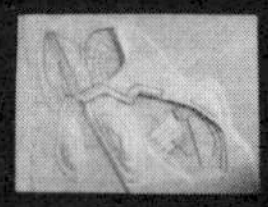

project_072
model_01
Mas Jordà Social
Housing, Palafolls,
Spain

Wood,
Cardboard
35x52x12
cm

2010

project_073 / models_01 - 05

Guggenheim Museum, Helsinki, Finland
60°10'15"N 24°56'15"E
pages 32, 208

project_073
model_01
Guggenheim Museum,
Helsinki, Finland

Wood
27x30x15
cm

project_073
model_02
Guggenheim Museum,
Helsinki, Finland

Enamelled
Welded
Wire
9x5x4 cm

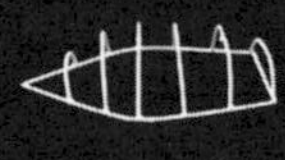

project_073
model_03
Guggenheim Museum,
Helsinki, Finland

Enamelled
Welded
Wire
7,5x4,5x2,5
cm

project_073
model_04_DHUB
Guggenheim Museum,
Helsinki, Finland

scale_1:500
Zinc Plated
Welded
Wire
41x21x5cm

project_073
model_05
Guggenheim Museum,
Helsinki, Finland

Enamelled
Welded
Wire
46x28x5
cm

1992

project_074 / model_01

Cultural Centre, Banyoles, Spain
41°24'48"N 02°12'06"E
pages 32

project_074
model_01
Cultural Centre,
Banyoles, Spain

Wood
65x50x12
cm

2018

project_075 / models_01 - 02

Zizkov Housing, Prague, Czech Republic
50°05'05"N 14°27'21"E
pages 33

project_075
model_01
Zizkov Housing, Prague, Czech Republic
White Matte Paper
120x85x18,5 cm

project_075
model_02
Zizkov Housing, Prague, Czech Republic
Enamelled Welded Wire
35x25x13,5 cm

2015

project_076 / models_01 - 02

Skylight Sports Centre, Port d'Envalira, Andorra
42°30'00"N 01°30'00"E
pages 9, 33

project_076
model_01
Skylight Sports Centre, Port d'Envalira, Andorra
Wood
12,5x36x50 cm

project_076
model_02
Skylight Sports Centre, Port d'Envalira, Andorra
White Cardboard
79x93x31 cm

2017

project_077 / models_01 - 02

KCP Convention Centre, Prague, Czech Republic
50°03'45"N 14°25'42"E
pages 33

2013

project_078 / models_01 - 07

Collider Activity Centre, Sofia, Bulgaria
41°42'00"N 23°19'48"E
pages 33

project_078
model_01
Collider Activity Centre, Sofia, Bulgaria
Enamelled Welded Wire
42x20x8 cm

project_078
model_02
Collider Activity Centre, Sofia, Bulgaria
Enamelled Welded Wire, Cardboard
61x33x14 cm

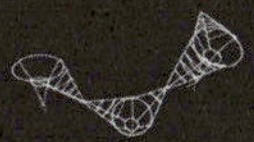

project_078
model_03
Collider Activity Centre, Sofia, Bulgaria
Enamelled Welded Wire
36x30x21 cm

project_078
model_04
Collider Activity Centre, Sofia, Bulgaria
Enamelled Welded Wire
28x18x10 cm

project_078
model_05
Collider Activity Centre, Sofia, Bulgaria
Zinc Plated Welded Wire
117x62x32 cm

project_078
model_06
Collider Activity Centre, Sofia, Bulgaria
3D Print
11,5x14,5x3 cm

project_079
model_02
Boa'an Culture and Art Centre, Shenzhen, China
Enamelled Welded Wire
17x17x41 cm

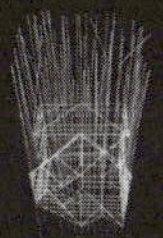

project_079
model_03
Boa'an Culture and Art Centre, Shenzhen, China
Cardboard
12x14x14 cm

2017

project_080 / models_01 - 02

Miño Still Water Confederation Headquarters, Ourense, Spain
42°20'08"N 07°51'51"W
pages 33

project_080
model_01
Miño Still Water Confederation Headquarters, Ourense, Spain
Wood, Welded Wire
60x98x16 cm

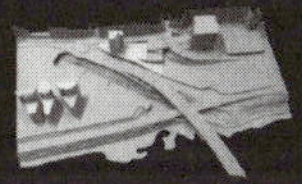

project_080
model_01
Miño Still Water Confederation Headquarters, Ourense, Spain
Wood, Cardboard
88x53x15,5 cm

2014

project_081 / model_01

Spanish Pavilion at Milan Exhibition, Milan, Italy
45°28'01"N 09°11'24"E
pages 33

project_081
model_01
Spanish Pavilion Milan at Exhibition, Milan, Italy
Enamelled Welded Wire
28x14x7 cm

2002

project_083 / model_01

La Salle Library, Barcelona, Spain
41°24'25"N 02°09'17"E
pages 34

project_083
model_01
La Salle Library, Barcelona, Spain
Wood
51x42x20 cm

2001

project_084 / model_01

Braus House, Olot, Spain
42°11'00"N 02°29'00"E
pages 34

project_084
model_01
Braus House, Olot, Spain
Wood
40x47x25 cm

2004 - 2006

project_085 / model_01

America Square and Public Space, L'Hospitalet De Llobregat, Spain
41°21'04"N 02°06'49"E
pages 8, 34

project_085
model_01
America Square and Public Space, L'Hospitalet De Llobregat, Spain
Wood
96x131x5 cm

2016

project_086 / models_01 - 02

Castle Attraction at Tibidabo Amusement Park, Barcelona, Spain
41°25'18"N 02°07'07"E
pages 34

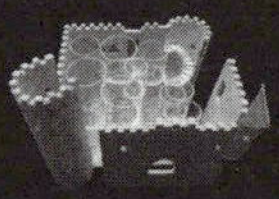

project_086
model_01
Castle Attraction at Tibidabo Amusement Park, Barcelona, Spain
Wood, Plexiglass
47 x 45 x 41 cm

project_086
model_02
Castle Attraction at Tibidabo Amusement Park, Barcelona, Spain
Welded Wire, Cardboard
18 x 14 x 18 cm

2000 - 2002

project_087 / models_01 - 04

Iberia Social Housing, Girona, Spain
41°58'46"N 02°48'52"E
pages 9, 34

project_087
model_01
Iberia Social Housing, Girona, Spain
Wood
47x33x18 cm

project_087
model_02
Iberia Social Housing, Girona, Spain
Wood
35x27x25 cm

project_087
model_03
Iberia Social Housing, Girona, Spain
Wood
20x22x46 cm

project_087
model_04
Iberia Social Housing, Girona, Spain
Wood
34x25x26 cm

2008

project_088 / models_01 - 02

Vilamarí Scout Centre, Barcelona, Spain
41°22'43"N 02°08'58"E
pages 34

project_088
model_01
Vilamarí Scout Centre, Barcelona, Spain
Wood
17,5x21x20 cm

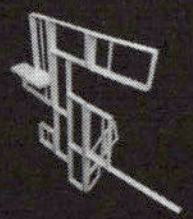

project_088
model_02
Vilamarí Scout Centre, Barcelona, Spain
Wood
40x22x35 cm

2006

project_089 / models_01 - 03

Raval Barceló Hotel, Barcelona, Spain
41° 22' 44.76"N 02°10'10"E
pages 34

project_089
model_01
Raval Barceló Hotel, Barcelona, Spain
Enamelled Welded Wire
8x8x8 cm

project_089
model_02
Raval Barceló Hotel, Barcelona, Spain
Wood
91x104x14 cm

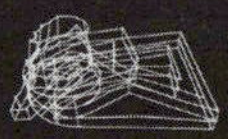

project_089
model_03
Raval Barceló Hotel, Barcelona, Spain
Enamelled Welded Wire
17x13x8,5 cm

2014

project_090 / model_01

Guinardó Market, Barcelona, Spain
41°25'09"N 02°10'41"E
pages 34

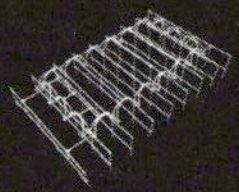

project_090
model_01
Guinardó Market, Barcelona, Spain
Enamelled Welded Wire
23x14x6 cm

2006

project_091 / model_01

Santa Maria Housing, Banyoles, Spain
42°07'08"N 02°45'57"E
pages 34

project_091
model_01
Santa Maria Housing, Banyoles, Spain
Wood , Cardboard
41x41x31 cm

2010

project_092 / model_01

Eixample Hotel, Barcelona, Spain
41°23'26"N 02°09'38"E
pages 34

project_092
model_01
Eixample Hotel, Barcelona, Spain
Wood
25x24x15 cm

2008

project_093 / models_01 - 04

Auditorium, Avila, Spain
40°39'00"N 04°41'00"W
pages 34-35

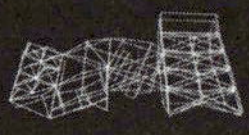

project_093
model_01
Auditorium, Avila, Spain
Enamelled Welded Wire
26x17x6 cm

project_093
model_02
Auditorium, Avila, Spain
Wood
28x22x5 cm

project_93
model_03
Auditorium, Avila, Spain
Wood
27x21x5 cm

project_093
model_04
Auditorium, Avila, Spain
Wood
28x22x5 cm

2007

project_094 / model_01

Elderly People Residence Centre, Granollers, Spain
41°36'00"N 02°00'00"E
pages 35

project_094
model_01
Elderly People Residence Centre, Granollers, Spain
Wood
120x70x21 cm

2008

project_095 / model_01

Social Housing, Bilbao, Spain
43°15'44"N 02°57'12"W
pages 35

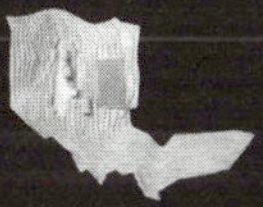

project_095
model_01
Social Housing, Bilbao, Spain
Wood
56x42x6 cm

2008

project_096 / model_01

Library, Pamplona, Spain
42°49'00"N 01°39'00"W
pages 35, 40

project_096
model_01
Library, Pamplona, Spain
Wood
16x13x6 cm

2008

project_097 / model_01

St. Lluis Housing, Palafolls, Spain
41°40'09"N 02°45'02"E
pages 35

project_097
model_01
St. Lluis Housing, Palafolls, Spain
Enamelled Welded Wire
22x10x8 cm

2004

project_098 / model_01

Catalan Pavilion, Guadalajara, Mèxico
20°40'36"N 103°20'51"W
pages 35, 40

project_098
model_01
Catalan Pavilion, Guadalajara, Mexico
Cardboard
85x43x18 cm

2014

project_099 / model_01

Zhengzhou Park, China
34°44'47"N 113°37'31"E
pages 35

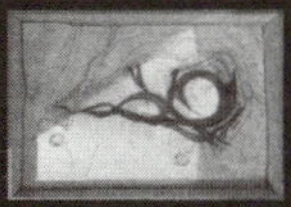

project_099
model_01
Zhengzhou Park, China
Wood
41x61x18 cm

2014

project_100 / model_01

Prčanj Resort, Kotor, Montenegro
42°47'00"N 19°28'00"E
pages 35

project_100
model_01
Prčanj Resort, Kotor, Montenegro
Cardboard
69,5x50x26 cm

2018

project_101 / models_01 - 03

Passeig de la Industria Public Space, Banyoles, Spain
42°06'57"N 02°45'46"E
pages 35

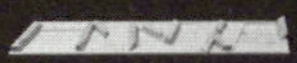

project_101
model_01
Passeig de la Industria Public Space, Banyoles, Spain
Wood
58x10x3 cm

project_101
model_02
Passeig de la Industria Public Space, Banyoles, Spain
Wood
23x10x2 cm

project_101
model_03
Passeig de la Industria Public Space, Banyoles, Spain
Plaster
95x26x6,5 cm

2008

project_102 / models_01 - 02

Eixample Housing, Barcelona, Spain
41°23'16"N 02°09'28"E
pages 35

project_102
model_01
Eixample Housing, Barcelona, Spain
Wood
40x22x10 cm

project_102
model_02
Eixample Housing, Barcelona, Spain
Wood
6x9x7,5 cm

2022

project_103 / models_01 - 04

Tibidabo Amusement Park Sign Landmark, Barcelona, Spain
41°25'17"N 02°07'11"E
pages 35

project_103
model_01
Tibidabo Amusement Park Sign Landmark, Barcelona, Spain
Enamelled Welded Wire
21x29x14,5 cm

project_103
model_02
Tibidabo Amusement Park Sign Landmark, Barcelona, Spain
Cardboard
150x30x5 cm

project_103
model_03
Tibidabo Amusement Park Sign Landmark, Barcelona, Spain
Cardboard
88x23x22,5 cm

project_103
model_04
Tibidabo Amusement Park Sign Landmark, Barcelona, Spain
Wood
25x130x3,5 cm

2022

project_104 / model_01

Gran Via Housing, Barcelona, Spain
41°23'32"N 02°10'19"E
pages 36

project_104
model_01
Gran Via Housing, Barcelona, Spain
Cardboard 64,5x53x4 cm

2019 - 2022

project_105 / model_01

Multiple Sclerosis Foundation Tamarit, Barcelona, Spain
41°22'43"N 2°09'39"E
pages 36

project_105
model_01
Multiple Sclerosis Foundation Tamarit, Barcelona, Spain
Wood, Printed Paper 60x66x5,5 cm

in progress

project_106 / model_01 – 07

Anis del Mono Factory Refurbishment, Badalona, Spain
41°26'33"N 02°14'47"E
pages 8, 36, 362-365

project_106
model_01
Anis del Mono Factory Refurbishment, Badalona, Spain
Wood 90x70x30 cm

project_106
model_02
Anis del Mono Factory Refurbishment, Badalona, Spain
Wood, Welded Wire 90x70x15 cm

project_106
model_03
Anis del Mono Factory Refurbishment, Badalona, Spain
White Matte Paper, Welded Wire

project_106
model_04
Anis del Mono Factory Refurbishment, Badalona, Spain
Cardboard

project_106
model_05
Anis del Mono Factory Refurbishment, Badalona, Spain
Gypsum

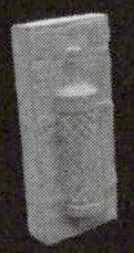

project_106
model_06
Anis del Mono Factory Refurbishment, Badalona, Spain
Gypsum

project_106
model_07
Anis del Mono Factory Refurbishment, Badalona, Spain
Gypsum

2016

project_107 / model_01

National Ceramic Museum, Seoul, South Korea
37°33'36"N 126°59'24"E
pages 9, 36, 40, 160, 208

project_107
model_01_DHUB
National Ceramic Museum, Seoul, South Korea
scale_1:600 Zinc plated Welded Wire 25x19x4cm

2016

project_108 / model_01

Kip Island Auditorium, Riga, Latvia
56°56'56"N 24°06'23"
pages 9, 36

project_108
model_01_DHUB
Kip Island Auditorium, Riga, Latvia
scale_1:200 Zin plated Welded Wire 27x34x14 cm

2009

project_109 / model_01

Market and Cultural Centre, Cuenca, Spain
40°04'18"N 02°08'06"W
pages 36, 40

project_109
model_01
Market and Cultural Centre, Cuenca, Spain
Wood, Cardboard, Welded Wire

in progress

project_110 / models_01 - 63

Vallcarca Industrial Area Transformation, Sitges, Spain
41°14'30"N 01°51'35"E
pages 8, 36-38, 41, 204-207, 366-369

project_110
model_01
Vallcarca Industrial Area Transformation, Sitges, Spain
scale_1:50 Wood

project_110
model_02
Vallcarca Industrial Area Transformation, Sitges, Spain
Wood

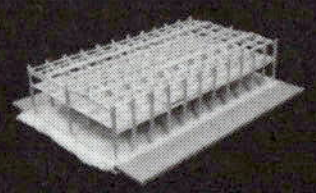

project_110
model_03
Vallcarca Industrial Area Transformation, Sitges, Spain
Wood

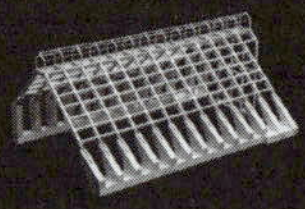

project_110
model_04
Vallcarca Industrial Area Transformation, Sitges, Spain
Wood

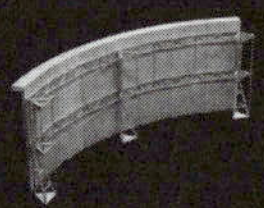

project_110
model_05
Vallcarca Industrial Area Transformation, Sitges, Spain
scale_1:50 Wood

project_110
model_06
Vallcarca Industrial Area Transformation, Sitges, Spain
Wood

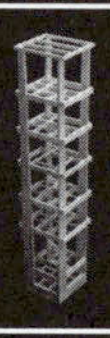

project_110
model_07
Vallcarca Industrial Area Transformation, Sitges, Spain
Wood

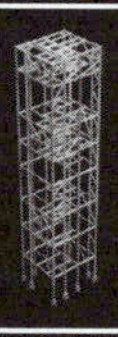

project_110
model_08
Vallcarca Industrial Area Transformation, Sitges, Spain
Wood

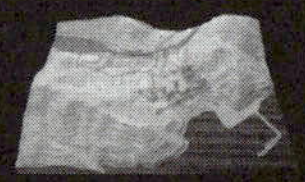

project_110
model_09
Vallcarca Industrial Area Transformation, Sitges, Spain
Wood, Enamelled Welded Wire

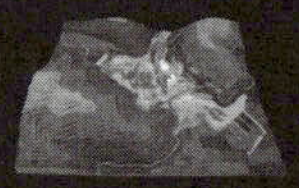

project_110
model_10
Vallcarca Industrial Area Transformation, Sitges, Spain
Wood, Enamelled Welded Wire

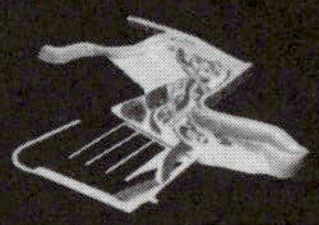

project_110
model_11
Vallcarca Industrial Area Transformation, Sitges, Spain
scale 1:2000 Wood

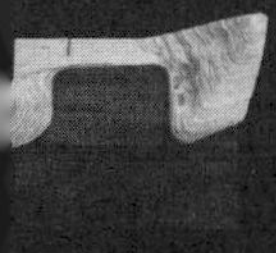

project_110
model_12
Vallcarca Industrial
Area Transformation,
Sitges, Spain
Wood

project_110
model_13
Vallcarca Industrial
Area Transformation,
Sitges, Spain
Welded
Wire

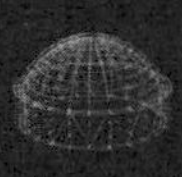

project_110
model_14
Vallcarca Industrial
Area Transformation,
Sitges, Spain
scale_1:200
Welded
Wire

project_110
model_15
Vallcarca Industrial
Area Transformation,
Sitges, Spain
scale_1:200
Welded
Wire

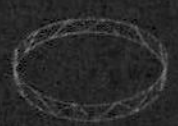

project_110
model_16
Vallcarca Industrial
Area Transformation,
Sitges, Spain
scale_1:200
Welded
Wire

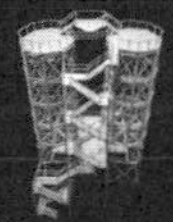

project_110
model_17
Vallcarca Industrial
Area Transformation,
Sitges, Spain
Wood

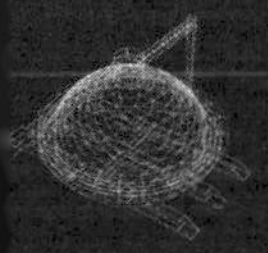

project_110
model_18
Vallcarca Industrial
Area Transformation,
Sitges, Spain
scale_1:200
Enamelled
Welded
Wire

project_110
model_19
Vallcarca Industrial
Area Transformation,
Sitges, Spain
scale_1:50
Welded
Wire

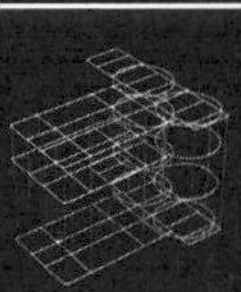

project_110
model_20
Vallcarca Industrial
Area Transformation,
Sitges, Spain
scale_1:200
Enamelled
Welded
Wire

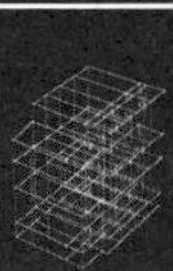

project_110
model_21
Vallcarca Industrial
Area Transformation,
Sitges, Spain
scale_1:200
Enamelled
Welded
Wire

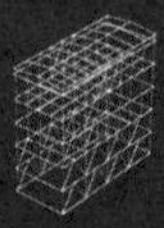

project_110
model_22
Vallcarca Industrial
Area Transformation,
Sitges, Spain
scale_1:200
Enamelled
Welded
Wire

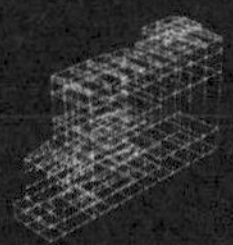

project_110
model_23
Vallcarca Industrial
Area Transformation,
Sitges, Spain
scale_1:200
Enamelled
Welded
Wire

project_110
model_24
Vallcarca Industrial
Area Transformation,
Sitges, Spain
scale_1:200
Enamelled
Welded
Wire

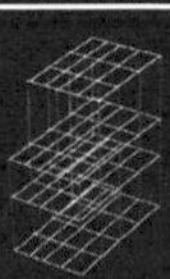

project_110
model_25
Vallcarca Industrial
Area Transformation,
Sitges, Spain
scale_1:200
Enamelled
Welded
Wire

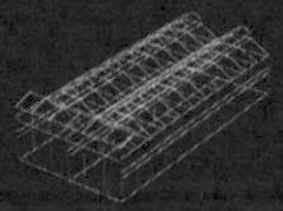

project_110
model_26
Vallcarca Industrial
Area Transformation,
Sitges, Spain
scale_1:200
Enamelled
Welded
Wire

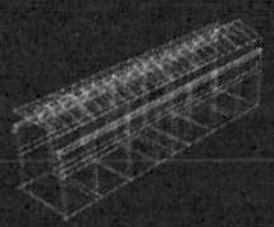

project_110
model_27
Vallcarca Industrial
Area Transformation,
Sitges, Spain
scale_1:200
Enamelled
Welded
Wire

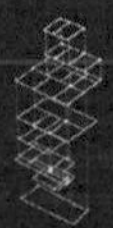

project_110
model_28
Vallcarca Industrial
Area Transformation,
Sitges, Spain
scale_1:200
Enamelled
Welded
Wire

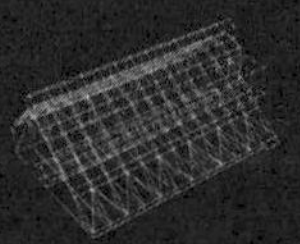

project_110
model_29
Vallcarca Industrial
Area Transformation,
Sitges, Spain
scale_1:200
Enamelled
Welded
Wire

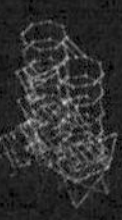

project_110
model_30
Vallcarca Industrial
Area Transformation,
Sitges, Spain
scale_1:200
Enamelled
Welded
Wire

project_110
model_31
Vallcarca Industrial
Area Transformation,
Sitges, Spain
scale_1:200
Enamelled
Welded
Wire

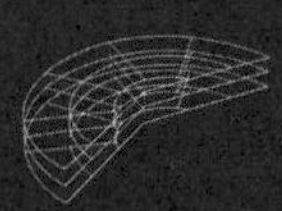

project_110
model_32
Vallcarca Industrial
Area Transformation,
Sitges, Spain
scale_1:200
Enamelled
Welded
Wire

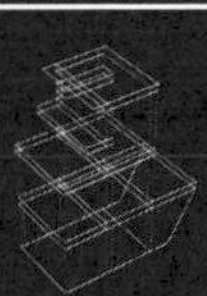

project_110
model_33
Vallcarca Industrial
Area Transformation,
Sitges, Spain
scale_1:200
Enamelled
Welded
Wire

project_110
model_34
Vallcarca Industrial
Area Transformation,
Sitges, Spain
scale_1:200
Enamelled
Welded
Wire

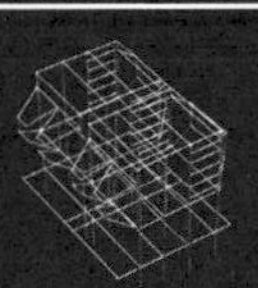

project_110
model_35
Vallcarca Industrial
Area Transformation,
Sitges, Spain
scale_1:200
Enamelled
Welded
Wire

project_110
model_36
Vallcarca Industrial
Area Transformation,
Sitges, Spain
scale_1:200
Enamelled
Welded
Wire

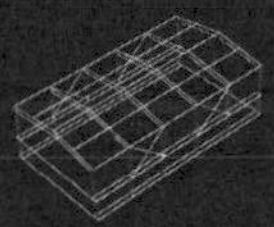

project_110
model_37
Vallcarca Industrial
Area Transformation,
Sitges, Spain
scale_1:200
Enamelled
Welded
Wire

project_110
model_38
Vallcarca Industrial
Area Transformation,
Sitges, Spain
scale_1:200
Enamelled
Welded
Wire

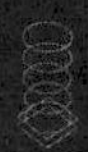

project_110
model_39
Vallcarca Industrial
Area Transformation,
Sitges, Spain
scale_1:200
Enamelled
Welded
Wire

project_110
model_40
Vallcarca Industrial
Area Transformation,
Sitges, Spain
scale_1:200
Enamelled
Welded
Wire

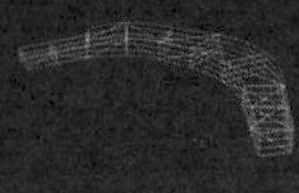

project_110
model_41
Vallcarca Industrial
Area Transformation,
Sitges, Spain
scale_1:200
Enamelled
Welded
Wire

project_110
model_42
Vallcarca Industrial Area Transformation, Sitges, Spain

scale_1:200
Enamelled Welded Wire

project_110
model_43
Vallcarca Industrial Area Transformation, Sitges, Spain

scale_1:200
Enamelled Welded Wire

project_110
model_44
Vallcarca Industrial Area Transformation, Sitges, Spain

scale_1:200
Enamelled Welded Wire

project_110
model_45
Vallcarca Industrial Area Transformation, Sitges, Spain

scale_1:200
Enamelled Welded Wire

project_110
model_46
Vallcarca Industrial Area Transformation, Sitges, Spain

scale_1:200
Enamelled Welded Wire

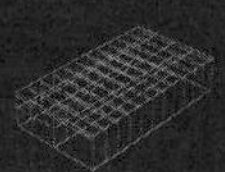

project_110
model_47
Vallcarca Industrial Area Transformation, Sitges, Spain

scale_1:200
Enamelled Welded Wire

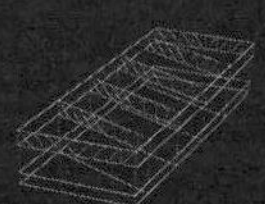

project_110
model_48
Vallcarca Industrial Area Transformation, Sitges, Spain

scale_1:200
Enamelled Welded Wire

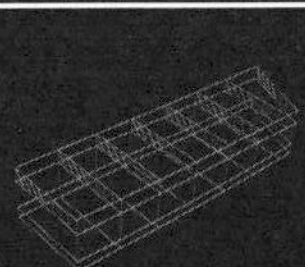

project_110
model_49
Vallcarca Industrial Area Transformation, Sitges, Spain

scale_1:200
Enamelled Welded Wire

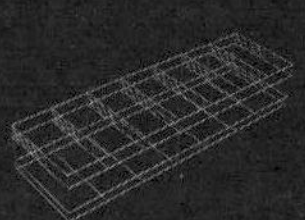

project_110
model_50
Vallcarca Industrial Area Transformation, Sitges, Spain

scale_1:200
Enamelled Welded Wire

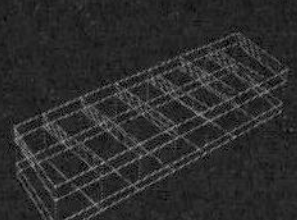

project_110
model_51
Vallcarca Industrial Area Transformation, Sitges, Spain

scale_1:200
Enamelled Welded Wire

project_110
model_52
Vallcarca Industrial Area Transformation, Sitges, Spain

scale_1:200
Enamelled Welded Wire

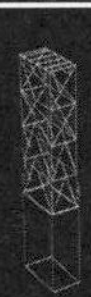

project_110
model_53
Vallcarca Industrial Area Transformation, Sitges, Spain

scale_1:200
Enamelled Welded Wire

project_110
model_54
Vallcarca Industrial Area Transformation, Sitges, Spain

scale_1:200
Enamelled Welded Wire

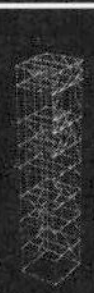

project_110
model_55
Vallcarca Industrial Area Transformation, Sitges, Spain

scale_1:200
Enamelled Welded Wire

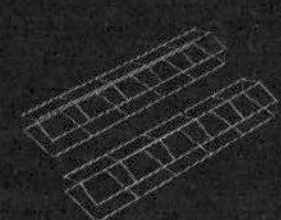

project_110
model_56
Vallcarca Industrial Area Transformation, Sitges, Spain

scale_1:200
Enamelled Welded Wire

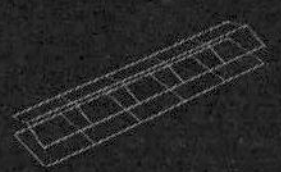

project_110
model_57
Vallcarca Industrial Area Transformation, Sitges, Spain

scale_1:200
Enamelled Welded Wire

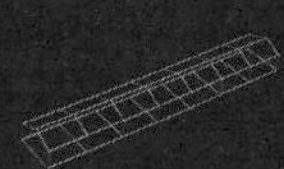

project_110
model_58
Vallcarca Industrial Area Transformation, Sitges, Spain

scale_1:200
Enamelled Welded Wire

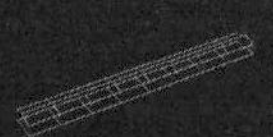

project_110
model_59
Vallcarca Industrial Area Transformation, Sitges, Spain

scale_1:200
Enamelled Welded Wire

project_110
model_60
Vallcarca Industrial Area Transformation, Sitges, Spain

scale_1:200
Enamelled Welded Wire

project_110
model_61
Vallcarca Industrial Area Transformation, Sitges, Spain

scale_1:200
Enamelled Welded Wire

project_110
model_62
Vallcarca Industrial Area Transformation, Sitges, Spain

scale_1:20
Enamelled Welded Wire

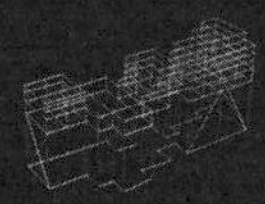

project_110
model_63
Vallcarca Industrial Area Transformation, Sitges, Spain

scale_1:20
Enamelled Welded Wire

2011

project_111 / models_01 - 02

Collserola Natural Park Phytoduct, Barcelona, Spain
41°24'44"N 02°04'26"E
pages 8, 38, 137

project_111
model_01
Collserola Natural Park Phytoduct, Barcelona, Spain

Enamelled Welded Wire
28x18x10 cm

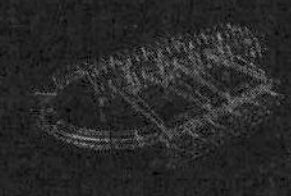

project_111
model_02_DHUB
Collserola Natural Park Phytoduct, Barcelona, Spain

scale_1:150
Zinc Plated Welded Wire
50x30x9cm

2017

project_112 / model_01

M.K. Čiurlionis International Concert Hall, Kaunas, Lithuania
54°53'50"N 23°53'10"E
pages 38, 208

project_112
model_01_DHUB
M.K. Čiurlionis International Concert Hall, Kaunas, Lithuania

scale_1:70
Zinc Plated Welded Wire
24x17x7cm

My work is much more complex than you might think. It's about lifting weights (weightlifting) and keeping the veins in your neck from swelling; it's about lifting the weight as if it doesn't weigh anything even though you know the effort you're making.

Projects are opportunities to develop subjects that interest you. Many of these are opinions about problems that arise, possibilities, nothing more. I like to express my discomfort towards the polite answers that are given nowadays.

The best way to approach the work of an architect is through your own work.

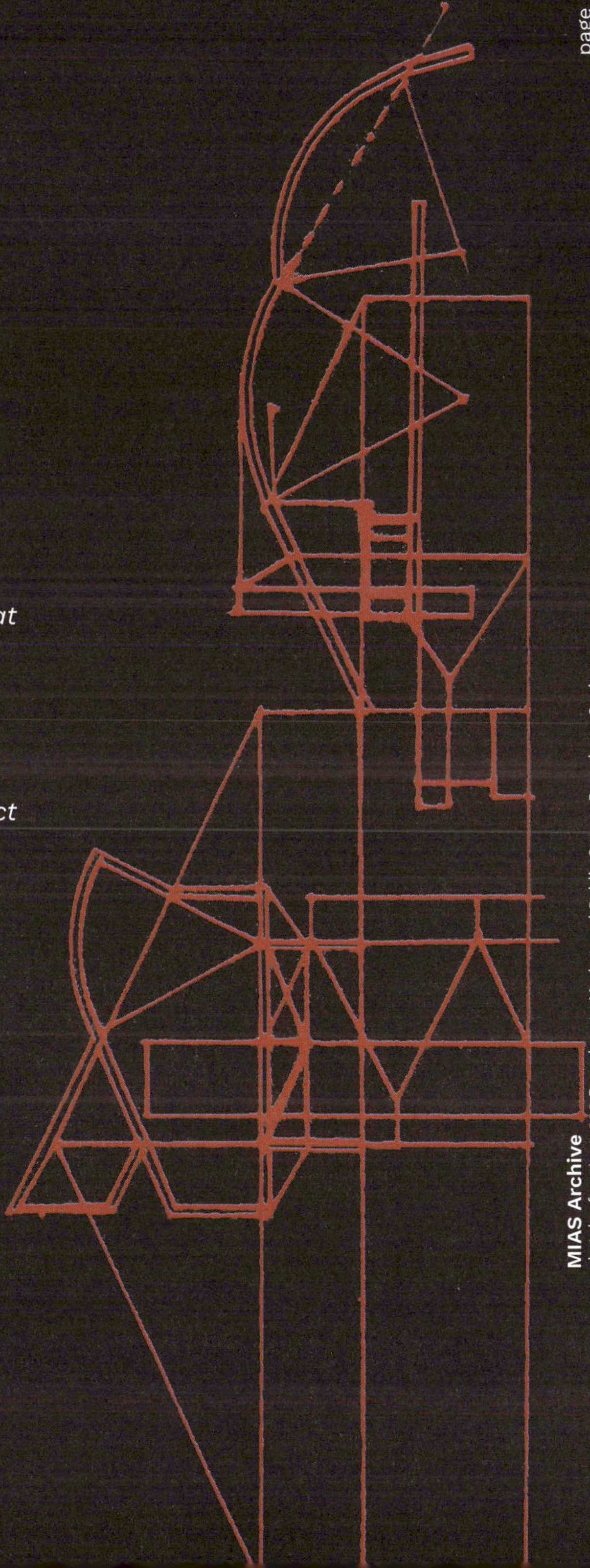

MIAS Archive
sketch of project_003 Barceloneta Market and Public Space, Barcelona, Spain

MIAS Archive

7.50x3.20m colour sketches on glass exhibited at 'MIAS The *Making* of Making (Architecture)' at DHUB Barcelona Design Museum in 2021-2022

MIAS Archive

7.50x3.20m colour sketches on glass exhibited at 'MIAS The *Making* of Making (Architecture)' at DHUB Barcelona Design Museum in 2021-2022

1999-2006 project_023 Old Town Public Space, Banyoles, Spain
Colour sketches printed on glass exhibited at 'MIAS The Making of Making (Architecture)' at DHUB Barcelona Design Museum in 2021-2022

1999-2006 project_023 Old Town Public Space, Banyoles, Spain
Colour sketches printed on glass exhibited at 'MIAS The *Making* of Making (Architecture)' at DHUB Barcelona Design Museum in 2021-2022

Banyoles Old Town Public Space

Open Competition, Winner
year: 1999-2006
location: Banyoles, Spain 42°07'05"N 02°45'53"E
surface: 18.000 m^2
client: Banyoles City Council

Awards
- 2015 AADIPA Architects Association for Defence and Intervention in Architectural Heritage Awards, Finalist
- 2015 Taipei City Government, International Design Awards, Finalist
- 2014 Piranesi Prix de Rome, Finalist
- 2013 International Stone Architecture Awards, Winner
- 2013 Taipei City Government, International Design Awards, Finalist
- 2010 FAD Awards, Public Space, Finalist
- 2009 Catalonia Construction Awards, Winner

1999-2006 project_023 Old Town Public Space. Banyoles, Spain

- 2008 CCCB Urban, European Prize for Public Space, Finalist
- 2008 Barcelona International Biennal of Landscape Architecture, Rosa Barba Prize, Finalist
- 2008 Urban Public Spaces European Prize, Finalist
- 2007 COAC Girona, Girona Area Architectural Awards for Public Space, Winner

Publications

- *Banyoles*, Miàs, Josep, Barcelona, Argra Trading S.L., 2013
- *Banyoles Old City Center*, Miàs, Josep, Barcelona, 2011

1999-2006 project_023 Old Town Public Space, Banyoles, Spain
7.50x3.20m line drawing on glass exhibited at 'MIAS The *Making* of Making (Architecture)' at DHUB Barcelona Design Museum in 2021-2022

1999-2006 project_023 Old Town Public Space, Banyoles, Spain
7.50x3.20m line drawing on glass exhibited at 'MIAS The *Making* of Making (Architecture)' at DHUB Barcelona Design Museum in 2021-2022

Banyoles Old Town Public Space

Open Competition, Winner
year: 1999-2006
location: Banyoles, Spain 42°07'05"N 02°45'53"E
surface: 1.000 m²
client: Banyoles City Council

1999-2006 project_023 Old Town Public Space, Banyoles, Spain

FERRETERIA
GENERAL
116
FLATO

2007-2013 project_015 Can Zariquiey Therapeutic Centre, Arenys de Munt, Spain
Collage exhibited at 14th Venice Biennale Catalan Pavilion

2007–2013 project_015 Can Zariquiey Therapeutic Centre, Arenys de Munt, Spain
Collage exhibited at 14th Venice Biennale Catalan Pavilion

Can Zariquiey Therapeutic Centre

year: 2007-2013
location: Arenys de Munt, Spain 41°35'57"N 02°32'38"E
surface: 1800 m²
client: Maresme Therapeutic Community

Awards
- 2015 Mies van der Rohe Awards, Nominated
- 2014 Venice Biennale of Architecture

I find Gaudí incredible for his ability not to answer the question, it's as though he wasn't interested in it. An entrance door in the shape of a dragon's wing, or rather, a dragon's wings in the shape of a door. Like those butterflies with folded wings resting on the walls of the crypt in Colònia Güell; in reality, this is an interplay of asymmetrical hinges and windows.
I find this way of using architecture to talk about other things fascinating.

To suddenly find a formal development as a result of a structural theme, by using the simplest systems for example, Catalan vaulted ceilings. This madness, or fantasy, is full of wisdom and knowledge. I find this geometric, structural and constructive rigour incredible, and suddenly, there's this leap towards something significant.
Something similar happens to me with Jujol, I find that world of contradictions, of ambiguities, fantastic.

Can Zariquiey Therapeutic Centre

year: 2007-2013
location: Arenys de Munt, Spain 41°35'57"N 02°32'38"E
surface: 1800 m^2
client: Maresme Therapeutic Community

2007-2013 project_015 Can Zariquiey Therapeutic Centre, Arenys de Munt, Spain

2013 project_013
Bus Stop,
Palafolls, Spain
41°40'13"N 02°44'57"E

2008-2009 project_012
Historical Building at Tibidabo Amusement Park,
Barcelona, Spain
41°25'17"N 02°07'08"E

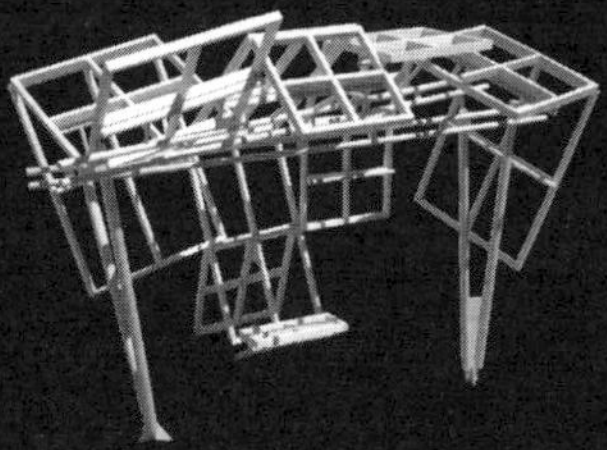

project_013
model_02

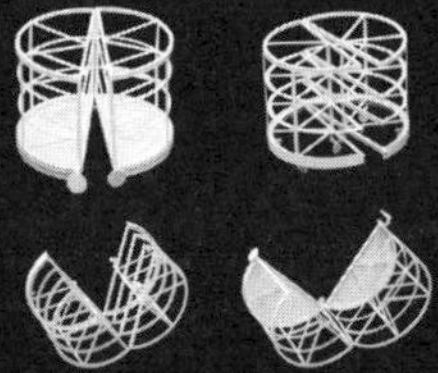

project_012
model_01

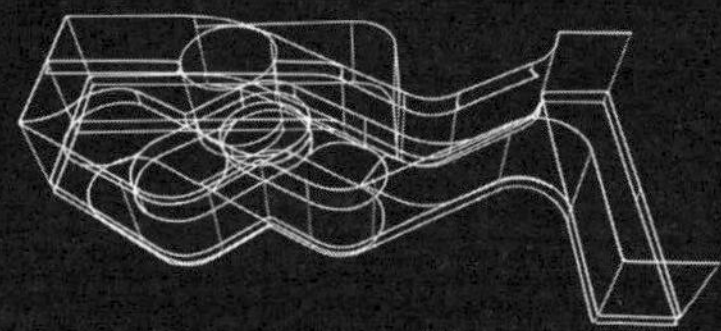

project_012
model_05

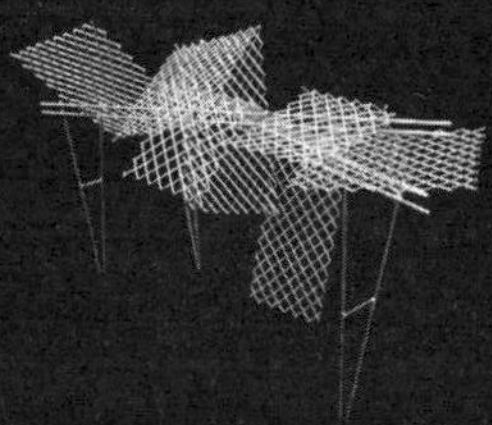

project_013
model_06

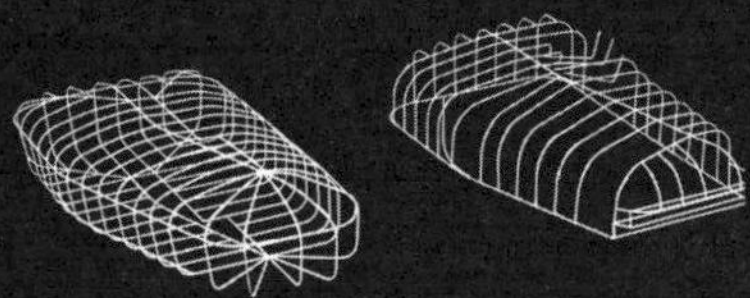

project_012
model_15

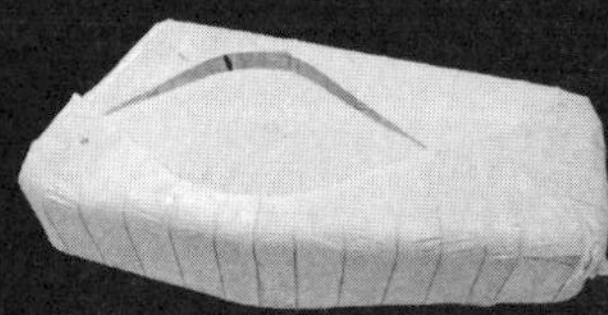

project_012
model_12

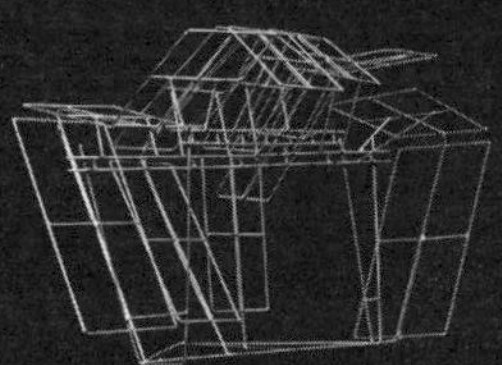

project_013
model_07_DHUB

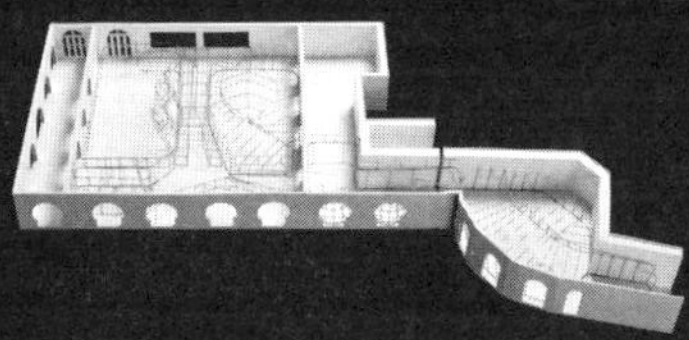

project_012
model_08

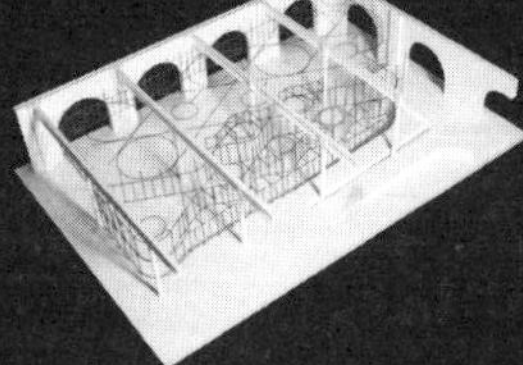

project_012
model_08

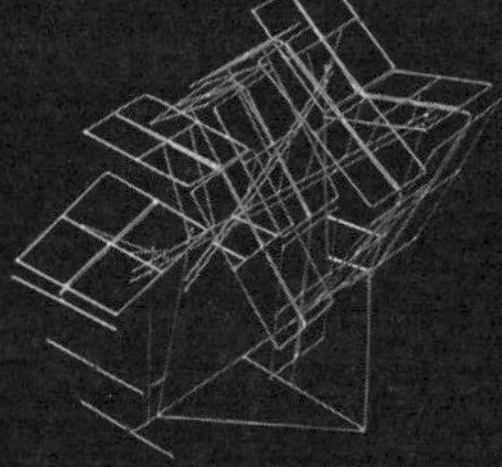

project_013
model_07_DHUB

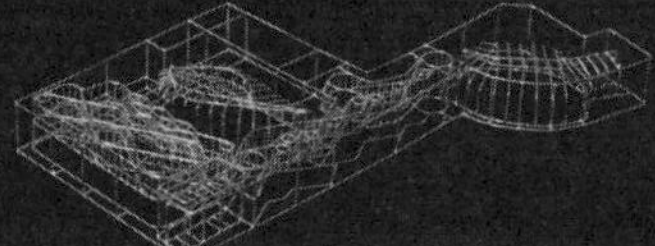

project_012
model_18_DHUB

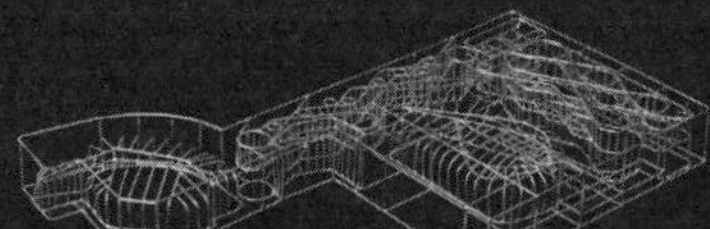

project_012
model_18_DHUB

2007-2008 project_009
Lower Funicular Station at Tibidabo Amusement Park,
Barcelona, Spain
41°24'59"N 02°07'51"E

project_009
model_09

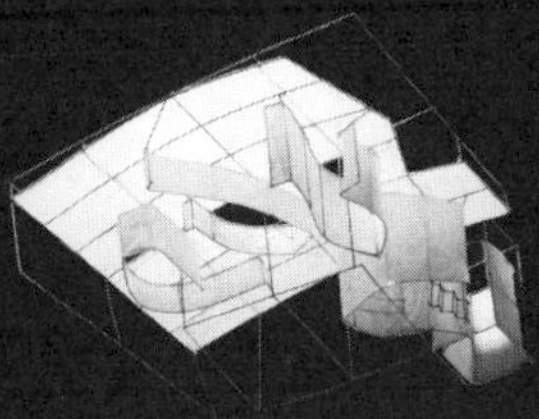

project_009
model_13

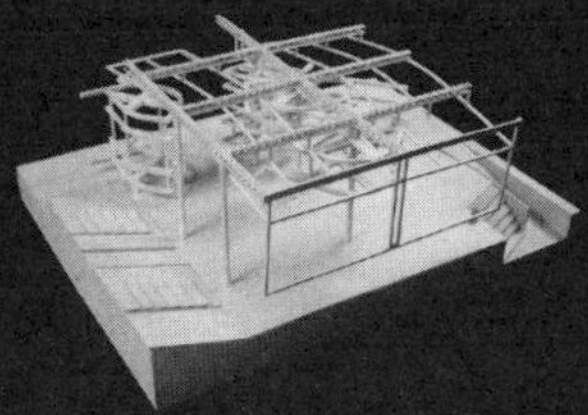

project_009
model_15

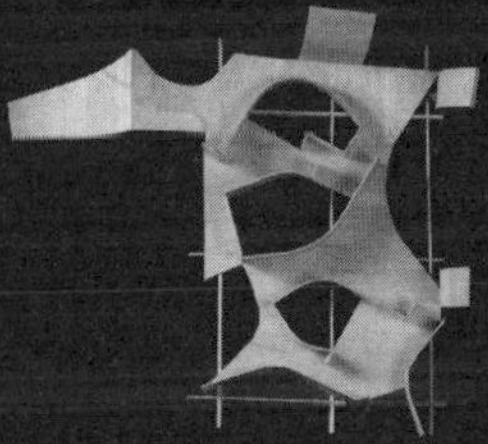

project_009
model_09

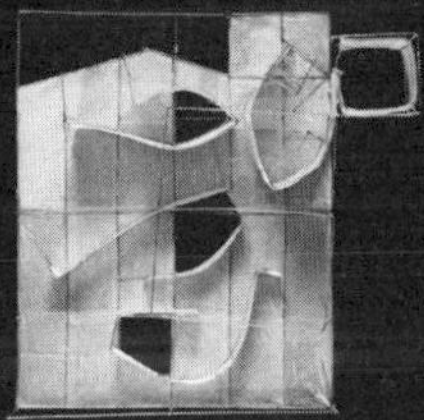

project_009
model_13

project_009
model_19_DHUB

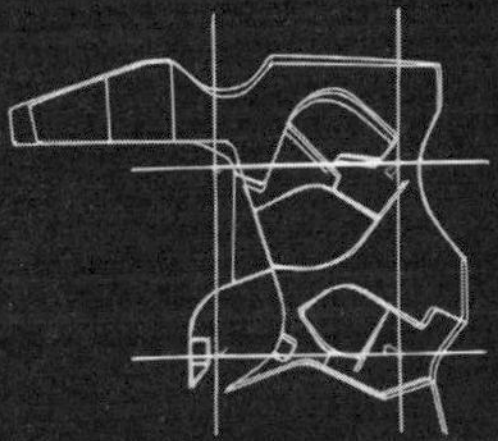

project_009
model_18
EC2020-2-AR49 Centre Pompidou
Permanent Collection

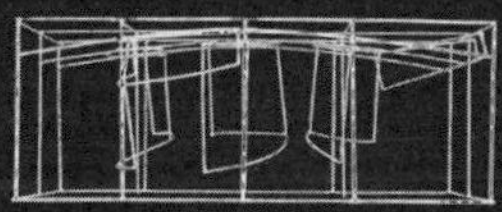

project_009
model_18
EC2020-2-AR49 Centre Pompidou
Permanent Collection

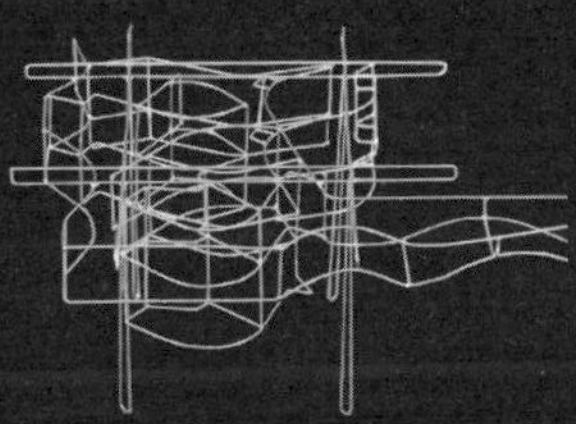

project_009
model_18
EC2020-2-AR49 Centre Pompidou
Permanent Collection

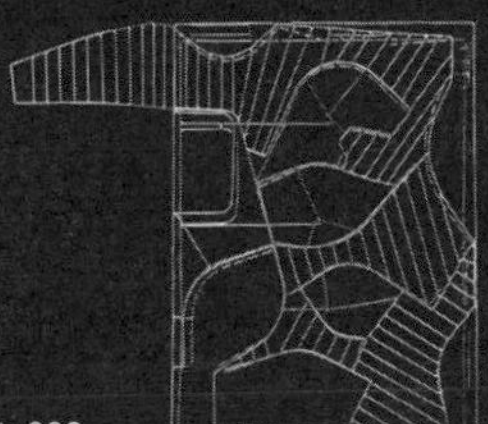

project_009
model_19_DHUB

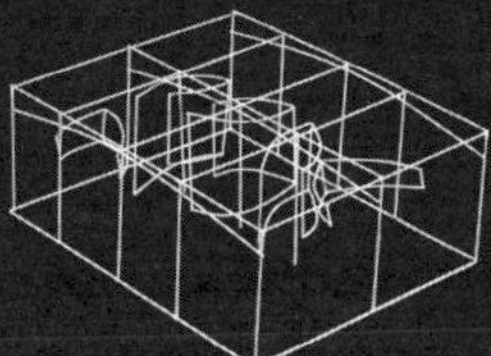

project_009
model_18
EC2020-2-AR49 Centre Pompidou
Permanent Collection

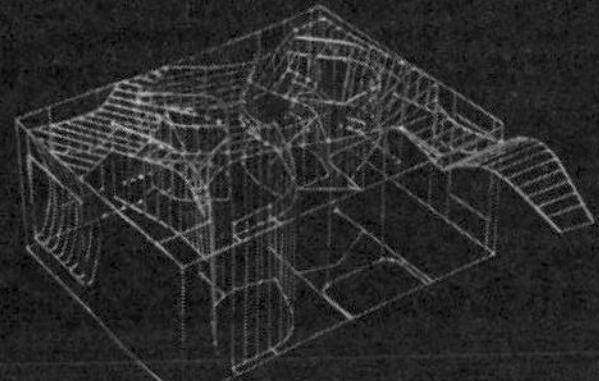

project_009
model_19_DHUB

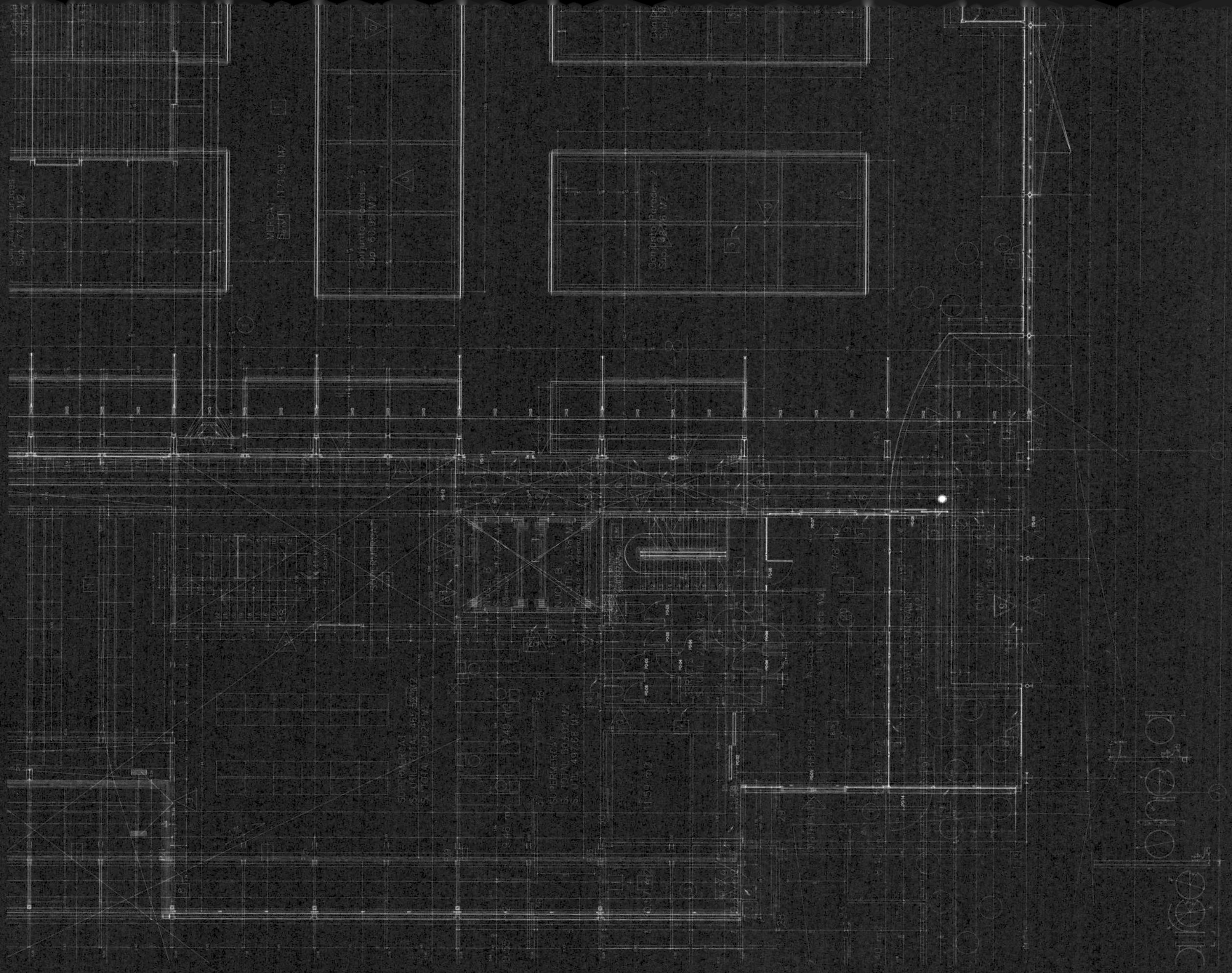

2001-2007 project_003 Barceloneta Market and Public Space, Barcelona, Spain
1.90x1.30m line drawing on glass exhibited at 'MIAS The *Making* of Making (Architecture)' at DHUB Barcelona Design Museum in 2021-2022

2001-2007 project_003 **Barceloneta Market and Public Space, Barcelona, Spain**
1.90x1.30m line drawing on glass exhibited at 'MIAS The *Making* of Making (Architecture)' at DHUB Barcelona Design Museum in 2021-2022

Barceloneta Market and Public Space

Open Competition, Winner
year: 2001-2007
location: Barcelona, Spain 41°22'49"N 02°11'21"E
surface: 5200 m²
client: Barcelona City Council, IMMB Institut Municipal de Mercats de Barcelona

Awards
- 2011 Archdaily Building of the Year, Selected
- 2011 Plataforma Arquitectura Work of the Year, Finalist
- 2008 Catalonia Construction Awards, Winner
- 2007 Barcelona City Prize for Architecture and Urbanism, Winner

2001-2007 project_003 Barcelona Market and Public Space, Barcelona, Spain

2001-2007 project_003 Barceloneta Market and Public Space, Barcelona, Spain
Detail of 7.50x3.20m line drawing on glass exhibited at 'MIAS The *Making* of Making (Architecture)' at DHUB Barcelona Design Museum in 2021-2022

2001-2007 project_003 Barceloneta Market and Public Space, Barcelona, Spain
Detail of 7.50x3.20m line drawing on glass exhibited at 'MIAS The *Making* of Making (Architecture)' at DHUB Barcelona Design Museum in 2021-2022

2001-2007 project_003 Barceloneta Market and Public Space, Barcelona, Spain

2001-2007 project_003 Barceloneta Market and Public Space, Barcelona, Spain
model_44 185x59x26m zinc plated welded wire, wood EC2020-2-AR48 Centre Pompidou Permanent Collection

2001-2007 project_003 Barceloneta Market and Public Space, Barcelona, Spain
model_44 185x59x26m zinc plated welded wire, wood EC2020-2-AR48 Centre Pompidou Permanent Collection

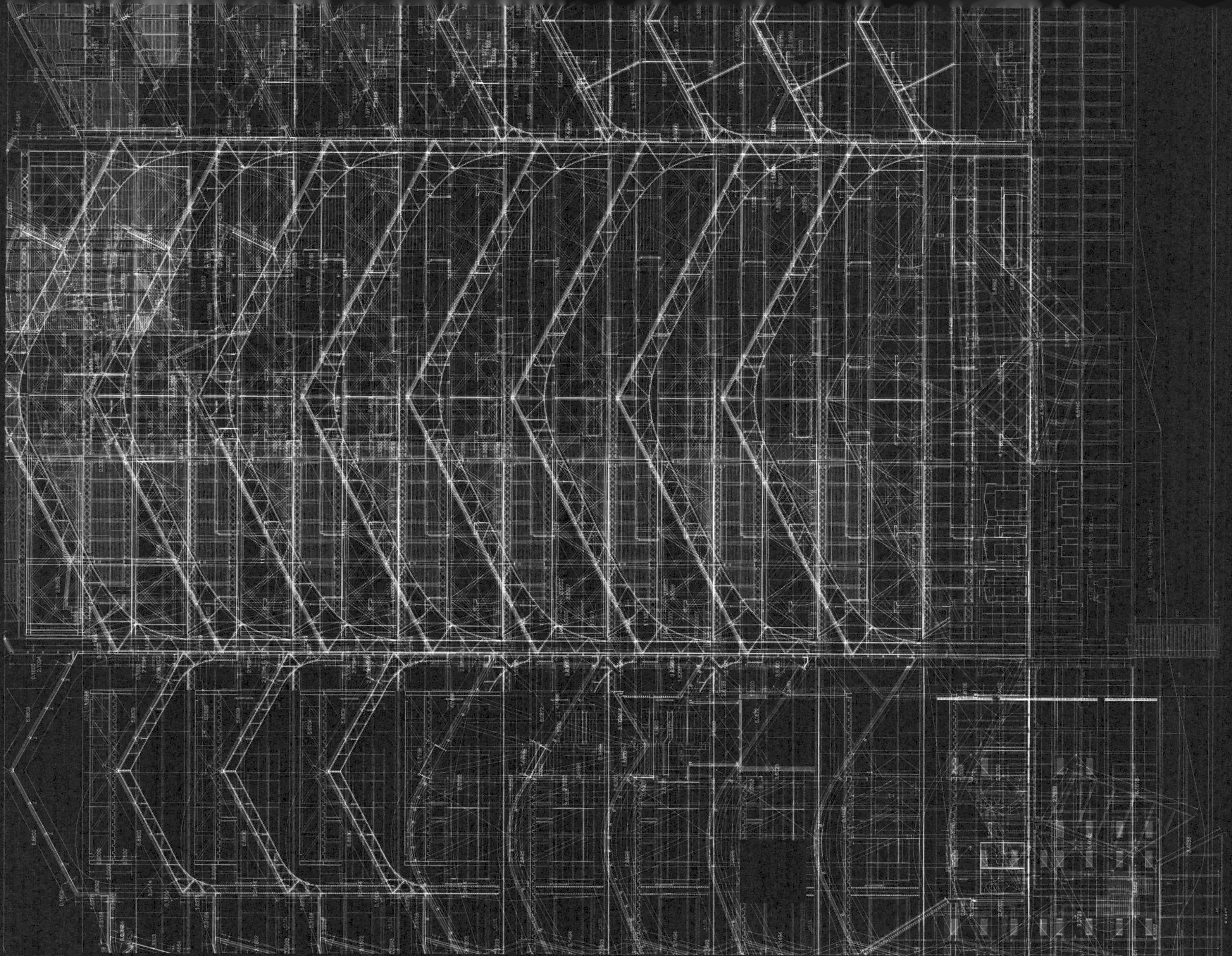

2001-2007 project_003 Barceloneta Market and Public Space, Barcelona, Spain
2.10x0.70m line drawing on glass exhibited at 'MIAS The *Making* of Making (Architecture)' at DHUB Barcelona Design Museum in 2021-2022

2001-2007 project_003 Barceloneta Market and Public Space, Barcelona, Spain
2.10x0.70m line drawing on glass exhibited at 'MIAS The *Making* of Making (Architecture)' at DHUB Barcelona Design Museum in 2021-2022

2001-2007 project_003
Barceloneta Market and Public Space,
Barcelona, Spain
41°22'49"N 02°11'21"E

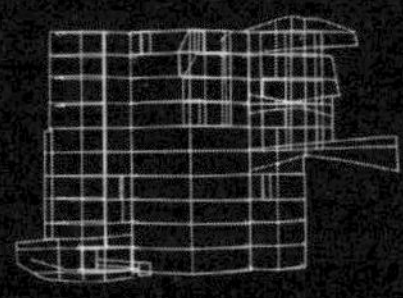

project_003
model_41
EC2020-2-AR85
Pompidou Collection

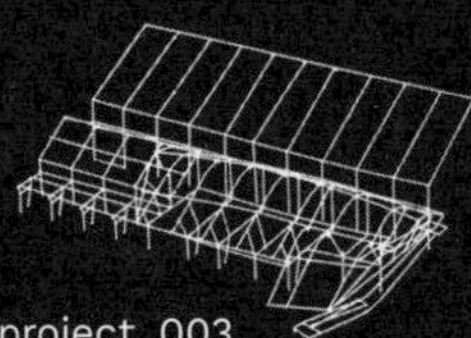

project_003
model_42
EC2020-2-AR84
Pompidou Collection

project_003
model_26

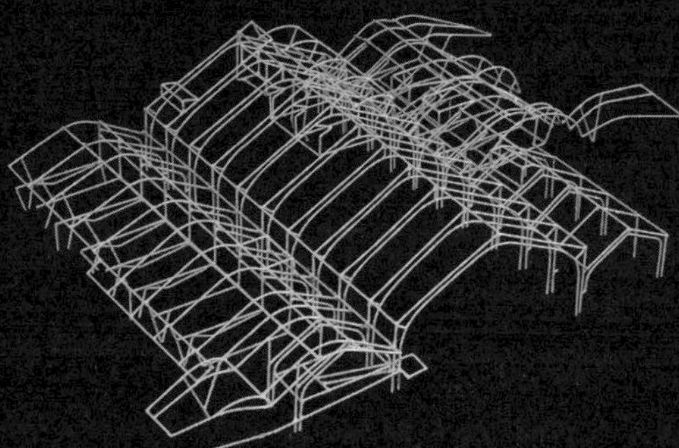

project_003
model_41
EC2020-2-AR85 Pompidou Collection

project_003
model_01

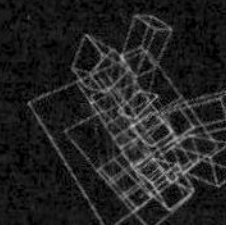

project_003
model_03

project_003
model_08

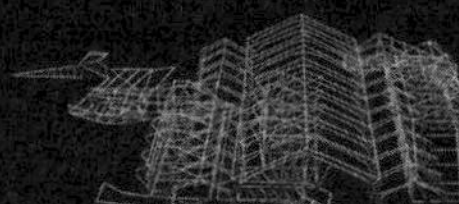

project_003
model_35

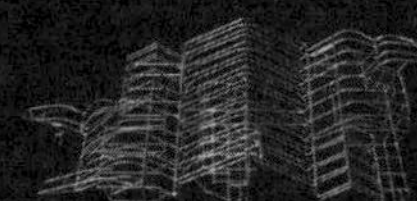

project_003
model_46

project_003
model_24

project_003
model_45
EC2020-2-AR47
Pompidou Collection

project_003
model_44
EC2020-2-AR48
Pompidou Collection

project_003
model_45
EC2020-2-AR47
Pompidou Collection

2001-2007 project_003
Barceloneta Market and Public Space,
Barcelona, Spain
41°22'49"N 02°11'21"E

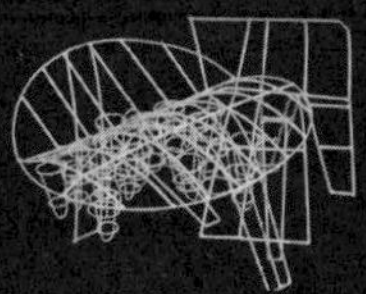

project_003
model_43
EC2020-2-AR46
Pompidou Collection

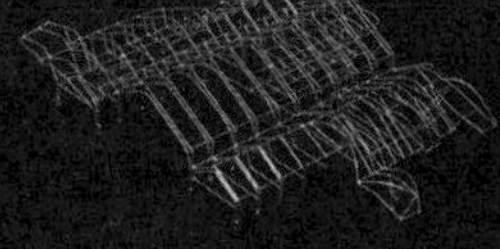

project_003
model_46

project_003
model_41
EC2020-2-AR85
Pompidou Collection

project_003
model_09

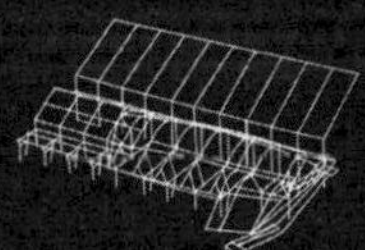

project_003
model_42
EC2020-2-AR84
Pompidou Collection

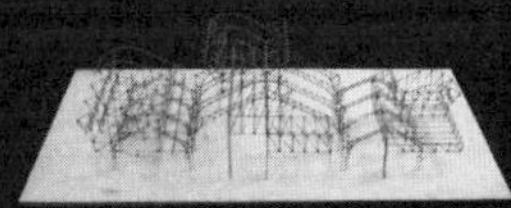

project_003
model_17

project_003
model_29

project_003
model_22

project_003
model_13

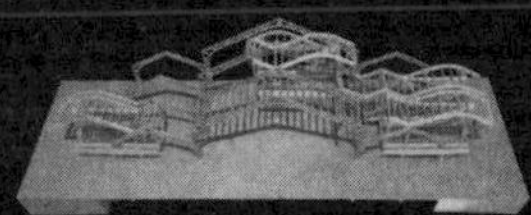

project_003
model_16

project_003
model_12

project_003
model_32

project_003
model_13

project_003
model_31

project_003
model_13

project_003
model_44
EC2020-2-AR48
Pompidou Collection

2000-2004 project_006 Golf Clubhouse and Sports Centre, Fontanals de Cerdanya, Spain
2.10x0.70m line drawing on glass exhibited at 'MIAS The *Making* of Making (Architecture)' at DHUB Barcelona Design Museum in 2021-2022

2000-2004 project 006 **Golf Clubhouse and Sports Centre, Fontanals de Cerdanya, Spain**

2.10x0.70m line drawing on glass exhibited at 'MIAS The *Making* of Making (Architecture)' at DHUB Barcelona Design Museum in 2021-2022

2000-2004 project_006 Golf Clubhouse and Sports Centre, Fontanals de Cerdanya, Spain
model_15 125x111x25cm balsa wood 1:100 EC2020-2-AR85 Centre Pompidou Permanent Collection

2000-2004 project_006 Golf Clubhouse and Sports Centre, Fontanals de Cerdanya, Spain

model_19 37x27x4cm 1:250 welded wire model exhibited at 'MIAS The *Making* of Making (Architecture)' at DHUB Barcelona Design Museum in 2021-2022

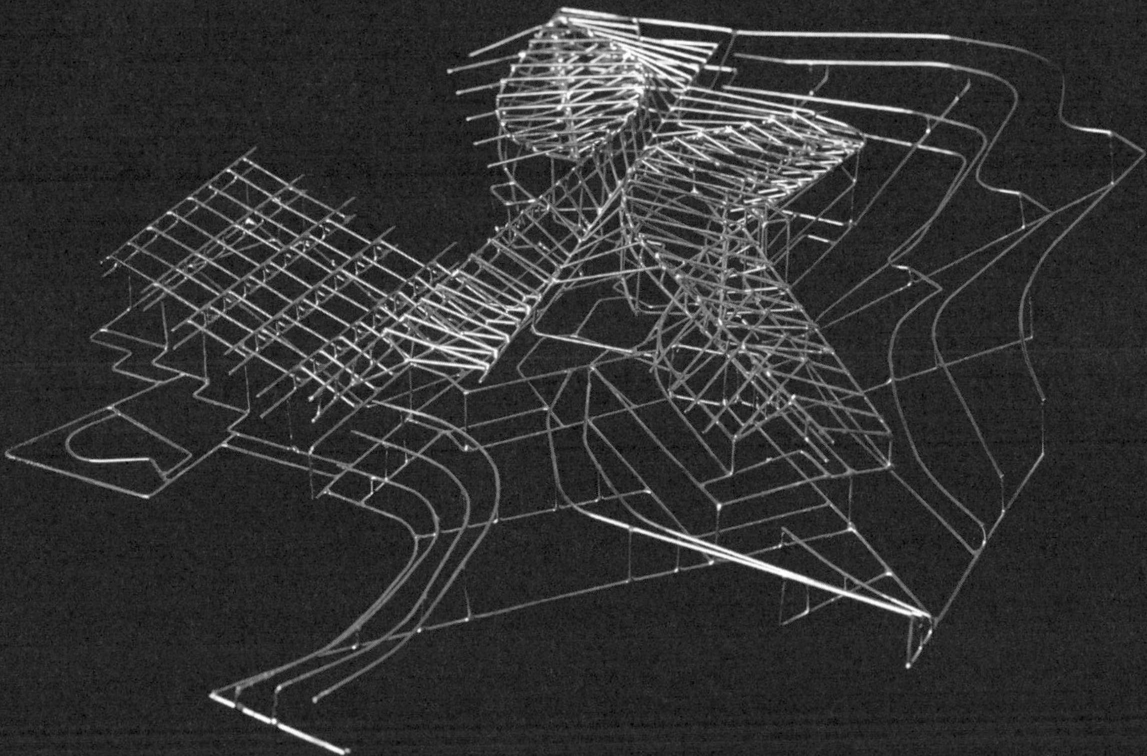

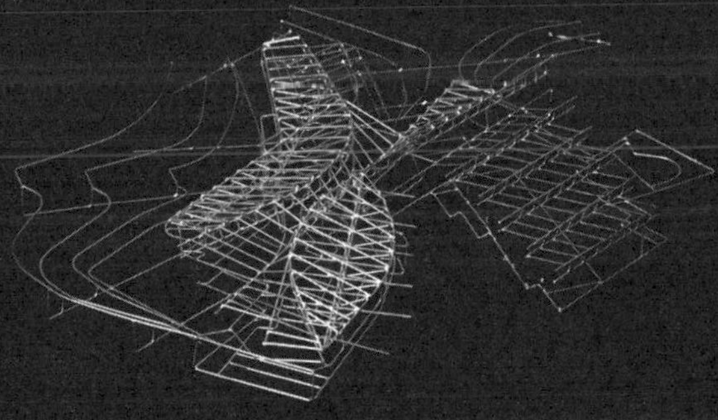

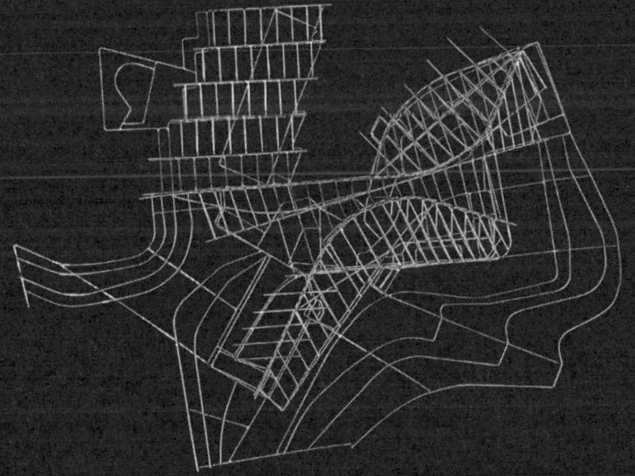

The Fontanals Golf Club originates from the knowledge of the place through the redrawing of the site. In reality, all the topography of a golf course is artificial, but the building is formed by this same topography. It obviously tries to camouflage itself, sticking close to the ground, and rising as much as necessary to allow a window or elongated space between the ground and the roof around its perimeter.

This enormous scheme required some fragmentation to reduce the impact on the site. All projects emerge from a rigorous analysis of the site, with the tools we have, and which are, I repeat, basically drawings. But they develop the aspects that concern or interest us. Of course, they always talk to each other and help each other out if necessary.

Golf Clubhouse and Sports Centre

Open Competition, Winner
year: 2000-2004
location: Fontanals de Cerdanya, Spain 42°23'48"N 01°52'37"E
surface: 2500 m^2
client: Fontanals Esportiva SL

Awards
- 2011 Archdaily Building of the Year, Selected
- 2011 Plataforma Arquitectura Work of the Year, Selected
- 2004 AJAC Young Architects Prize to Best Young Architect under 40 for Built Work, Winner
- 2003 COAC Girona, Girona Area Architectural Awards, Finalist

Publications
- *Fontanals Pyrenees Golf Centre*, Miàs, Josep, Barcelona, 2011

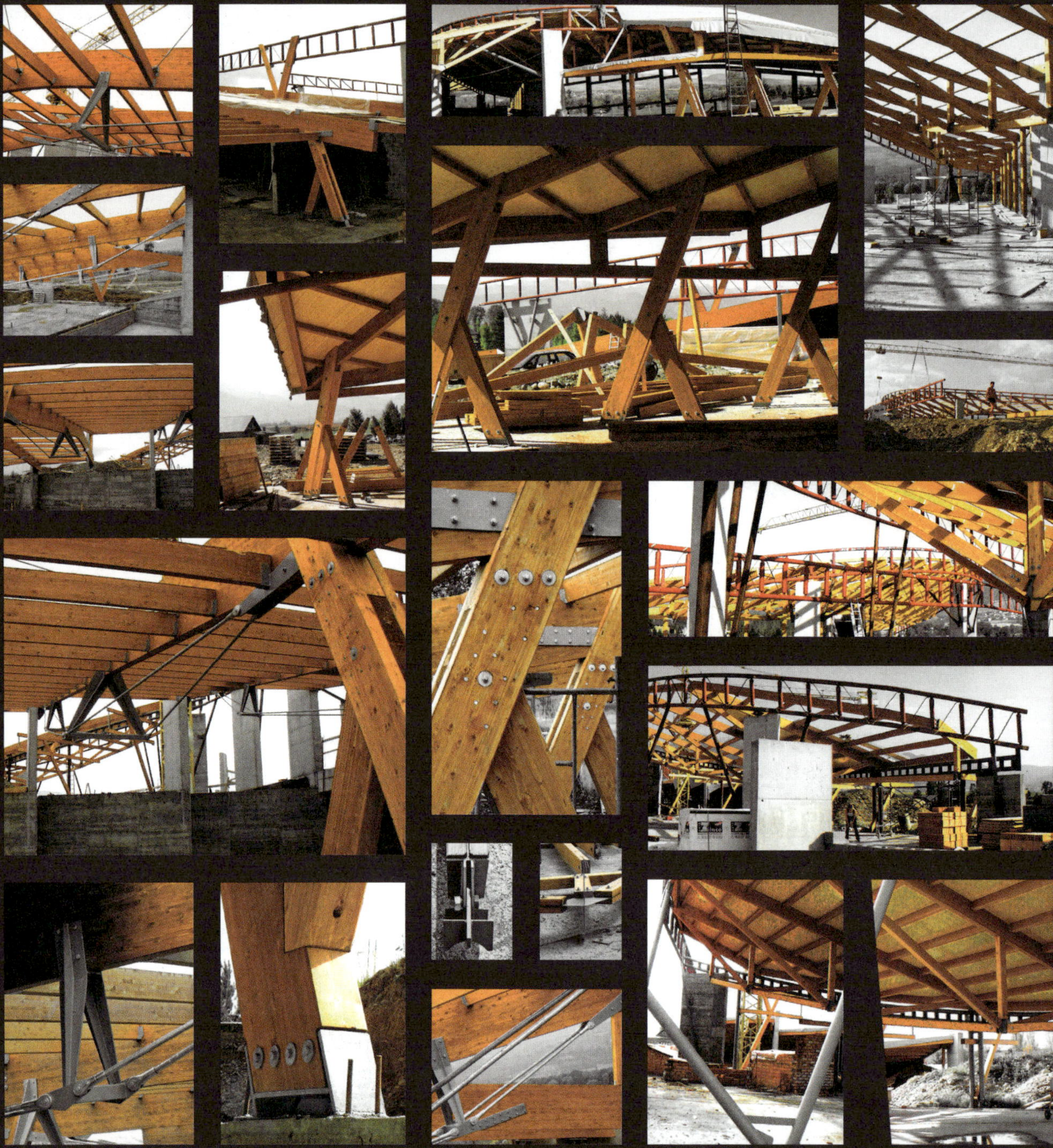

2000–2004 project_006 Golf Clubhouse and Sports Centre, Fontanals de Cerdanya, Spain

2000–2004 project_006 Golf Clubhouse and Sports Centre, Fontanals de Cerdanya, Spain

1995 project_001
Banys Vells Swimming Club and Bar,
Banyoles, Spain
42°07'16"N 02°45'29"E

2000-2004 project_006
Golf Clubhouse and Sports Centre,
Fontanals de Cerdanya, Spain
42°23'48"N 01°52'37"E

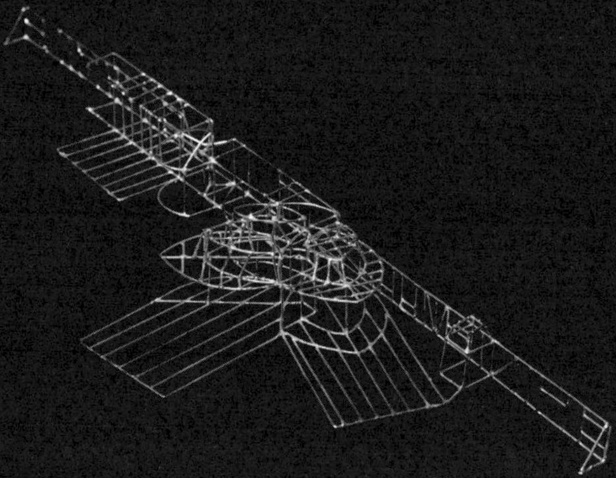

project_001
model_05_DHUB

project_006
model_13

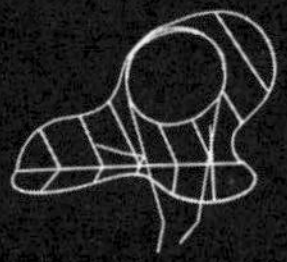

project_006
model_14

project_006
model_16

project_006
model_16

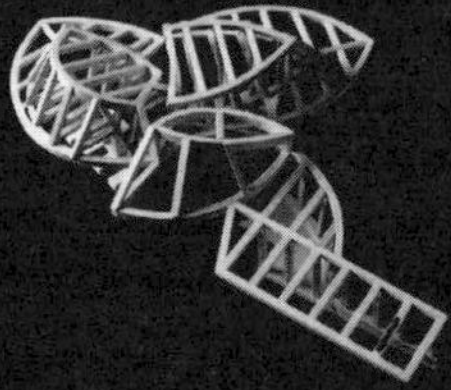

project_001
model_03

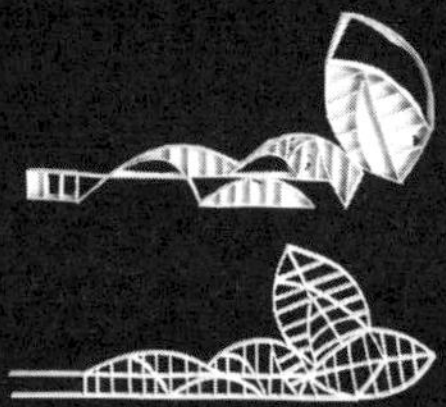

project_001
model_03

project_006
model_16

project_006
model_16

project_001
model_01

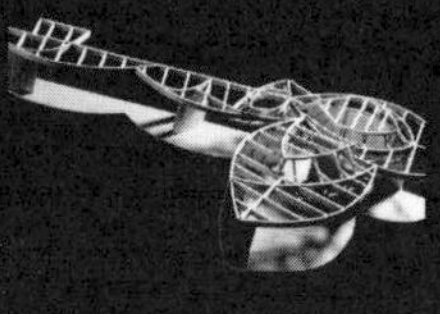

project_001
model_03

project_006
model_11

project_006
model_11

2000-2004 project_006
Golf Clubhouse and Sports Centre,
Fontanals de Cerdanya, Spain
42°23'48"N 01°52'37"E

project_006
model_01

project_006
model_06

project_006
model_17

project_006
model_17

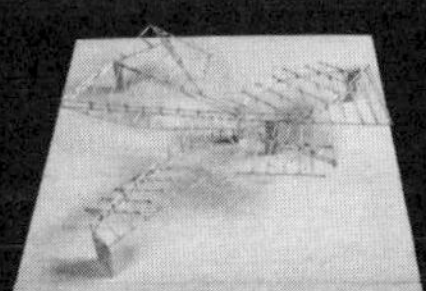

project_006
model_02

project_006
model_07

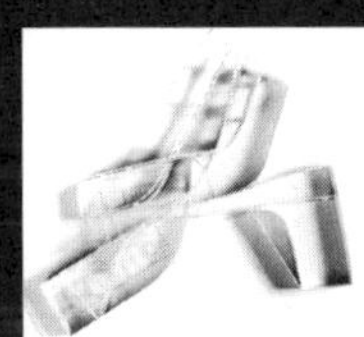

project_006
model_04

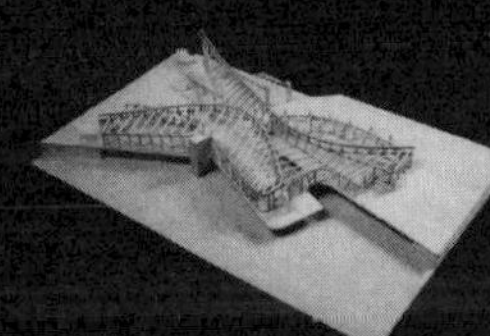

project_006
model_18

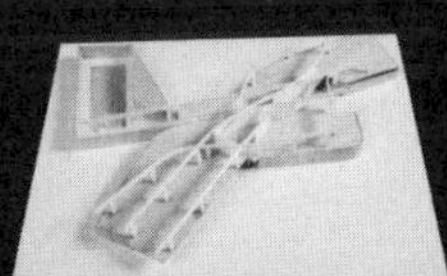

project_006
model_03

project_006
model_08

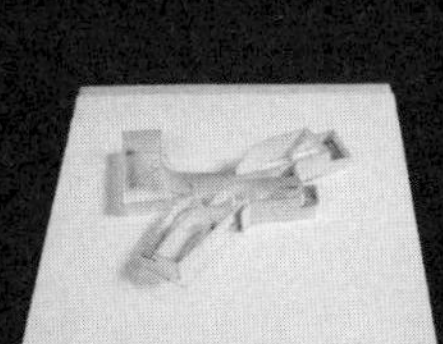

project_006
model_04

project_006
model_10

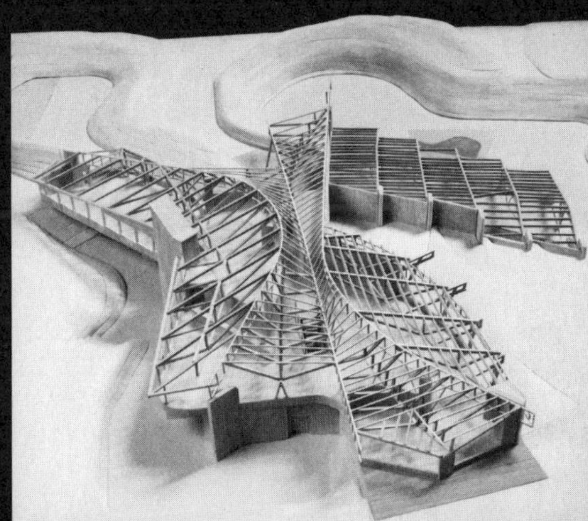

project_006
model_15
EC2020-2-AR85
Pompidou Collection

2005-2006 project_008 Butterfly House, Besalú, Spain
Detail of 7.50x3.20m line drawing on glass exhibited at 'MIAS The *Making* of Making (Architecture)' at DHUB Barcelona Design Museum in 2021-2022

2011-2012 project_005 Topographic House, Llavaneres, Spain
Detail of 7.50x3.20m line drawing on glass exhibited at 'MIAS The *Making* of Making (Architecture)' at DHUB Barcelona Design Museum in 2021-2022

DHUB Barcelona Design Museum

'MIAS The *Making* of Making (Architecture)'

Butterfly House

2005-2006 project_008 Butterfly House, Besalú, Spain

year: 2005-2006
location: Besalú, Spain 42°12'00"N 02°41'43"E
surface: 220 m^2
client: Private

2005-2006 project_008 Butterfly House, Besalú, Spain

Topographic House

year: 2011-2012
location: Llavaneres, Spain 41°34'32"N 02°28'59"E
surface: 700 m²
client: Private

Awards
- 2011 Archdaily Building of the Year, Selected
- 2011 Plataforma Arquitectura Work of the Year, Selected

2005 - 2006 project_008
Butterfly House,
Besalú, Spain
42°12'00"N 02°41'43"E

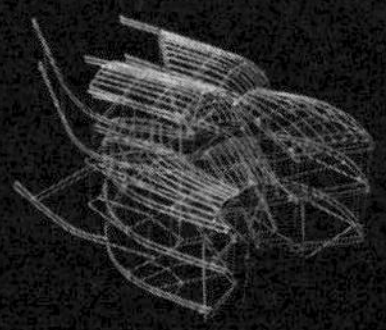

project_008
model_19_DHUB

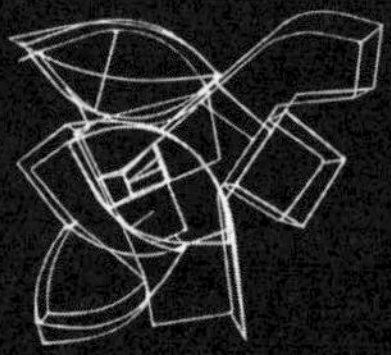

project_008
model_13

project_008
model_03

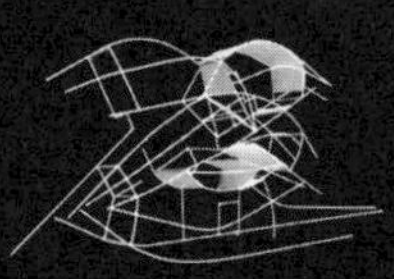

project_008
model_05

project_008
model_12

project_008
model_19_DHUB

project_008
model_07

project_008
model_13

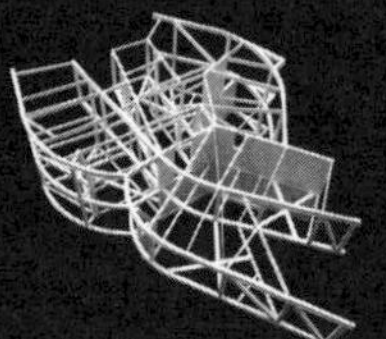

project_008
model_01

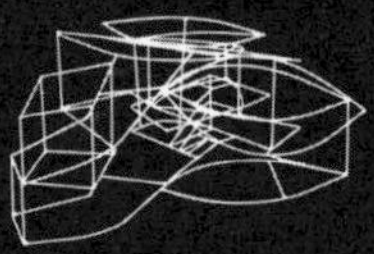

project_008
model_13

project_008
model_08

project_008
model_08

project_008
model_14

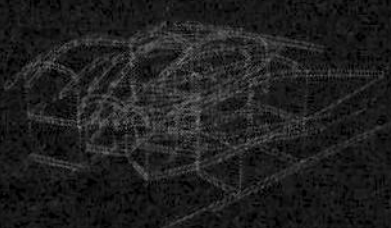

project_008
model_17

project_008
model_12

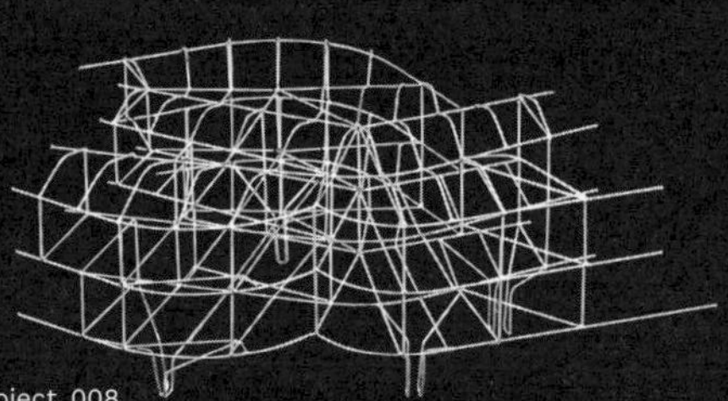

project_008
model_18
EC2020-2-AR60
Pompidou Collection

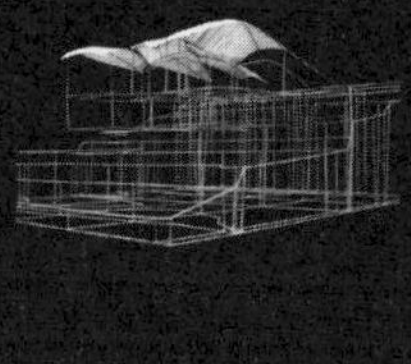

project_008
model_16

project_008
model_13

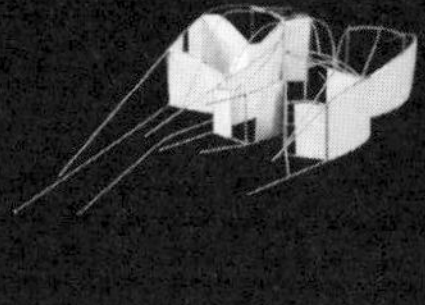

project_008
model_12

2011 - 2012 project_005
Topographic House,
Llavaneres, Spain
41°34'32"N 02°28'59"E

project_005
model_06

project_005
model_06

project_005
model_06

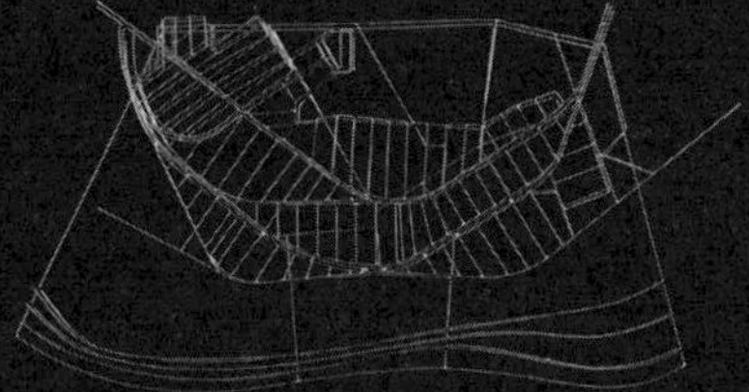

project_005
model_10
EC2020-2-AR58
Pompidou Collection

project_005
model_07

project_005
model_07

project_005
model_07

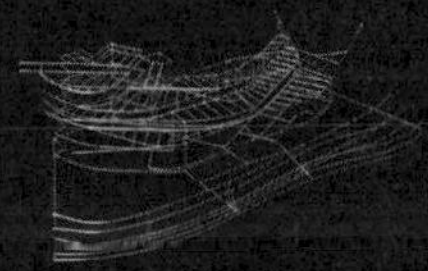

project_005
model_10
EC2020-2-AR58
Pompidou Collection

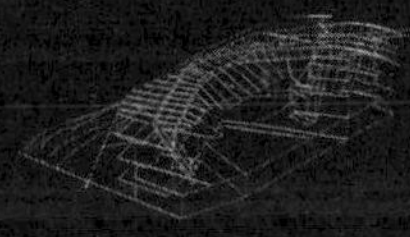

project_005
model_10
EC2020-2-AR58
Pompidou Collection

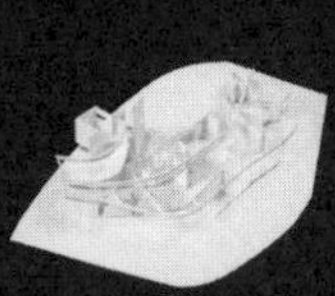

project_005
model_08

project_005
model_08

project_005
model_05

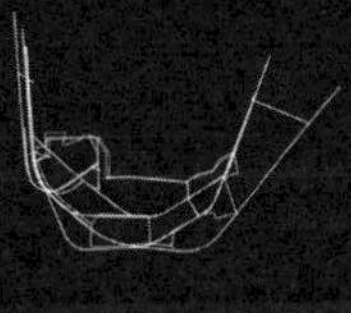

project_005
model_03

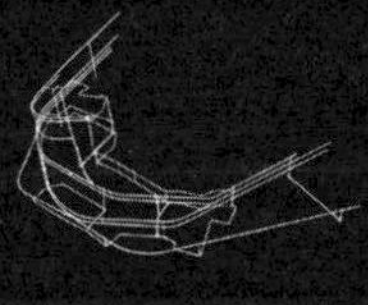

project_005
model_03

project_005
model_01

project_005
model_01

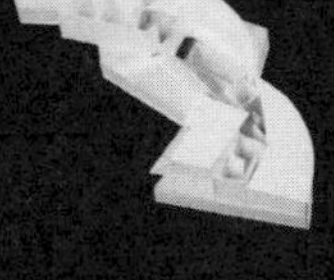

project_005
model_01

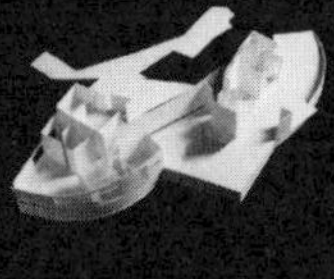

project_005
model_02

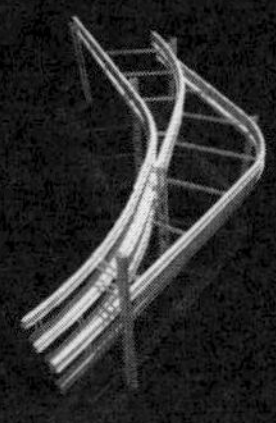

project_005
model_06

I think of infrastructure as places offering even greater interaction than the buildings themselves.

2007–2012 project_007 Pedestrian Bridge, Palafolls, Spain

2007-2012 **project_007**
Pedestrian Bridge,
Palafolls, Spain
41°39'50"N 02°44'50"E

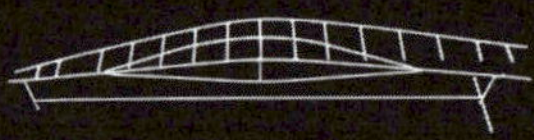

project_007
model_08

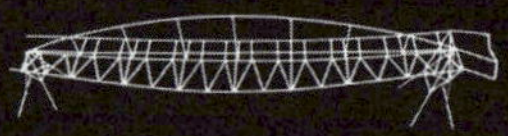

project_007
model_09

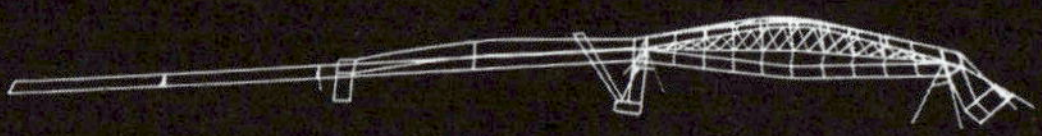

project_007
model_10

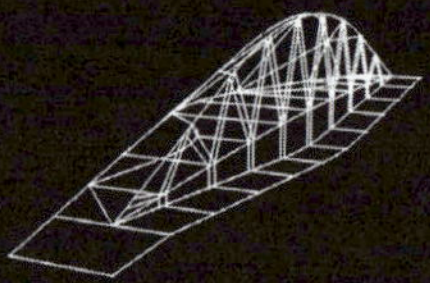

project_007
model_08

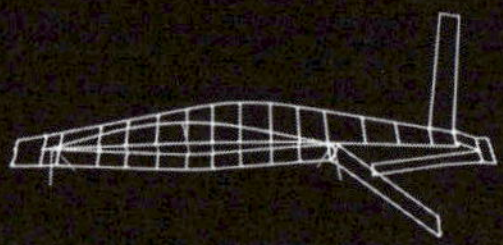

project_007
model_09

project_007
model_02

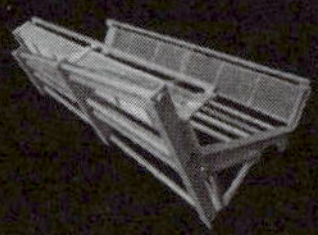

project_007
model_02

project_007
model_17
EC2020-2-AR40
Pompidou Collection

project_007
model_18
EC2020-2-AR41
Pompidou Collection

project_007
model_02

project_007
model_03

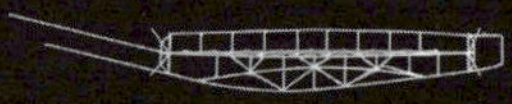

project_007
model_17
EC2020-2-AR40
Pompidou Collection

project_007
model_18
EC2020-2-AR41
Pompidou Collection

project_007
model_03

project_007
model_03

project_007
model_17
EC2020-2-AR40
Pompidou Collection

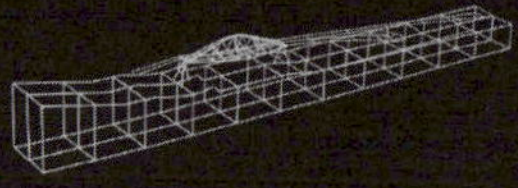

project_007
model_18
EC2020-2-AR41
Pompidou Collection

project_007
model_03

2007-2012 **project_007**
Pedestrian Bridge,
Palafolls, Spain
41°39'50"N 02°44'50"E

2013 project_064
Baltic Sea Park,
Pärnu, Estonia
58°23'17"N 24°29'54"E

project_007
model_04

project_007
model_04

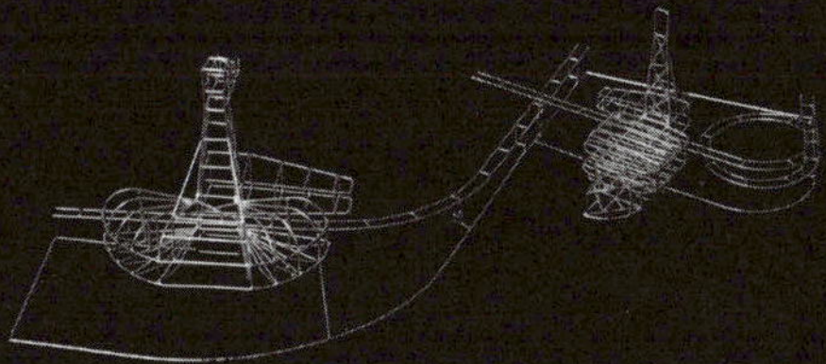

project_064
model_10_DHUB

project_007
model_07

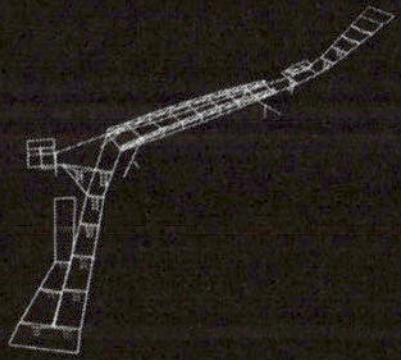

project_007
model_07

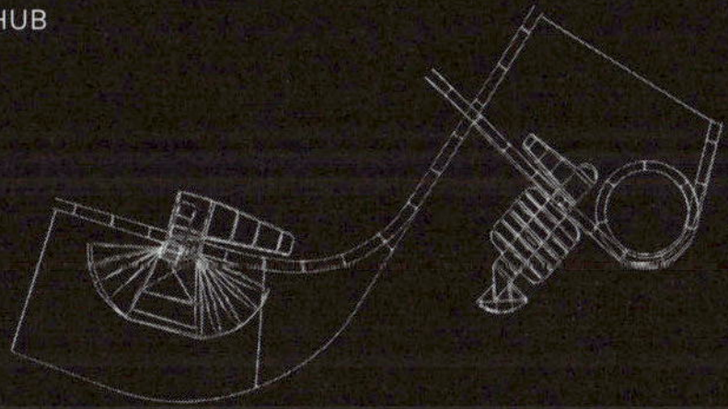

project_064
model_10_DHUB

project_007
model_08

project_007
model_07

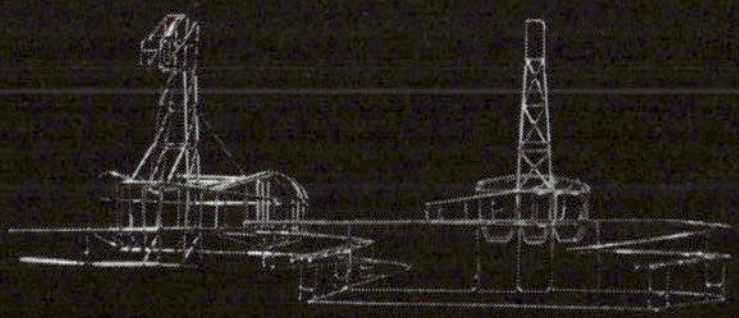

project_064
model_10_DHUB

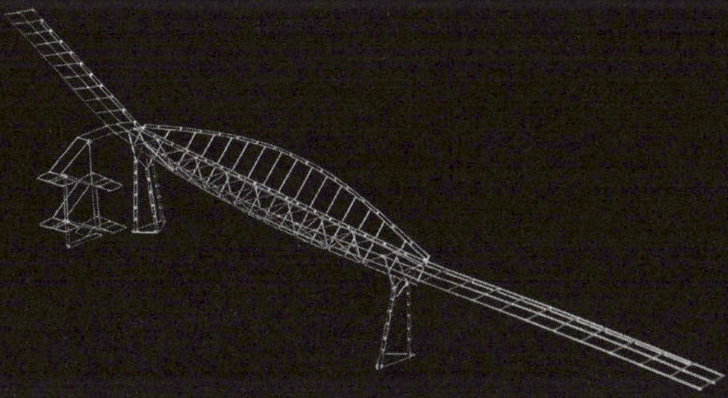

project_007
model_13

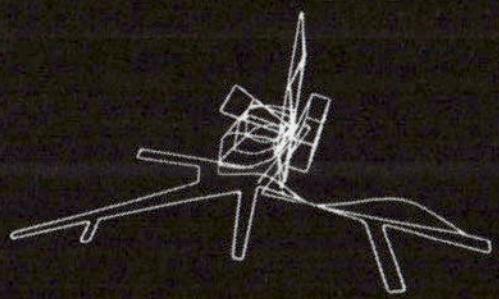

project_064
model_08

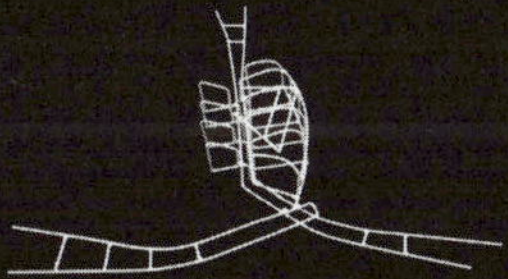

project_064
model_05

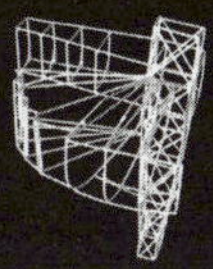

project_064
model_07

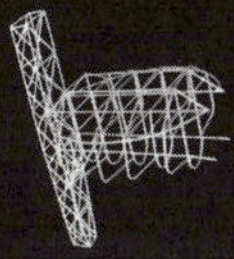

project_064
model_07

2017-2021 project_035 Cucadellum Funicular to Tibidabo Amusement Park, Barcelona, Spain
Colour sketches printed on glass exhibited at 'MIAS The Making of Making (Architecture)' at DHUB Barcelona Design Museum in 2021-2022

2017-2021 project_035 Cucadellum Funicular to Tibidabo Amusement Park, Barcelona, Spain

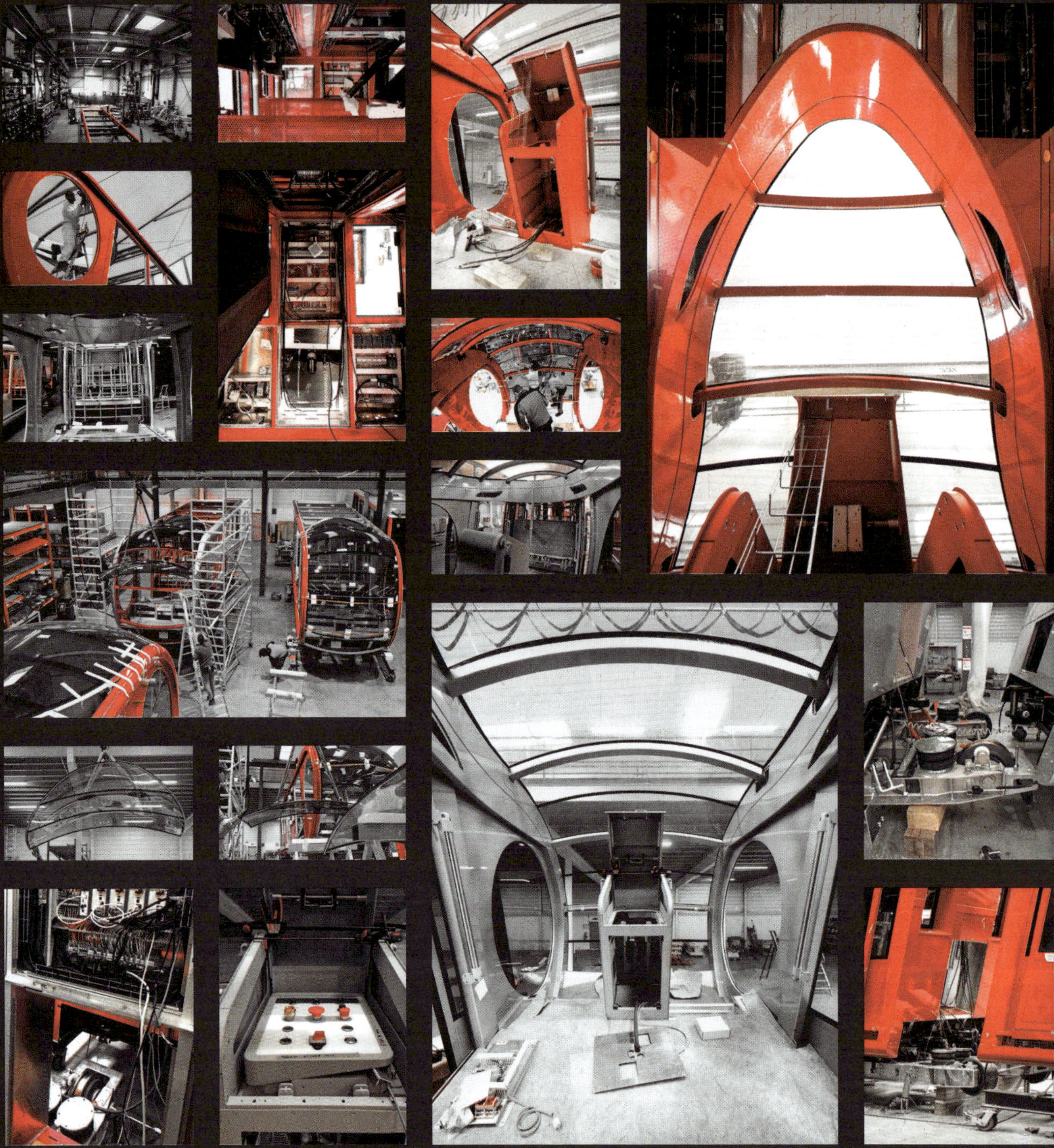

We believe that large infrastructures really transform cities. This idea of infrastructural buildings have a little bit to do with the ambition to engage with and get involved in the city. That involvement with the city, being actively part of it, clearly introduces a civic sense to architecture.

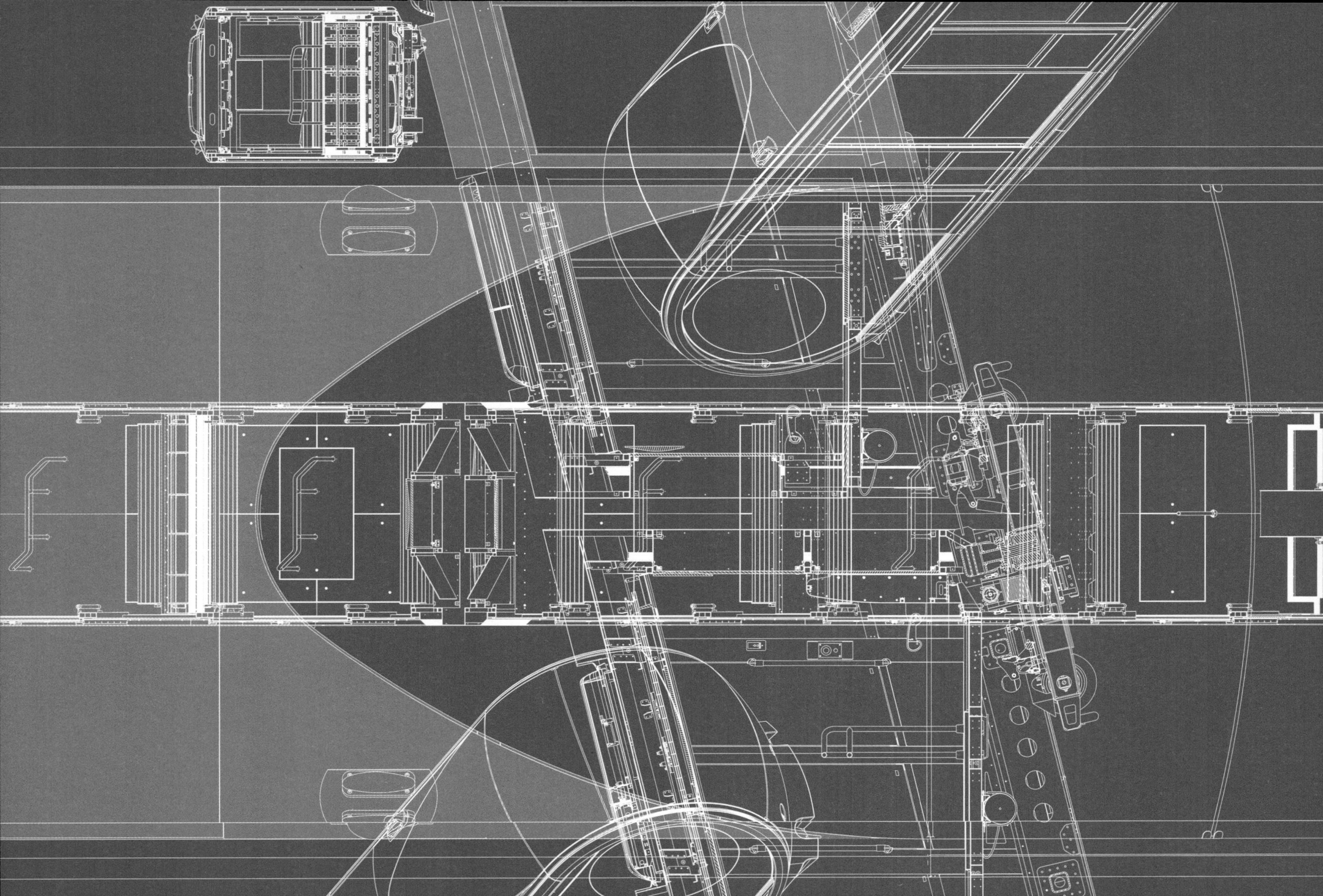

2017-2021 project_035 Cucadellum Funicular to Tibidabo Amusement Park, Barcelona, Spain
7.50x3.20m line drawing on glass exhibited at 'MIAS The *Making* of Making (Architecture)' at DHUB Barcelona Design Museum in 2021-2022

2017-2021 project_035 Cucadellum Funicular to Tibidabo Amusement Park, Barcelona, Spain
7.50x3.20m line drawing on glass exhibited at 'MIAS The *Making* of Making (Architecture)' at DHUB Barcelona Design Museum in 2021-2022

Cucadellum Funicular to Tibidabo Amusement Park

year: 2017-2021
location: Barcelona, Spain 41°24'59"N 02°07'51"
client: Barcelona City Council, Tibidabo Amusement Park

Awards
- 2023 LOOP Design Awards, Landscape, Urban Design category, Winner
- 2023 German Design Awards, Nominated
- 2023 DNA Paris Design Awards, Infrastructures & Transportation category, Winner
- 2023 Architizer A+ Awards, Sustainable Transportation category, Winner
- 2022 Dux Award to Sustainability

2017-2021 project_035 Cucadellum Funicular to Tibidabo Amusement Park, Barcelona, Spain

I am very interested in the ambiguity between public and private spaces, their occupation and appropriation, even when it is conflictive. So, some spaces in our projects question their public-private nature, not in the sense of ownership but rather in the sense of use of space.

Even the vocabulary we use to talk about the spaces inside our buildings are characteristic of the public space outside: street, square, passageway, etc. And the same is true the other way round. With the occupation of public space using terms related to an interior space: living room,

corridor, etc. The aim is to provide buildings with certain urban conditions. In the 22@ Plug-in office building the interior spaces are open-plan spaces that open out onto the city; they are really exterior spaces.

I think that architecture needs the commitment of its inhabitants, and it must be the inhabitants who interpret this. And I say this when it is the project itself that rigorously defines any element.

COMARCAS CATALANAS, S.

2006-2011 project_025 Plug-in Building at 22@, Barcelona, Spain

Plug-in Building at 22@

Restricted Competition, Winner
year: 2006-2011
location: Barcelona, Spain 41°23'44"N 02°11'**31"E**
surface: 7000 m^2
client: 22@ Poblenou

2006–2011 project_025 Plug-in Building at 22@, Barcelona, Spain

2007-2010 project_024
Annexa Joan Puigbert School,
Girona, Spain
41°58'42"N 02°49'38"E

2006-2011 project_025
Plug-in Building at 22@,
Barcelona, Spain
41°23'44"N 02°11'31"E

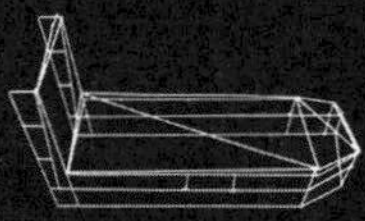

project_024
model_05

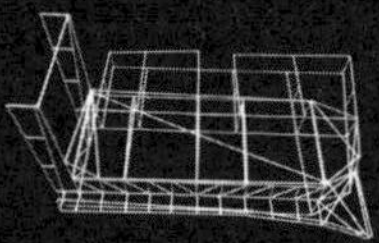

project_024
model_06

project_025
model_11

project_025
model_11

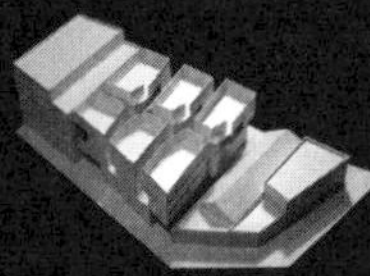

project_025
model_11

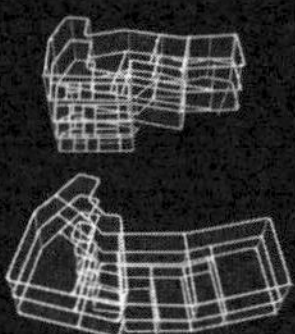

project_024
model_11

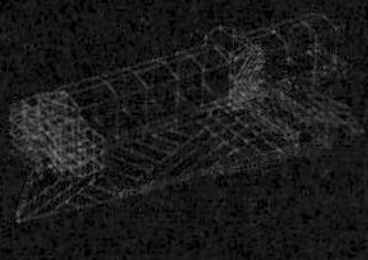

project_024
model_13_DHUB

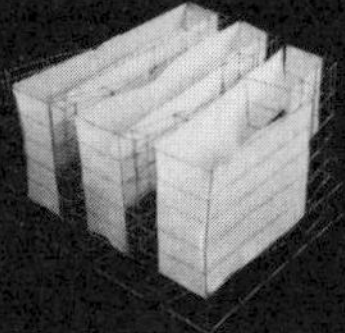

project_025
model_15

project_025
model_15

project_025
model_05

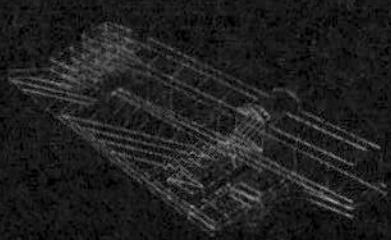

project_024
model_13_DHUB

project_024
model_13_DHUB

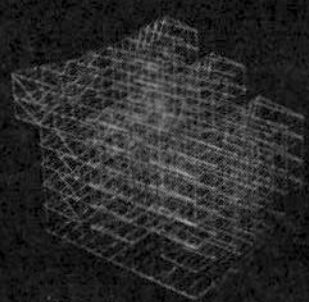

project_025
model_17

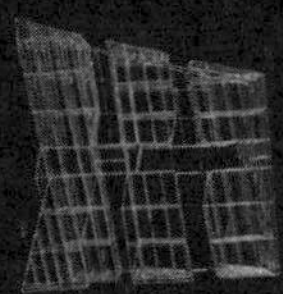

project_025
model_17

project_025
model_17

project_024
model_07

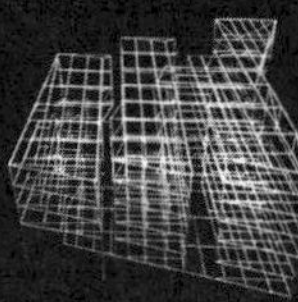

project_025
model_16
EC2020-2-AR83
Pompidou Collection

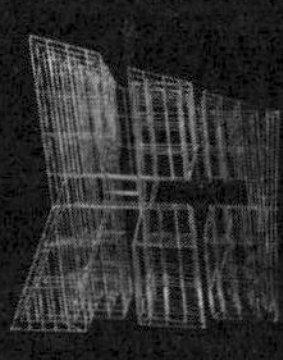

project_025
model_16
EC2020-2-AR83
Pompidou Collection

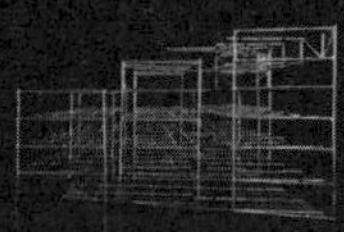

project_025
model_16
EC2020-2-AR83
Pompidou Collection

2007 project_061
Llull Travel Lodge Hotel at 22@,
Barcelona, Spain
41°23'00" N 02°11'00" E

project_061
model_05

project_061
model_05

project_061
model_05

project_061
model_01

project_061
model_02

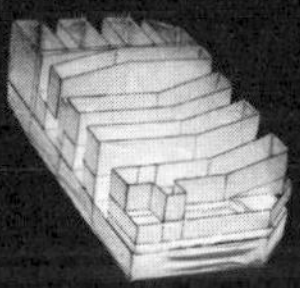

project_061
model_06

project_061
model_06

project_061
model_06

project_061
model_04

project_061
model_04

project_061
model_10

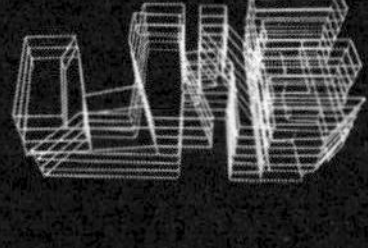

project_061
model_03

project_061
model_06

project_061
model_04

project_061
model_04

project_061
model_10

project_061
model_11

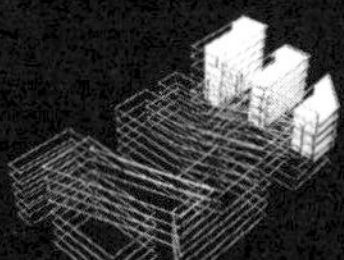

project_061
model_06

project_061
model_12

project_061
model_12

2017-2022 project_038 Can Vidalet Market, Esplugues de Llobregat, Spain

1.30x1.5m line drawing on glass exhibited at 'MIAS The *Making* of Making (Architecture)' at DHUB Barcelona Design Museum in 2021-2022

Moreover, we see innovation not only as a technical and quality improvement, but also as an economic improvement. In our case, innovation has almost always been linked to an economic problem, or to cost reduction.

2017-2022 project_039 La Plana Market, Esplugues de Llobregat, Spain
1.30x1.15m line drawing on glass exhibited at 'MIAS The *Making* of Making (Architecture)' at DHUB Barcelona Design Museum in 2021-2022

project_038

Can Vidalet Market

Open Competition, Winner
year: 2017-2022
location: Esplugues de Llobregat, Spain 41°22'26"N 02°06'02"E31"E
surface: 10.115 m^2
client: Esplugues de Llobregat City Council

2017-2022 project_38 Can Vidalet Market, Esplugues de Llobregat, Spain

La Plana Market

Open Competition, Winner
year: 2017-2022
location: Esplugues de Llobregat, Spain 41°22'22"N 02°05'03"E1"E
surface: 7776 m²

2017-2022 project_039 La Plana Market, Esplugues de Llobregat, Spain

2017-2022 / project_038 / models_01 - 13
Can Vidalet Market,
Esplugues de Llobregat, Spain
41°22'26"N 02°06'02"E

2017-2022 / project_039 / models_01 - 04
La Plana Market,
Esplugues de Llobregat, Spain
41°22'22"N 02°05'03"E

project_038
model_05

project_038
model_06

project_039
model_04

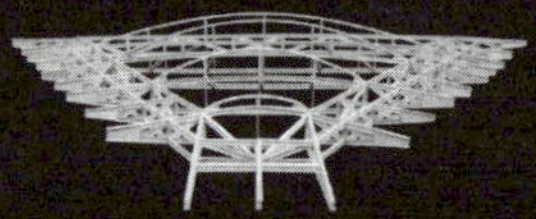

project_039
model_04

project_038
model_12_DHUB

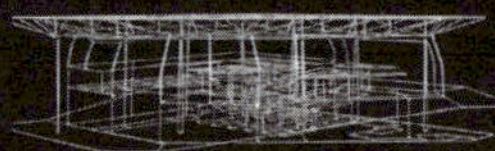

project_038
model_11
EC2020-2-AR57
Pompidou Collection

project_039
model_03

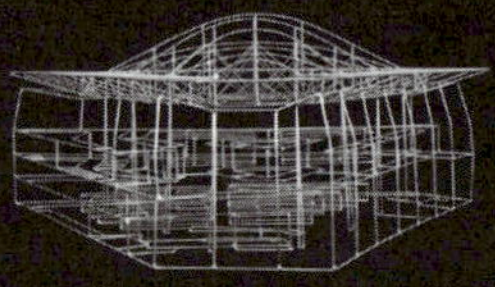

project_039
model_02
EC2020-2-AR64
Pompidou Collection

project_038
model_12_DHUB

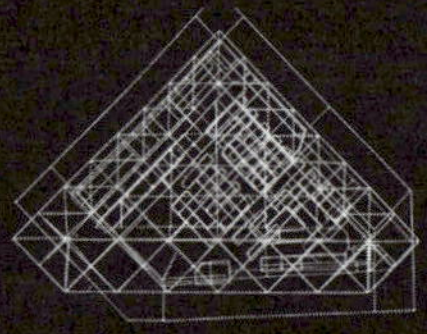

project_038
model_11
EC2020-2-AR57
Pompidou Collection

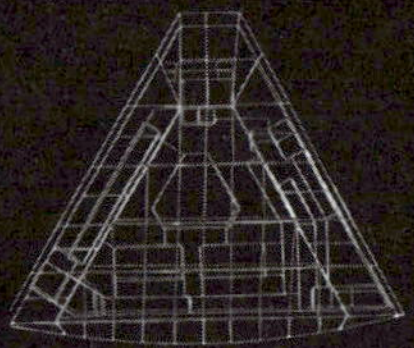

project_039
model_03

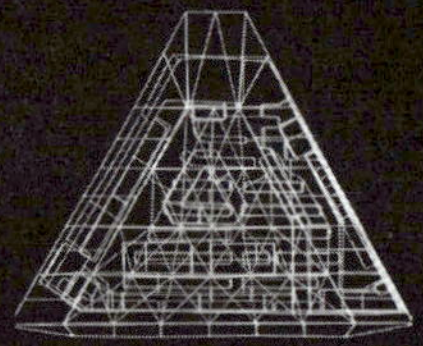

project_039
model_02
EC2020-2-AR64
Pompidou Collection

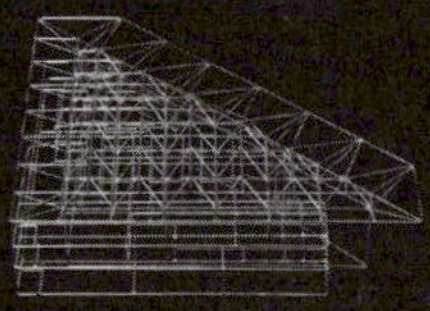

project_038
model_12_DHUB

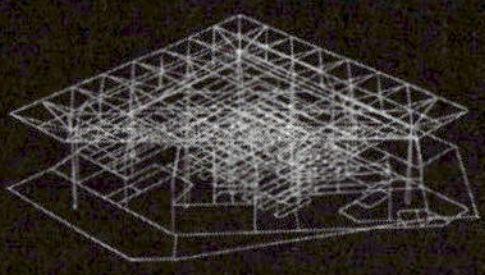

project_038
model_11
EC2020-2-AR57
Pompidou Collection

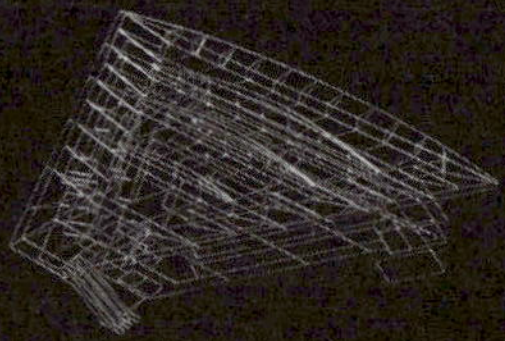

project_039
model_03

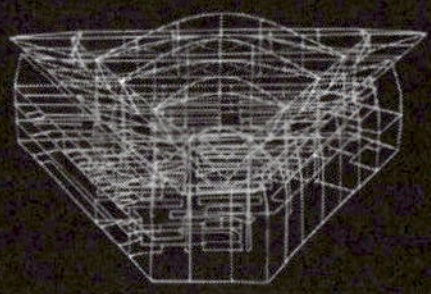

project_039
model_02
EC2020-2-AR64
Pompidou Collection

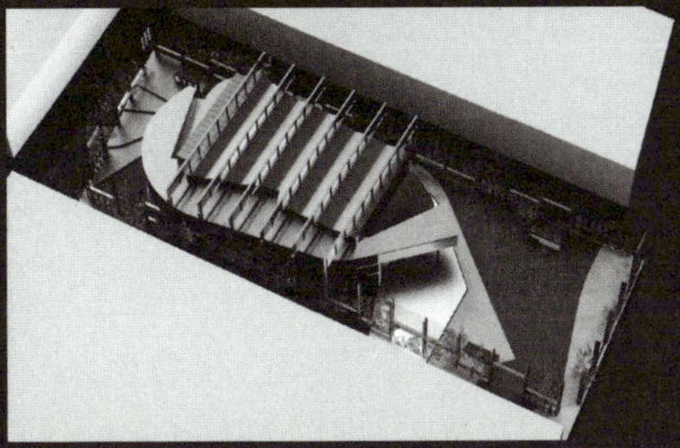

2009 / project_044 / models_01 - 09
Elx Auditorium, Elx, Spain
38°16'14"N 00°42'28"W

2011 / project_111 / models_01 - 02
Phytodut, Portes de Collserola Park, Barcelona, Spain
41°24'44"N 02°04'26"E

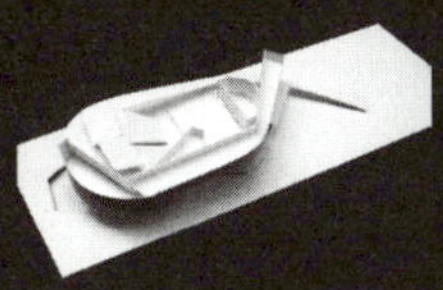

project_044
model_01

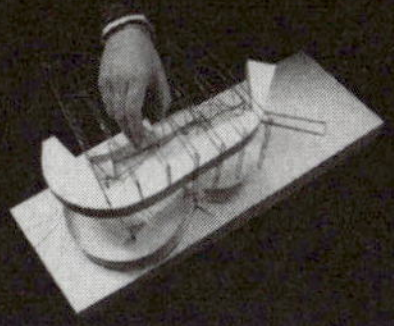

project_044
model_01

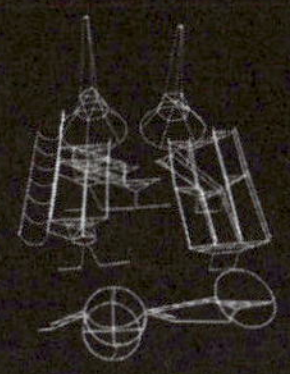

project_111
model_01

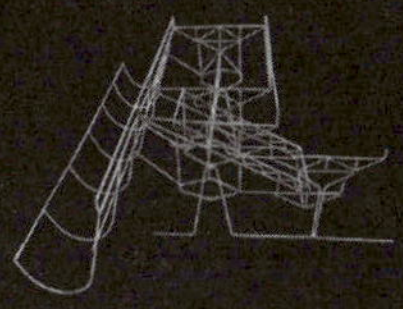

project_111
model_01

project_044
model_02

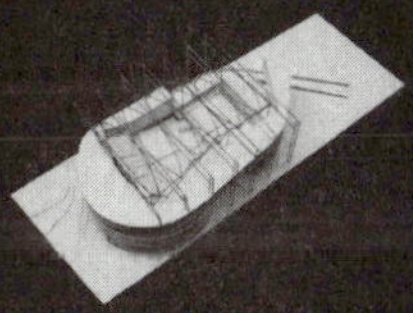

project_044
model_01

project_111
model_01

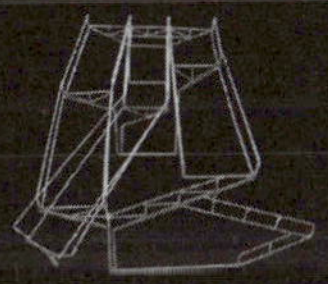

project_111
model_01

project_044
model_04_DHUB

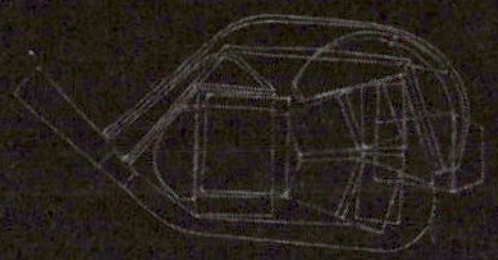

project_044
model_03

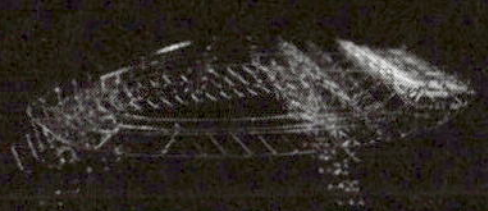

project_111
model_02

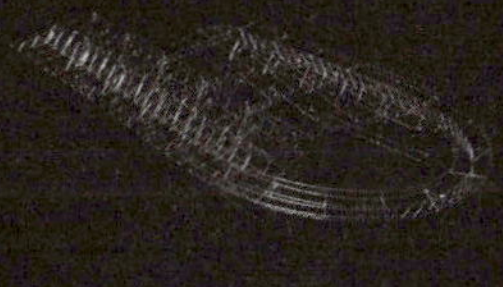

project_111
model_02_DHUB

project_044
model_04_DHUB

project_044
model_04_DHUB

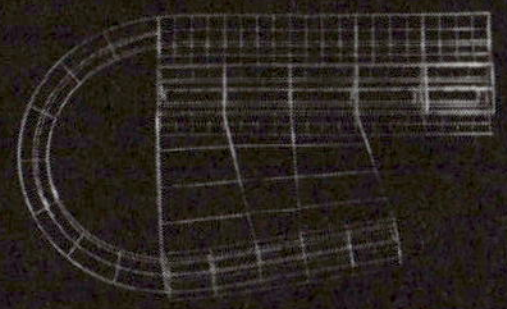

project_111
model_02_DHUB

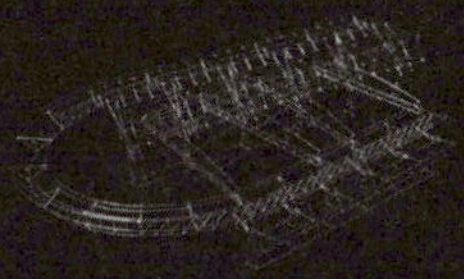

project_111
model_02_DHUB

2009-2012 project_027 Torrebaró Social Housing, Barcelona, Spain
Colour sketches printed on glass exhibited at 'MIAS T[illegible] Making of Making (Architecture)' at DHUB Barcelona Design Museum in 2021-2022

2009-2012 project_027 Torrebaró Social Housing, Barcelona, Spain
Colour sketches printed on glass exhibited at 'MIAS The *Making* of Making (Architecture)' at DHUB Barcelona Design Museum in 2021-2022

2009-2012 project_027 Torrebaró Social Housing, Barcelona, Spain

model_02 65x54x87cm balsa wood exhibited at 'MIAS The *Making* of Making (Architecture)' at DHUB Barcelona Design Museum in 2021-2022

2009-2012 project_027 Torrebaró Social Housing, Barcelona, Spain
model_02 65x54x87cm balsa wood exhibited at 'MIAS The *Making* of Making (Architecture)' at DHUB Barcelona Design Museum in 2021-2022

We have approached each new project as a challenge, so that the same materials and construction system take a further step forward, improving on the features of the previous one. And all of this with the aim of becoming as industrialised as possible and, therefore, reducing costs. I am very interested in the application of systems from one building element to another, causing moments of tension, doubt and response to occur at the same time.

Torrebaró Social Housing

page 142

Open Competition, Winner
year: 2009-2012
location: Barcelona, Spain 41°27'36"N 02°10'50"E1"E
surface: 5000 m^2
client: Barcelona City Council, BAGURSA, REGESA

Awards
- 2012 Barcelona City Prize for Architecture and Urbanism, Selected

Publications
- *Torrebaró Housing Building*, Miàs, Josep, Barcelona, 2011

2009-2012 **project_027**
Torrebaró Social Housing,
Barcelona, Spain
41º27'36"N 02º10'50"E

project_027
model_03

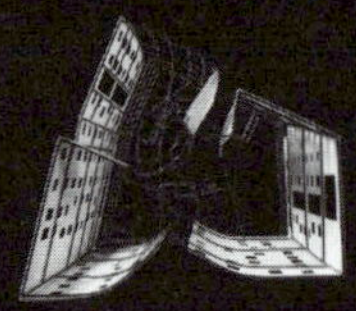
project_027
model_04

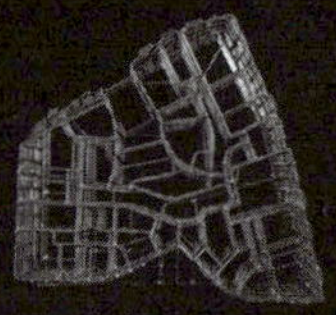
project_027
model_10_DHUB

project_027
model_09

project_027
model_09

project_027
model_03

project_027
model_04

project_027
model_10_DHUB

project_027
model_08

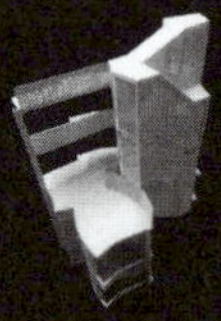
project_027
model_01

project_027
model_03

project_027
model_07

project_027
model_06

project_027
model_03

project_027
model_02

project_027
model_05

project_027
model_03

project_027
model_10_DHUB

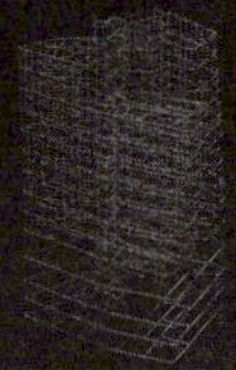
project_027
model_10_DHUB

project_027
model_02

in progress project_028
Cocobolo Centre,
Panama City, Panama
09°00'00"N 79°30'00"W

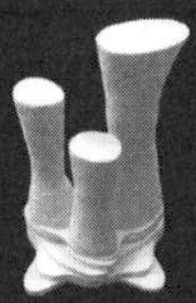

project_028
model_05

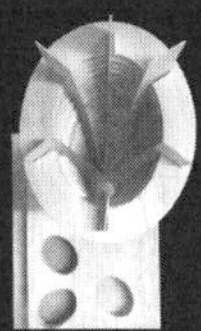

project_028
model_02

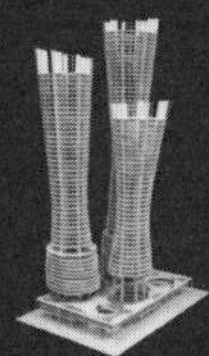

project_028
model_04

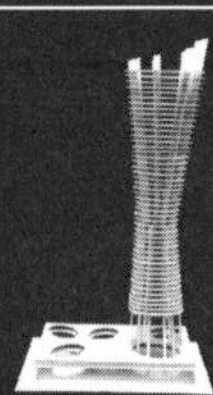

project_028
model_02

project_28
model_04

project_028
model_04

project_028
model_06

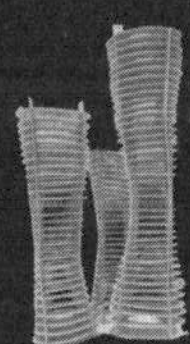

project_028
model_02

project_028
model_02

project_028
model_01

project_028
model_09_DHUB

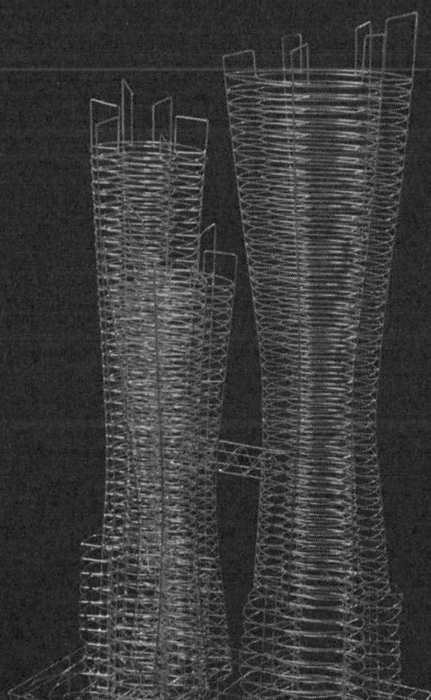

project_028
model_09_DHUB

project_028
model_04

in progress project_028 Cocobolo Centre, Panama City, Panama
model_04 61x42x80cm 1:100 wood model exhibited at 'MIAS The *Making* of Making (Architecture)' at DHUB Barcelona Design Museum in 2021-2022

in progress project_028 Cocobolo Centre, Panama City, Panama
model_04 61x42x80cm 1:100 wood model exhibited at 'MIAS The *Making* of Making (Architecture)' at DHUB Barcelona Design Museum in 2021-2022

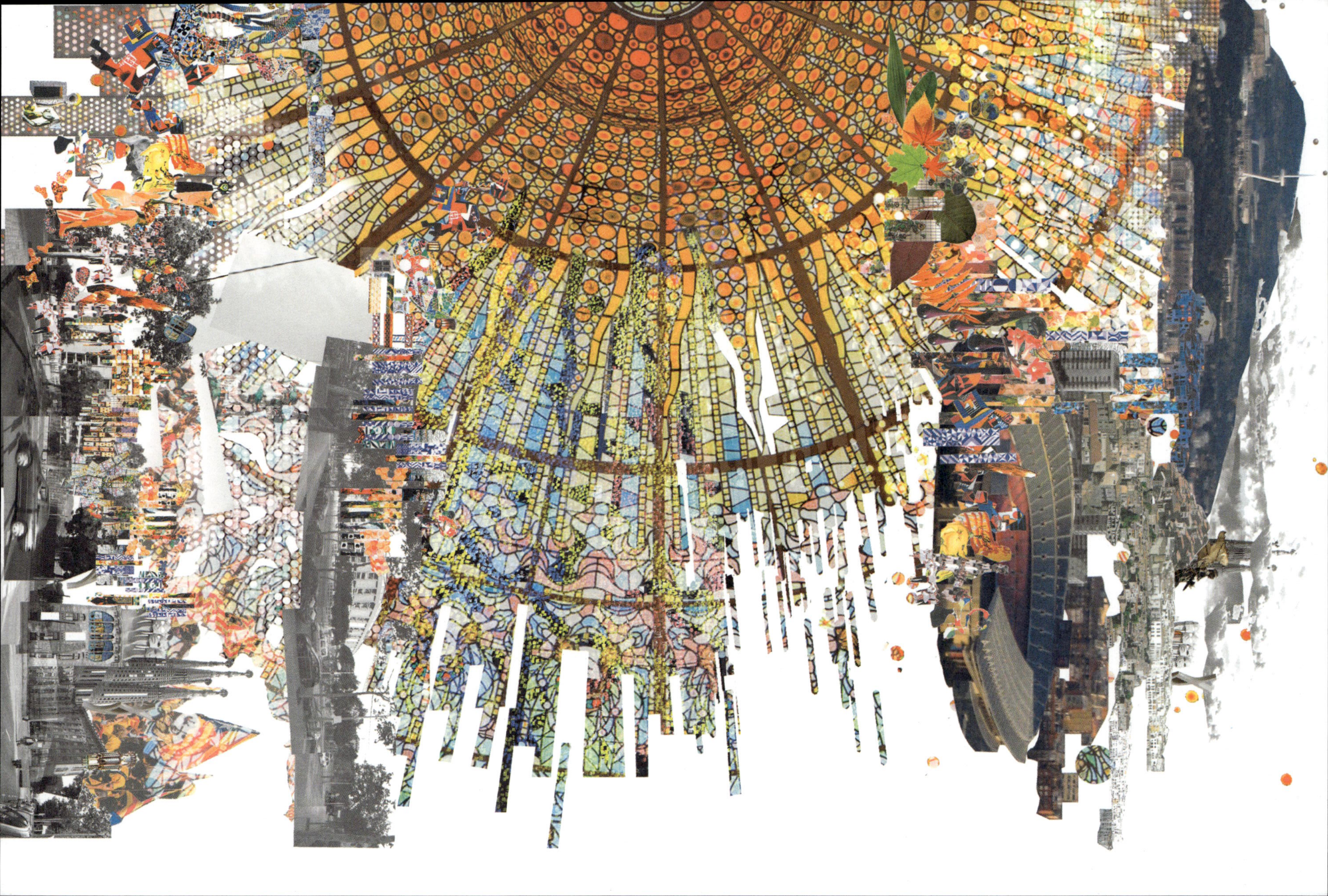

FCB

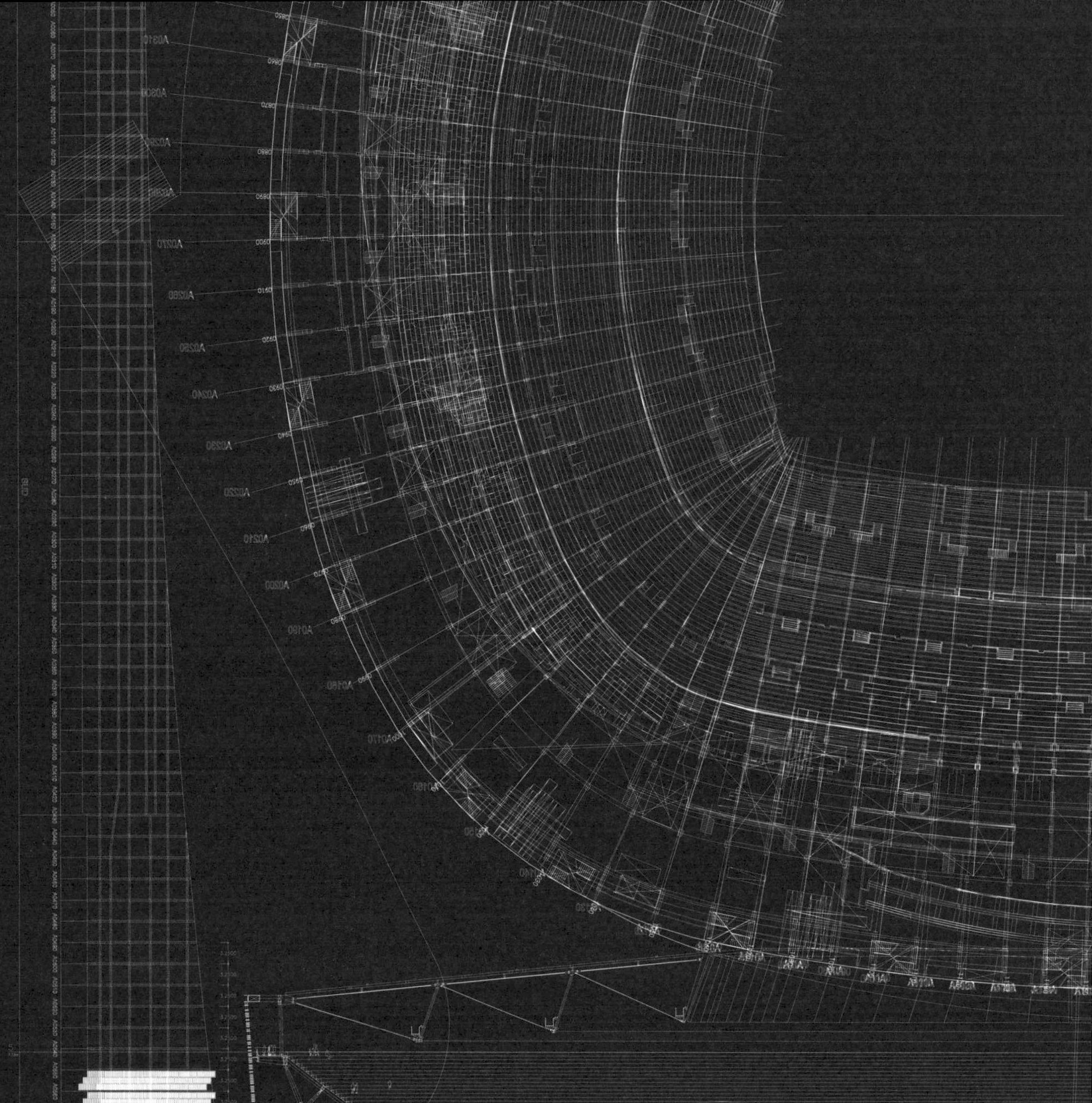

2015-2016 project_040 New Camp Nou FC Barcelona, Barcelona, Spain
1.80x1.80m line drawing on glass exhibited at 'MIAS The *Making* of Making (Architecture)' at DHUB Barcelona Design Museum in 2021-2022

The new Camp Nou stadium desired two very different aspects: to complete an asymmetrical stadium with a different structure from the existing one and to build a roof and a façade.
The collages we made of the stadium, with cut-outs of other buildings, places and people in the city, were to enable us to identify the character of this new façade and its colours. As we were aware at all times that the truly interesting façade is the one that is produced on the inside when we see the stands full, we decided

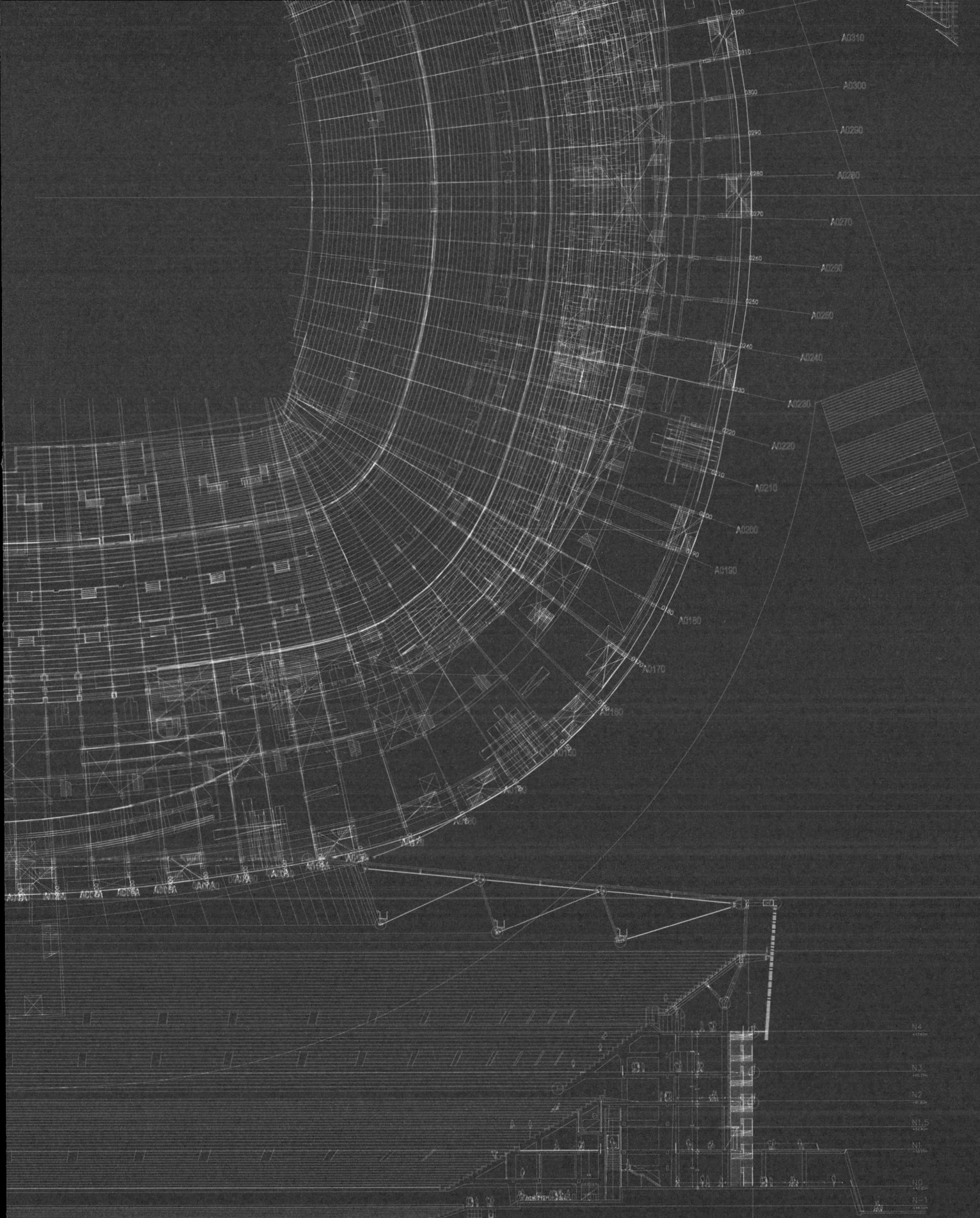

2015-2016 project_040 New Camp Nou FC Barcelona, Barcelona, Spain
1.80x1.80m line drawing on glass exhibited at 'MIAS The *Making* of Making (Architecture)' at DHUB Barcelona Design Museum in 2021-2022

to transfer the interior image to the exterior. Hence, the use of coloured ceramic pieces on a human scale, incorporating LED technology, interactive sensors for the public from the outside, etc. Another part of the proposal involves the use of public space around the stadium, and its relationship with the immediately surrounding city, which has been called the Espai Barça.

2015-2016 project_040 New Camp Nou FC Barcelona, Barcelona, Spain
model 08 150x165x115cm 1:75 wood model exhibited at 'MAS The Making of Making (Architecture)' at DHUB Barcelona Design Museum in 2021-2022

2015–2016 project_040 New Camp Nou FC Barcelona, Barcelona, Spain
model_08 150x165x115cm 1:75 wood model exhibited at 'MIAS The *Making* of Making (Architecture)' at DHUB Barcelona Design Museum in 2021-2022

2015-2016 project_040
New Camp Nou FC Barcelona,
Barcelona, Spain
41°22'51"N 02°07'22"E

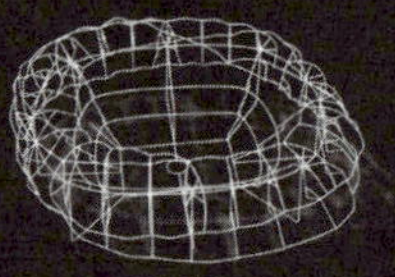

project_040
model_02

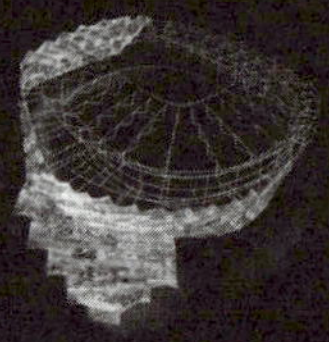

project_040
model_06

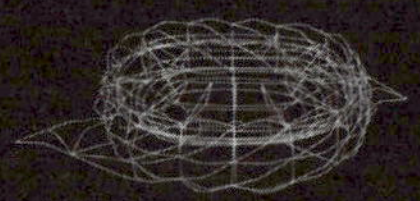

project_040
model_03_DHUB

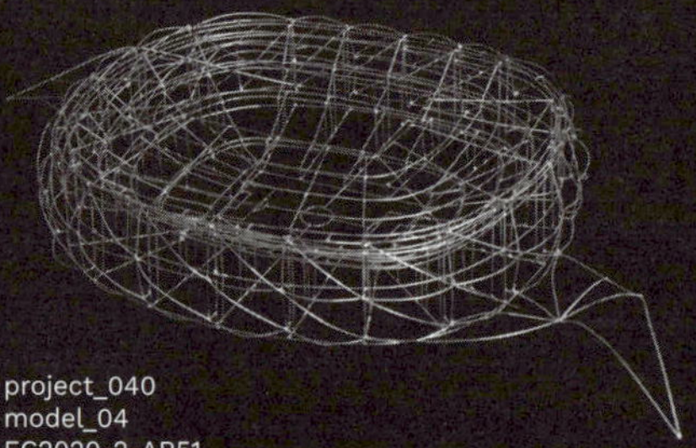

project_040
model_04
EC2020-2-AR51
Pompidou Collection

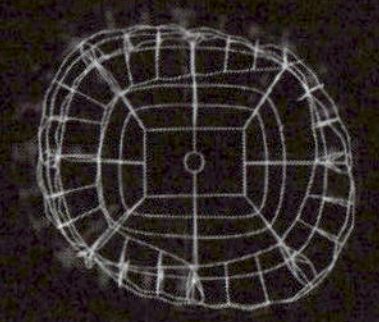

project_040
model_02

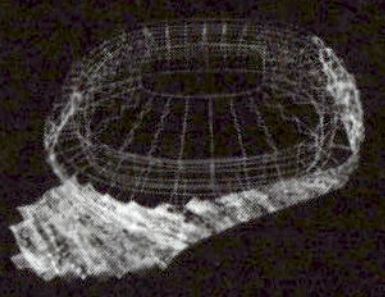

project_040
model_06

project_040
model_03_DHUB

project_040
model_04
EC2020-2-AR51
Pompidou Collection

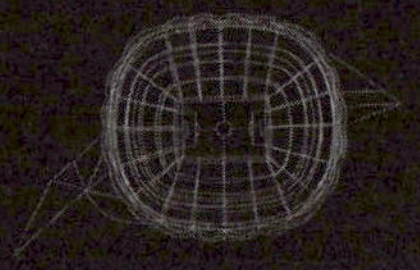

project_040
model_04
EC2020-2-AR51
Pompidou Collection

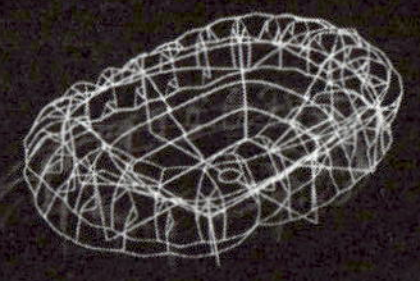

project_040
model_02

project_040
model_06

project_040
model_03

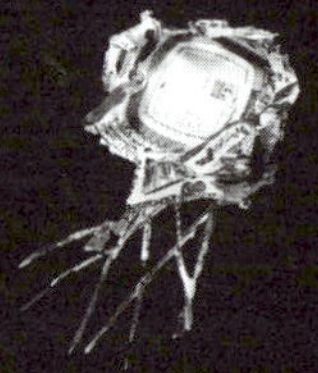

project_040
model_01

project_040
model_01

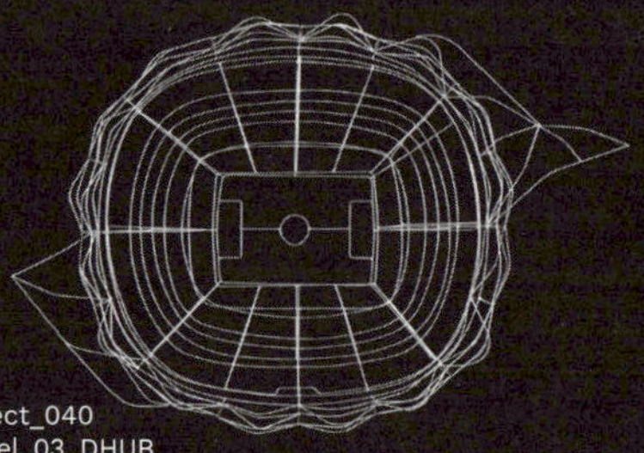

project_040
model_03_DHUB

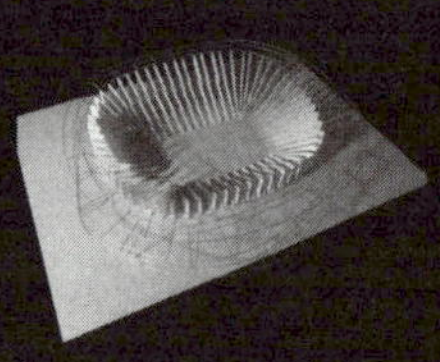

project_040
model_07

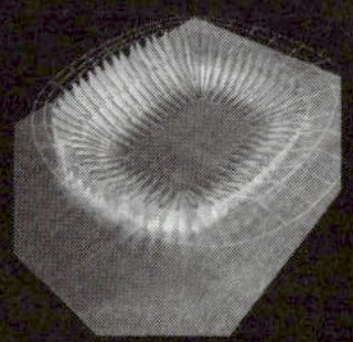

project_040
model_07

project_040
model_02

2017 project_031
Nebula Caixa Forum,
Valencia, Spain
39°27'14"N 00°20'59"W

2013 project_034
Brazilian Antarctic Station,
South Sethland Islands, Antarctica
62°05'06"S 58°23'28"W

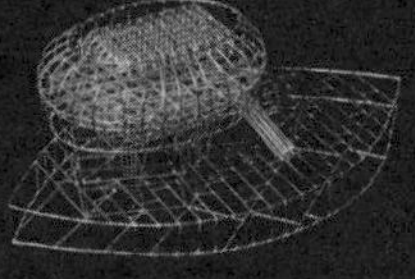

project_031
model_04

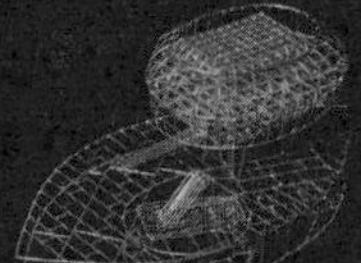

project_031
model_04

project_034
model_01

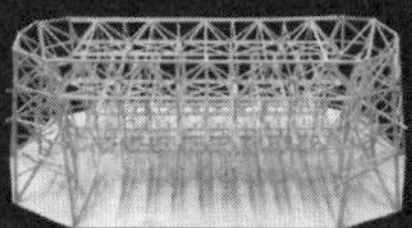

project_034
model_01

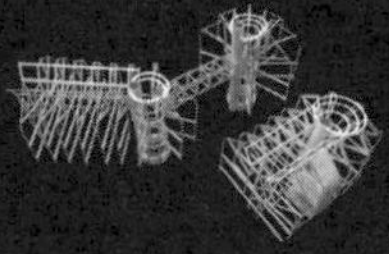

project_034
model_02

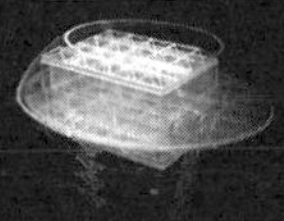

project_031
model_01

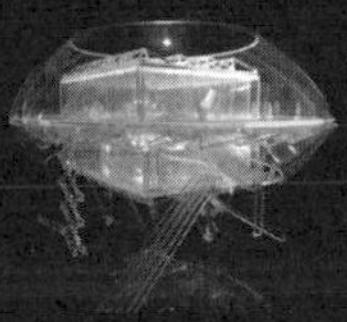

project_031
model_01

project_034
model_04

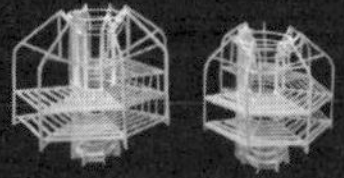

project_034
model_04

project_034
model_04

project_031
model_02

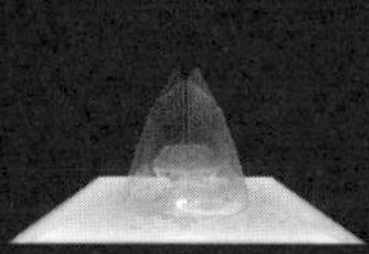

project_031
model_02

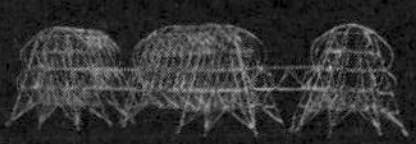

project_034
model_07_DHUB

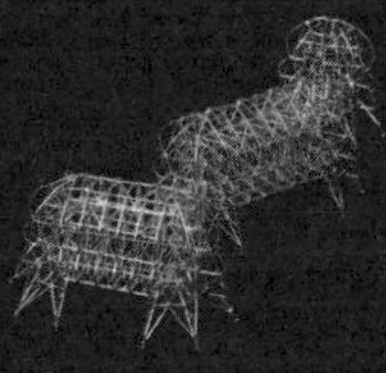

project_034
model_07_DHUB

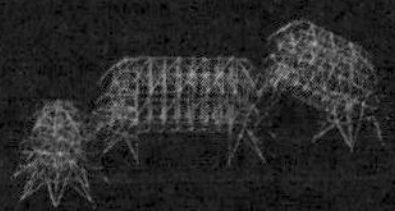

project_034
model_07_DHUB

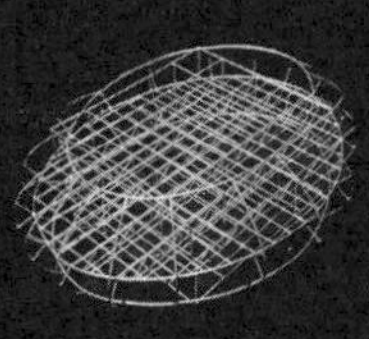

project_031
model_03_DHUB

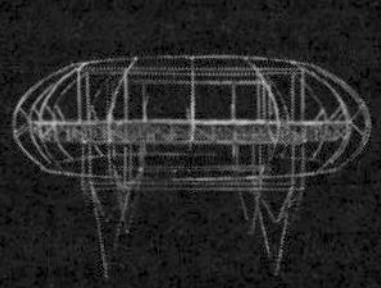

project_031
model_03_DHUB

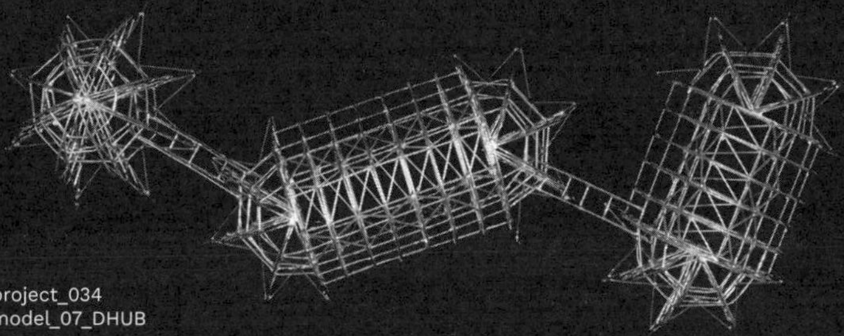

project_034
model_07_DHUB

in progress project_028 Cocobolo Centre, Panama City, Panama
2016 project_107 National Ceramic Museum, Seoul, South Korea

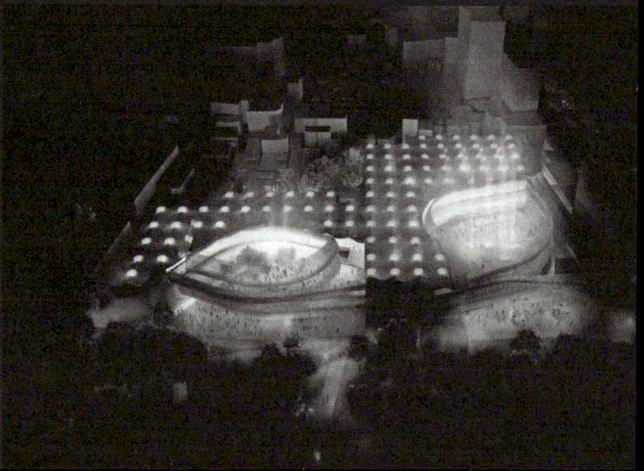

2017 project_031 Nebula Caixa Forum, Valencia, Spain
2015 project_079 Bao'an Culture and Art Centre, Shenzhen, China

in progress project_030 The Cloud Andorra Telecom Headquarters, Andorra La Vella, Andorra
model_69 welded wire 39x120x56cm EC2020-2-AR73 Centre Pompidou Permanent Collection

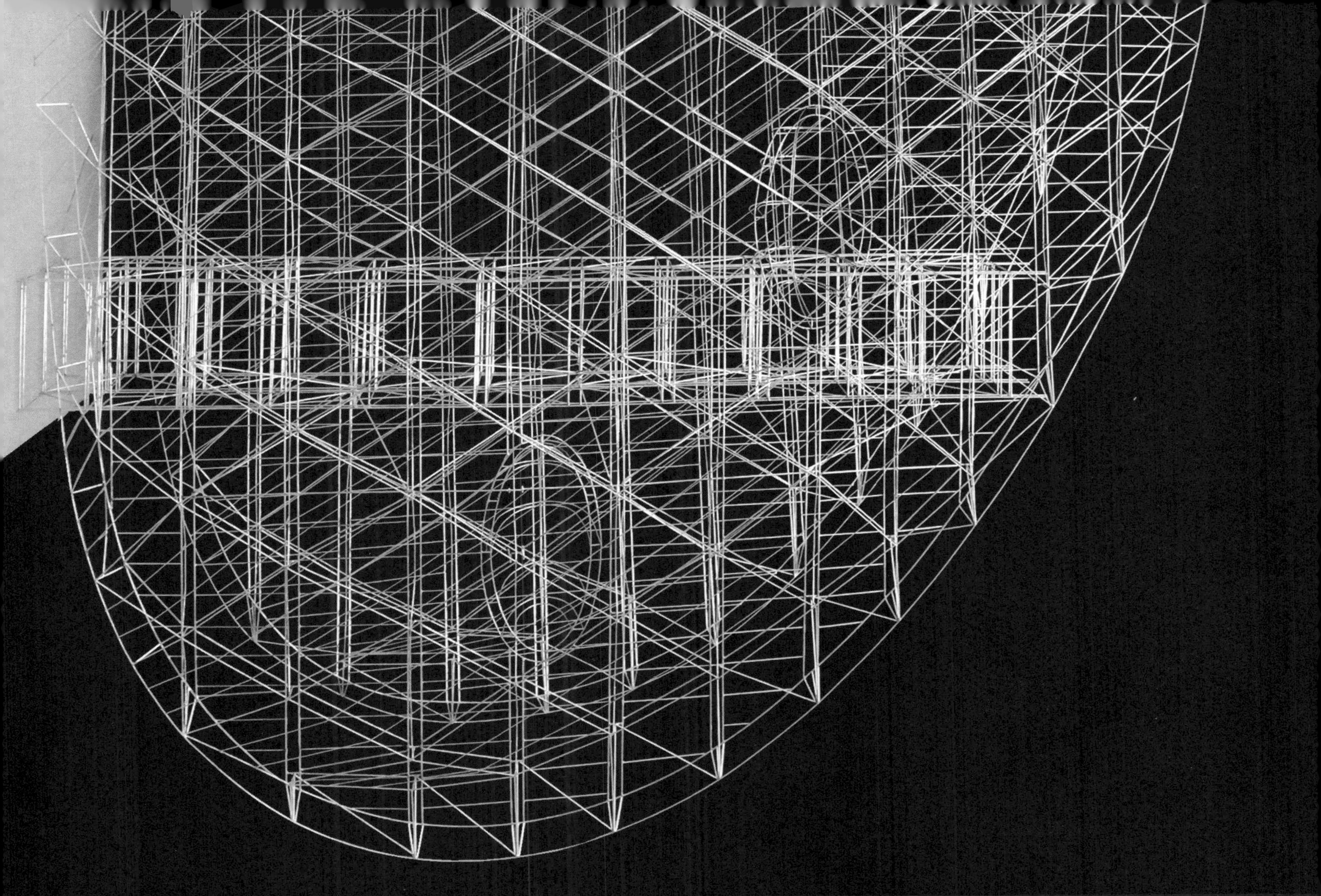

in progress project_030 The Cloud Andorra Telecom Headquarters, Andorra La Vella, Andorra
model_69 welded wire 39x120x56cm EC2020-2-AR73 Centre Pompidou Permanent Collection

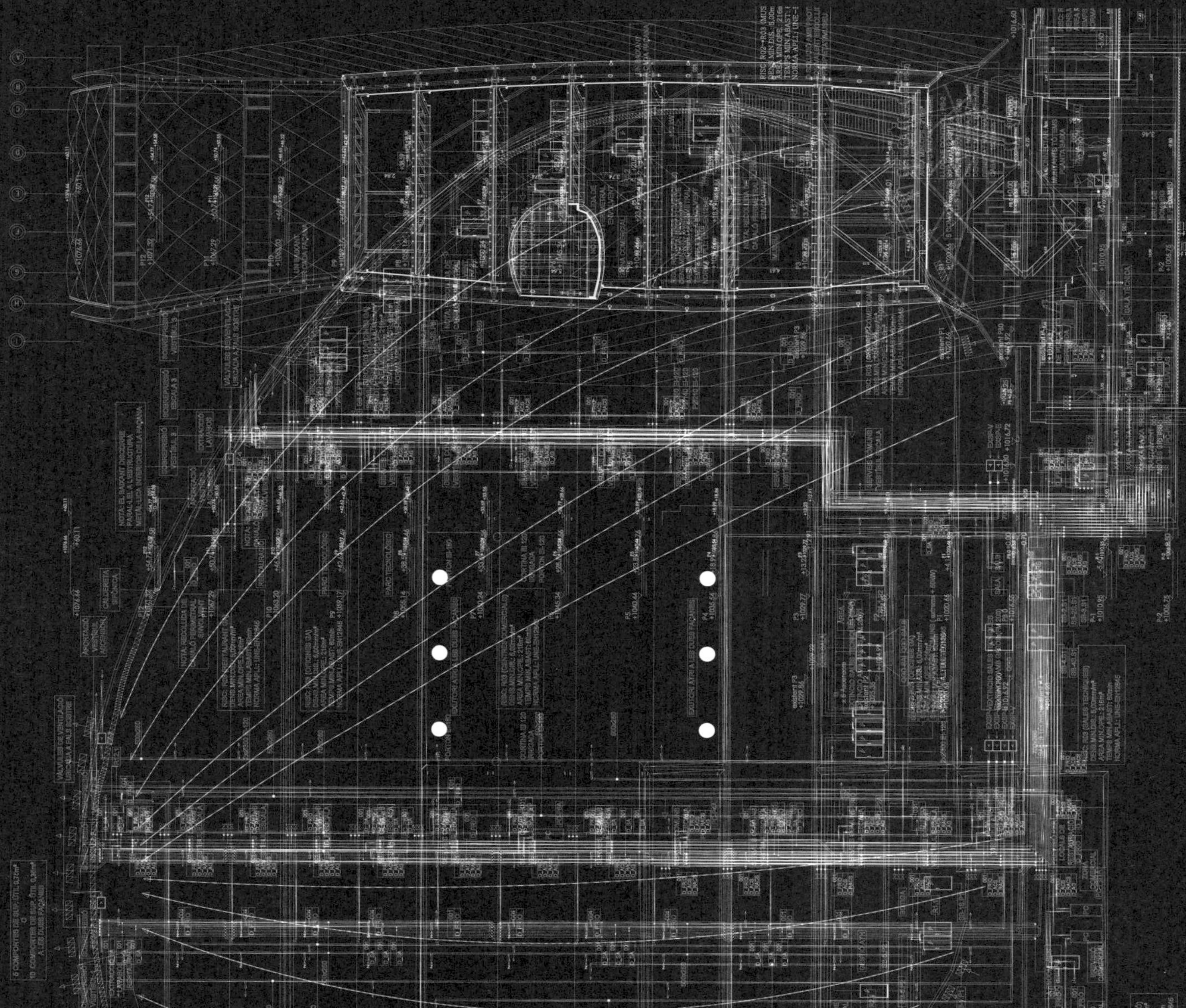

in progress project_030 The Cloud Andorra Telecom Headquarters, Andorra La Vella, Andorra
1.95x2.10m line drawing on glass exhibited at 'MIAS The *Making* of Making (Architecture)' at DHUB Barcelona Design Museum in 2021-2022

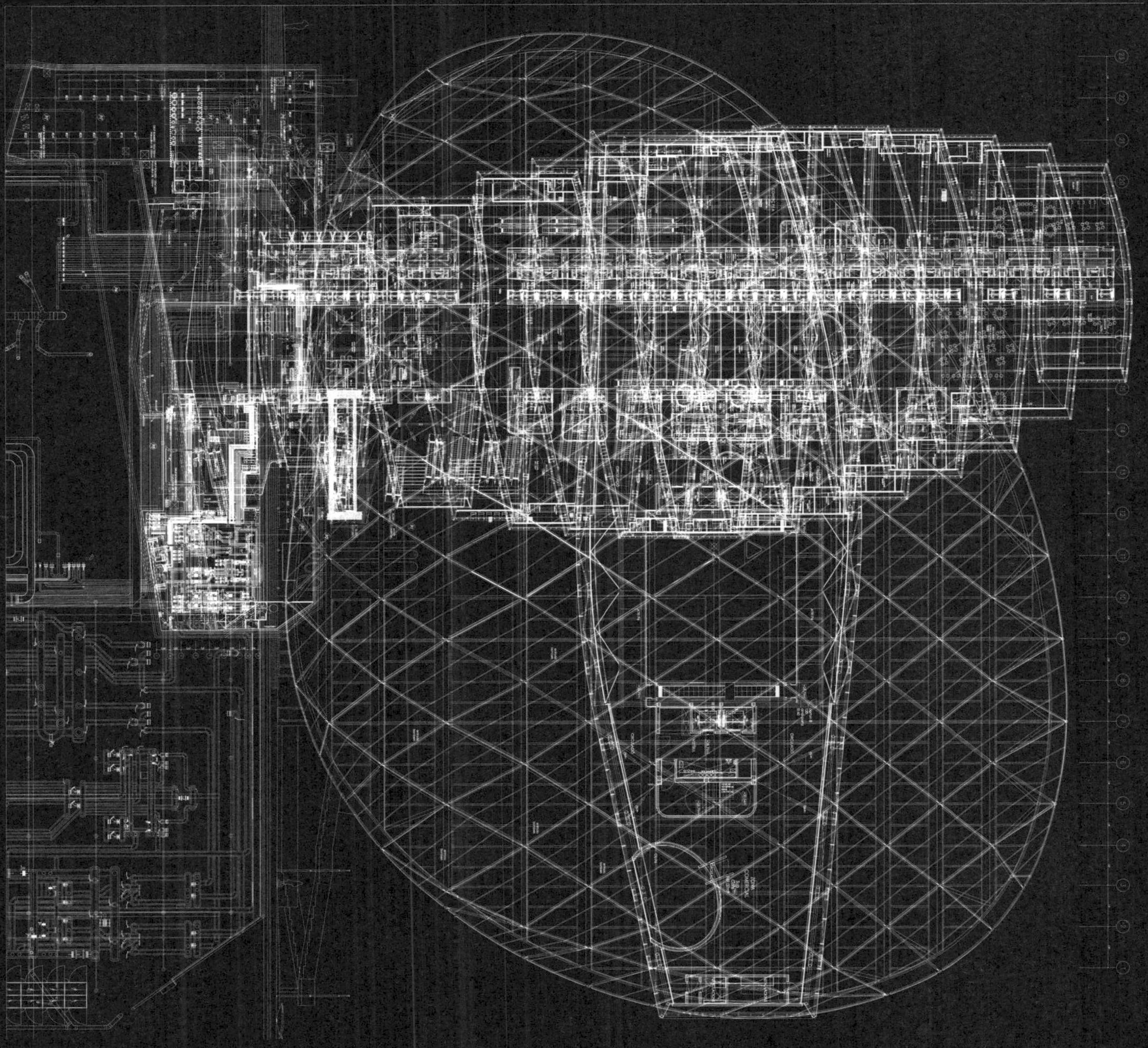

in progress project_030 The Cloud Andorra Telecom Headquarters, Andorra La Vella, Andorra
1.95x2.10m line drawing on glass exhibited at 'MIAS The *Making* of Making (Architecture)' at DHUB Barcelona Design Museum in 2021-2022

in progress project_030 The Cloud Andorra Telecom Headquarters, Andorra La Vella, Andorra

in progress project_030 The Cloud Andorra Telecom Headquarters, Andorra La Vella, Andorra

'MIAS The *Making* of Making (Architecture)'

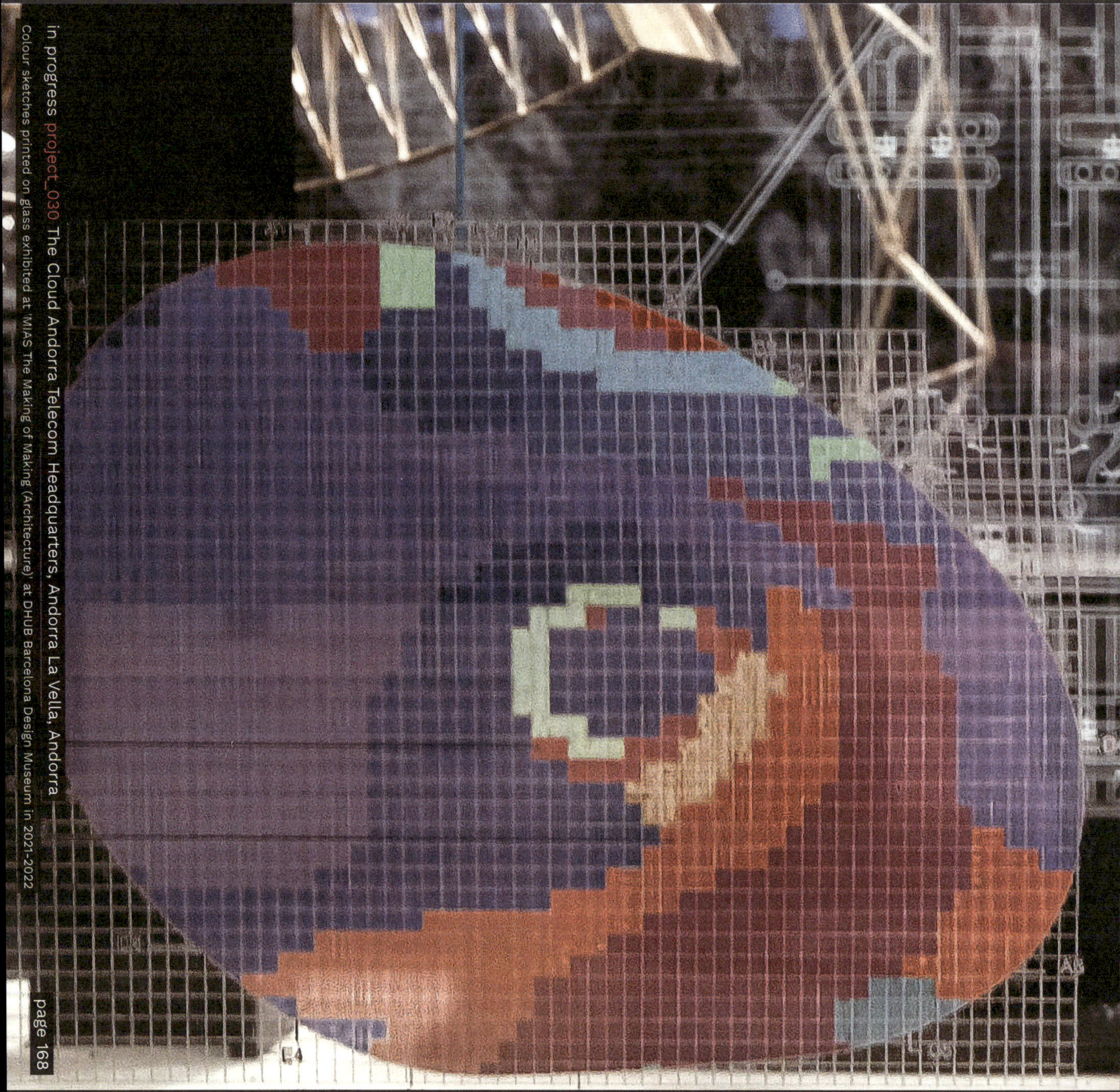

in progress project_030 The Cloud Andorra Telecom Headquarters, Andorra La Vella, Andorra

Colour sketches printed on glass exhibited at 'MIAS The Making of Making (Architecture)' at DHUB Barcelona Design Museum in 2021-2022

In Andorra, we wanted to construct a building that would free up as much public space as possible in a place that was already very built-up. That's why the project is lifted off the ground, offering the public all the space that the building itself occupies in height.

The existing building is included in its interior, using the previous roof as a habitable surface of an interior space in a five-storey hall, in such a way that this floor level of the hall coincided with the level of the neighbouring buildings' roofs. The cross-sectional

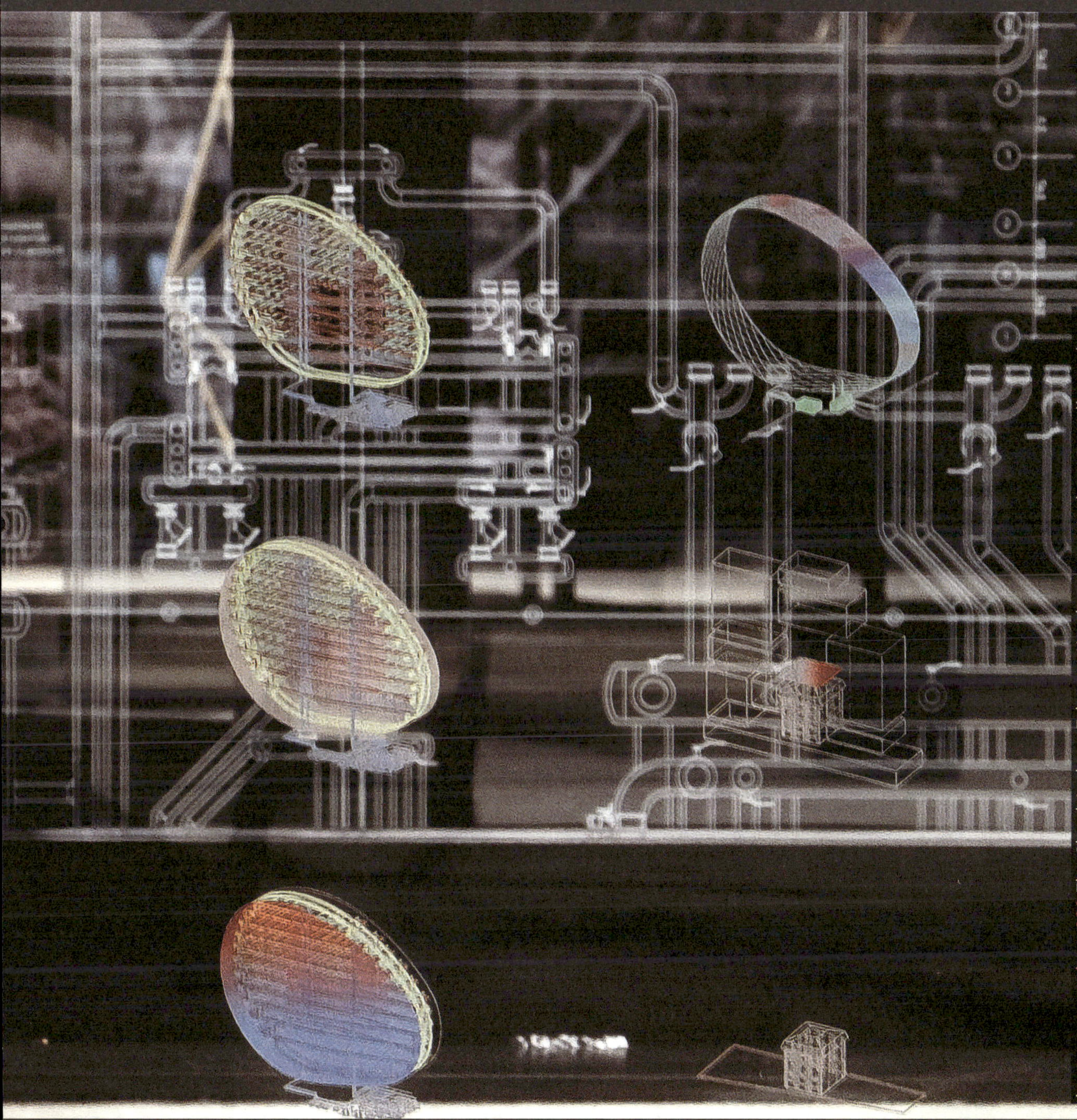

Colour sketches printed on glass exhibited at 'MIAS The Making of Making (Architecture)' at DHUB Barcelona Design Museum in 2021-2022

dimension, less than 15 metres, allows natural light to enter all the spaces and a view through the building itself. The most relevant aspect of the project is that it was designed like a machine, with a 1.5-metre-thick perimeter ring where all the installations are located.

The double glass façade acts as a thermal cushion to avoid the need to air-condition the interiors. This feature can be structural and the interior free of any structure, leaving the spaces without any pillars.

in progress **project_030**
The Cloud Andorra Telecom Headquarters,
Andorra La Vella, Andorra
42°30'29"N 01°31'57"E

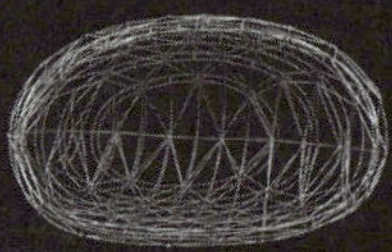

project_030
model_08

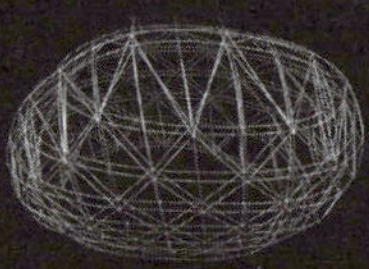

project_030
model_08

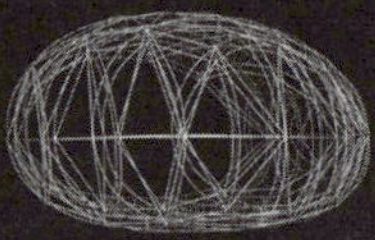

project_030
model_08

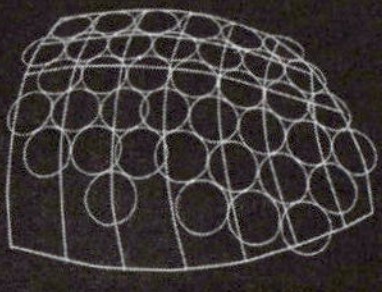

project_030
model_04

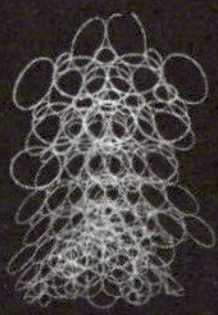

project_030
model_20

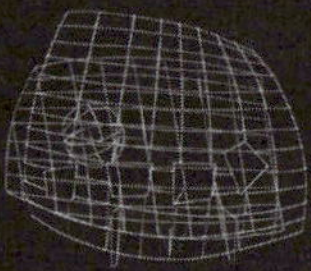

project_030
model_24
EC2020-2-AR52
Pompidou Collection

project_030
model_24
EC2020-2-AR52
Pompidou Collection

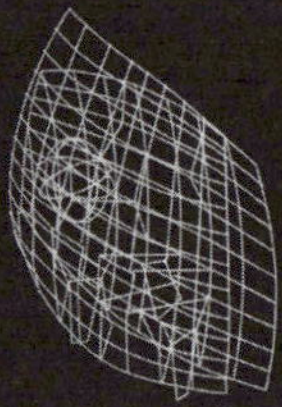

project_030
model_24
EC2020-2-AR52
Pompidou Collection

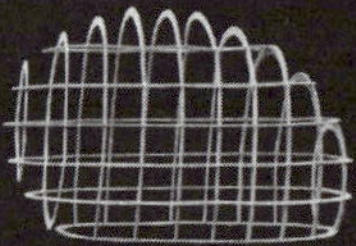

project_030
model_17

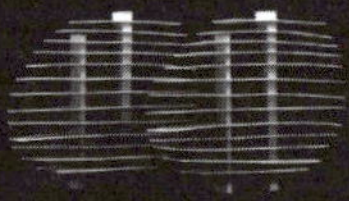

project_030
model_09

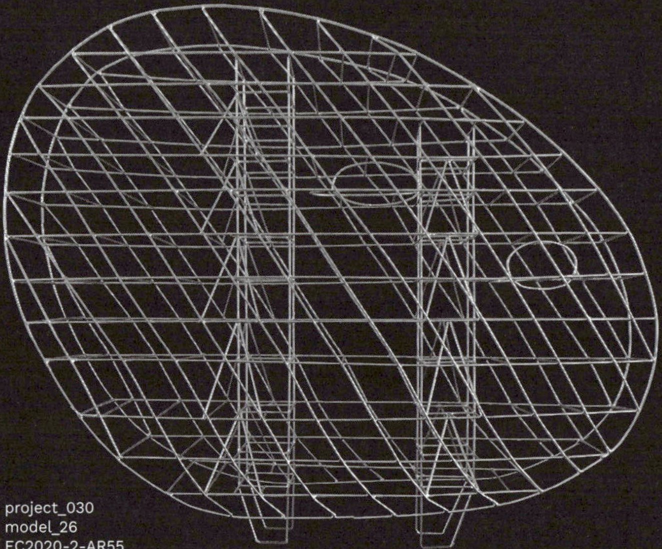

project_030
model_26
EC2020-2-AR55
Pompidou Collection

project_030
model_27
EC2020-2-AR55
Pompidou Collection

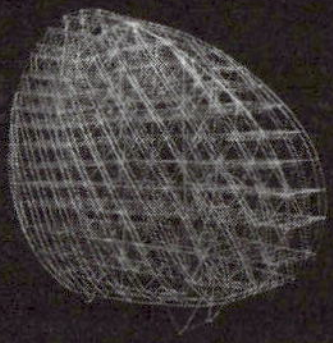

project_030
model_27
EC2020-2-AR55
Pompidou Collection

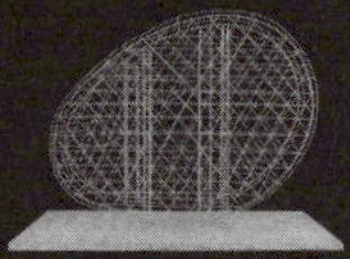

project_030
model_25
EC2020-2-AR53
Pompidou Collection

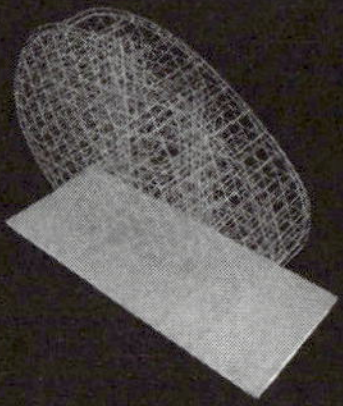

project_030
model_25
EC2020-2-AR53
Pompidou Collection

in progress **project_030**
The Cloud Andorra Telecom Headquarters,
Andorra La Vella, Andorra
42°30'29"N 01°31'57"E

2014 **project_037**
Passenger Terminal and Service Centre,
Kinmen, Taiwan
24°25'3"N 118°17'36"E

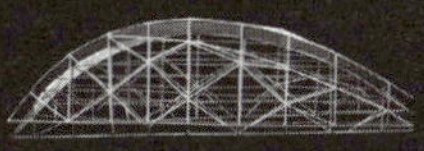

project_030
model_01

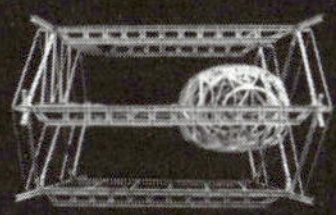

project_030
model_21

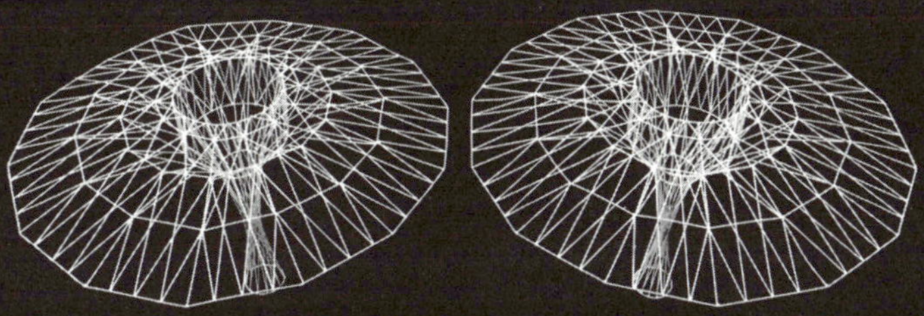

project_037
model_02

project_030
model_07

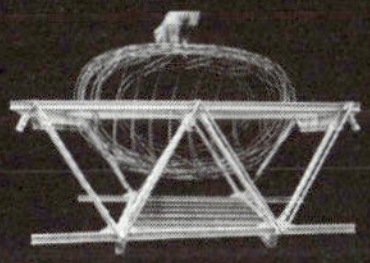

project_030
model_21

project_037
model_10

project_037
model_10

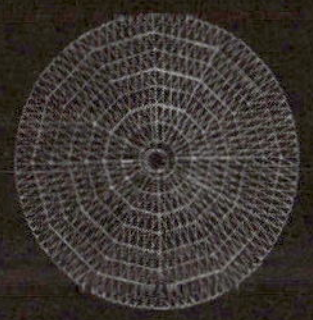

project_037
model_10

project_030
model_07

project_030
model_07

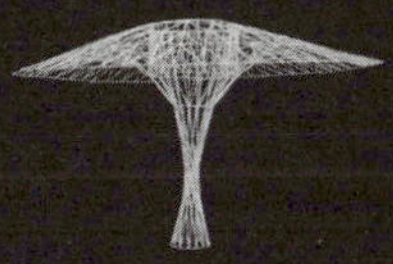

project_037
model_02

project_037
model_02

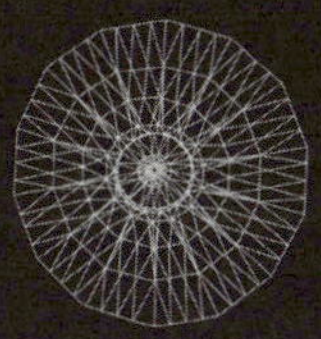

project_037
model_02

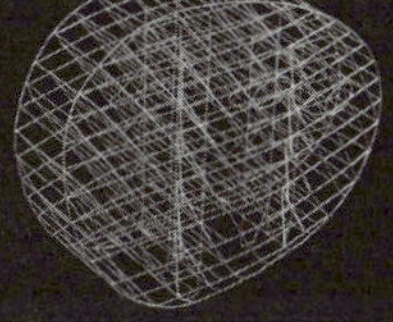

project_030
model_26
EC2020-2-AR55
Pompidou Collection

project_030
model_26
EC2020-2-AR55
Pompidou Collection

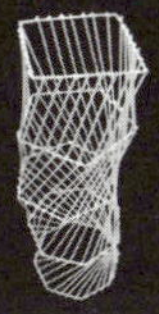

project_037
model_05

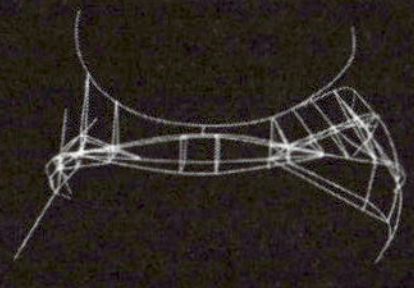

project_037
model_04

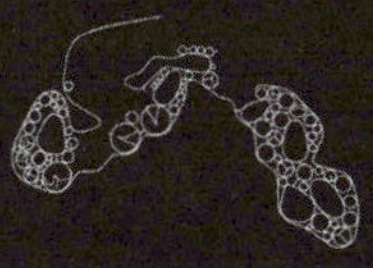

project_037
model_01

2014 project_037 Passenger Terminal and Service Centre, Kinmen, Taiwan
model_03 170x170x20cm balsa wood exhibited at 'MIAS The *Making* of Making (Architecture)' at DHUB Barcelona Design Museum in 2021-2022

2014 project_037 Passenger Terminal and Service Centre, Kinmen, Taiwan
model_03 170x170x20cm balsa wood exhibited at 'MIAS The *Making* of Making (Architecture)' at DHUB Barcelona Design Museum in 2021-2022

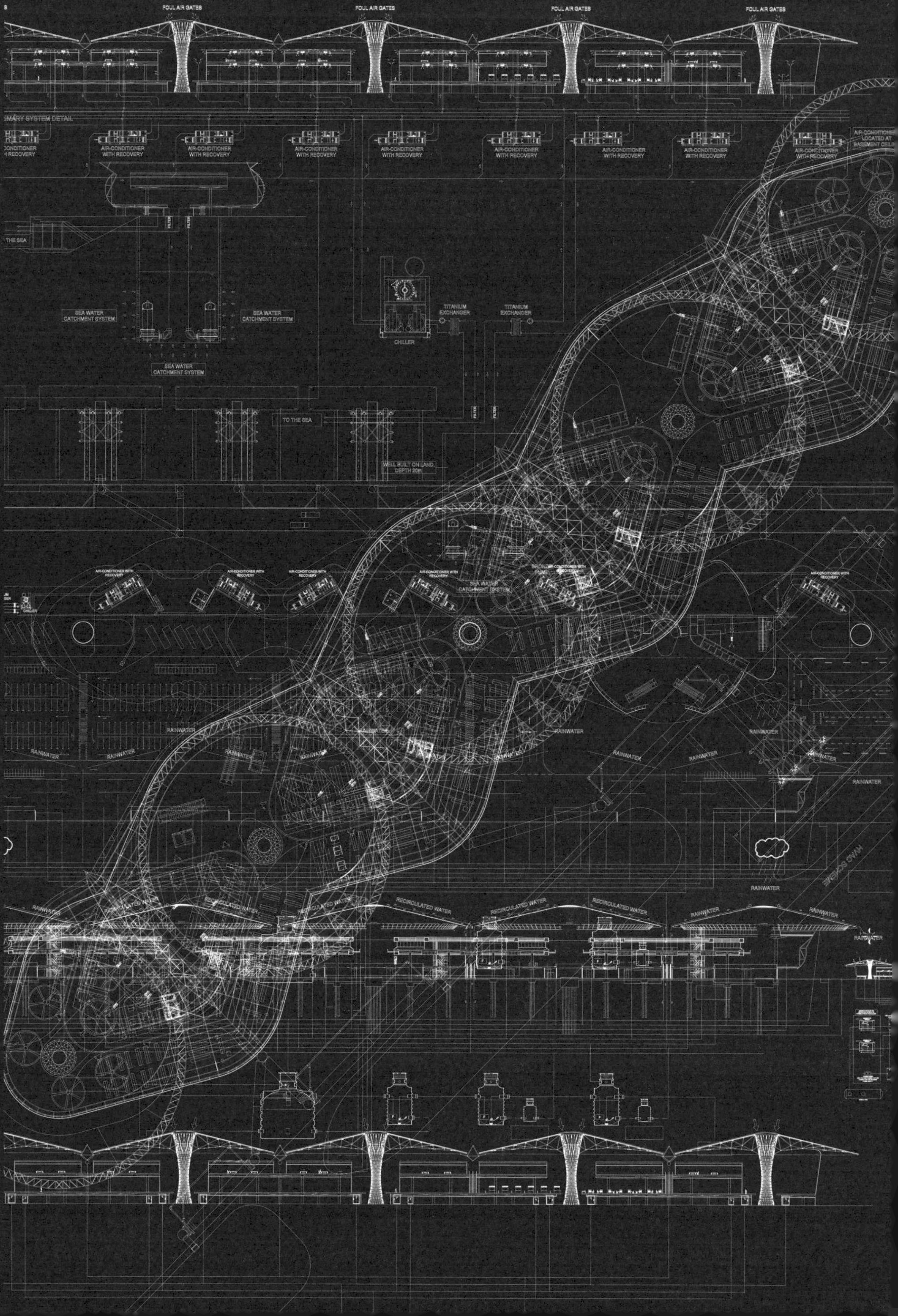

2014 project_037 Passenger Terminal and Service Centre, Kinmen, Taiwan

1.95x2.10m line drawing on glass exhibited at 'MIAS The *Making* of Making (Architecture)' at DHUB Barcelona Design Museum in 2021-2022

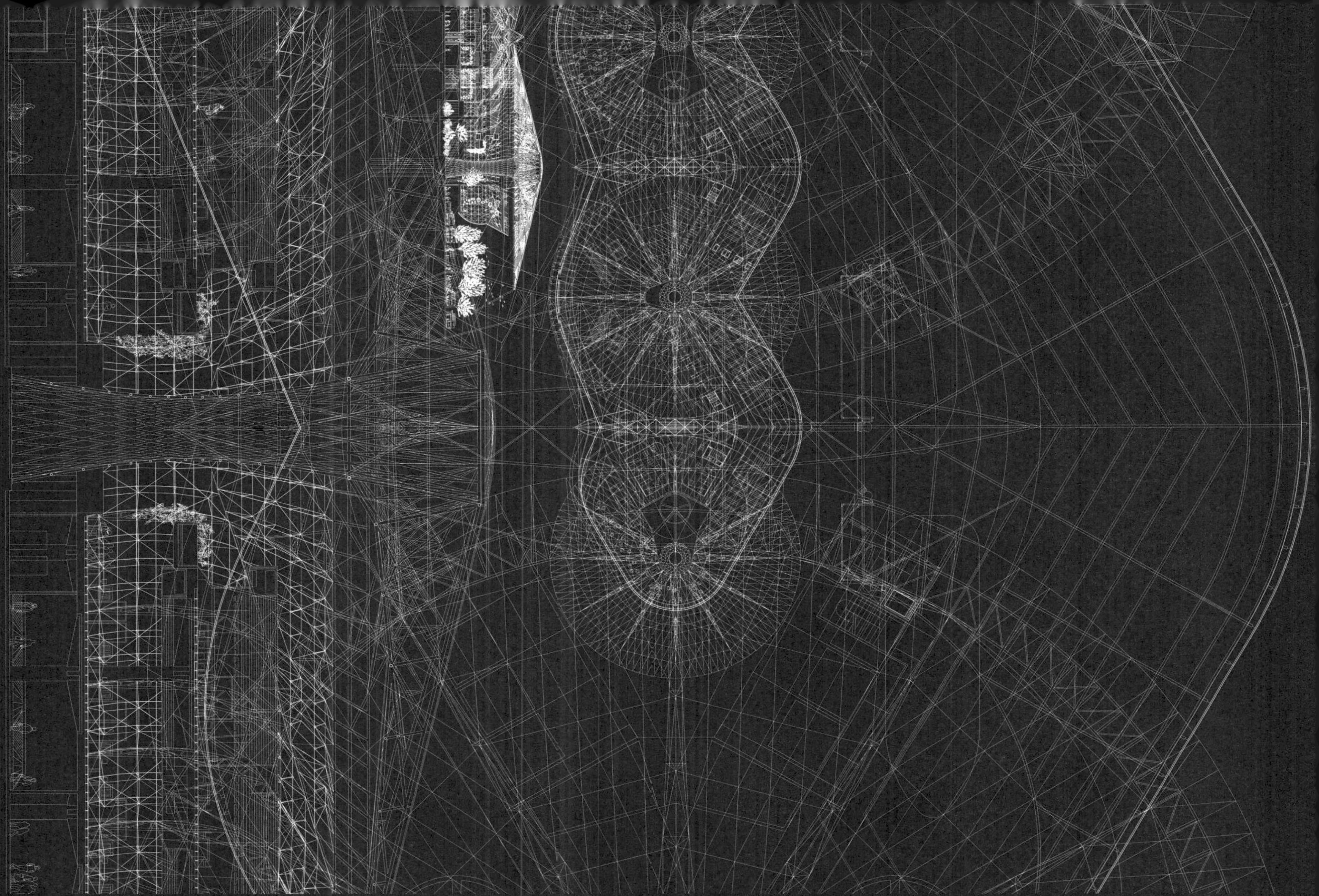

2014 project_037 Passenger Terminal and Service Centre, Kinmen, Taiwan
1.95x2.10m line drawing on glass exhibited at 'MIAS The *Making* of Making (Architecture)' at DHUB Barcelona Design Museum in 2021-2022

RESTAURANT
PORT OF KINMEN
RESTAURANT

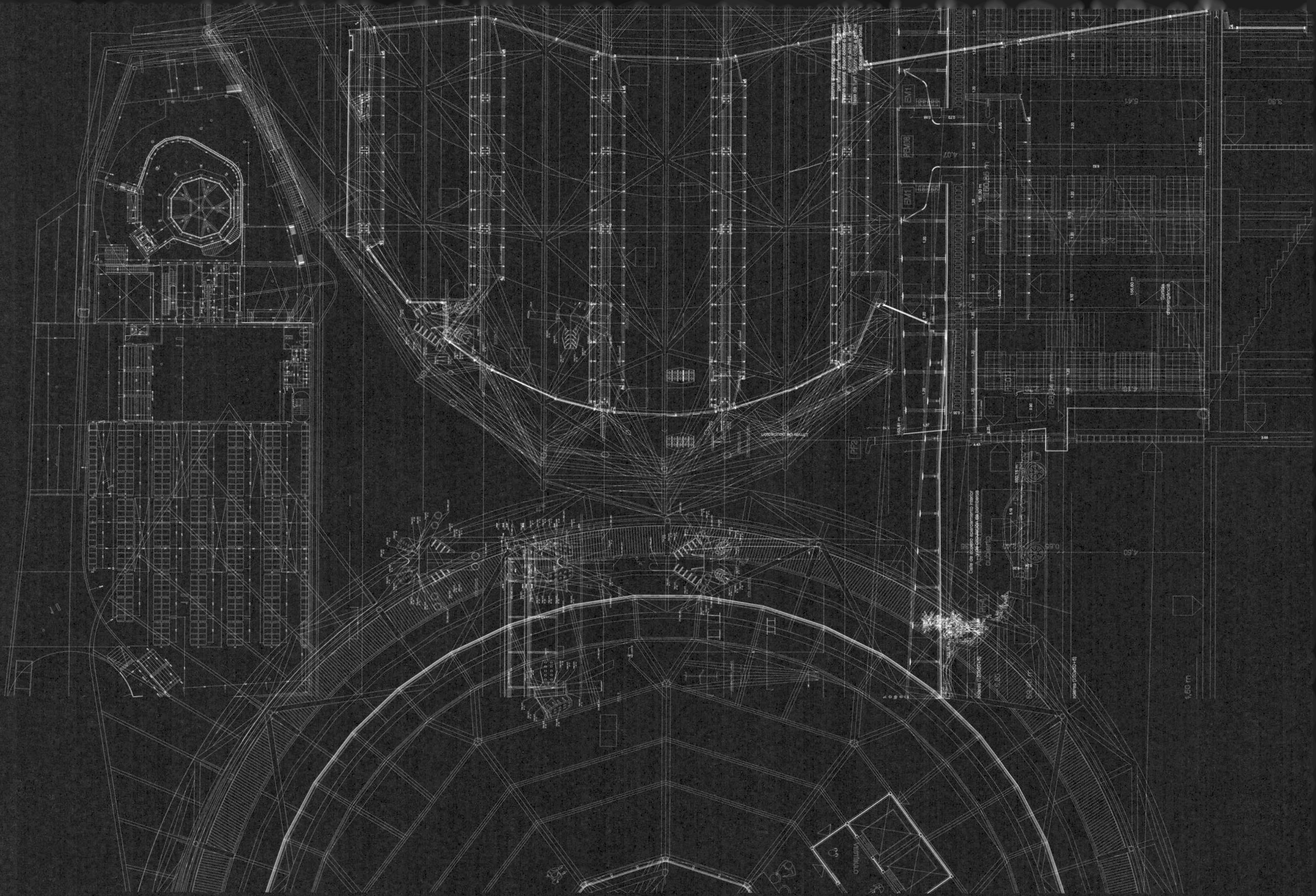

2007-2011 project_029 iGuzzini Lighting Iberian Headquarters, Sant Cugat del Vallès, Spain
1.50x2.10m line drawing on glass exhibited at 'MIAS The *Making* of Making (Architecture)' at DHUB Barcelona Design Museum in 2021-2022

2007-2011 project_029 iGuzzini Lighting Iberian Headquarters, Sant Cugat del Vallès, Spain
1.50x2.10m line drawing on glass exhibited at 'MIAS The *Making* of Making (Architecture)' at DHUB Barcelona Design Museum in 2021-2022

iGuzzini Lighting Iberian Headquarters

Restricted Competition, Winner
year: 2007-2011
location: Sant Cugat del Vallès, Spain 41°29'28"N 02°03'27" "E
surface: 9000 m^2
client: iGuzzini Lighting Iberian

Awards
- 2013 Architizer A+ Awards, Winner
- 2013 WAN Awards to Façades, Finalist
- 2012 Catalonia Construction Awards, Selected
- 2012 WAF World Architecture Festival of Singapore Awards, Shortlisted
- 2011 Archdaily Building of the Year, Winner
- 2011 Plataforma Arquitectura Work of the Year, Finalist

2007-2011 project_029 iGuzzini Lighting Iberian Headquarters, Sant Cugat del Vallès, Spain

Exhibitions
- Venice Biennale 2012
- "iGuzzini BCN Corporate Building", The Bartlett School of Architecture, 2012
- "Il Cielo iGuzzini", COAC Barcelona, 2008

Publications
- *iGuzzini Barcelona Corporate Building*, Miàs, Josep, Barcelona, Actar Publishers, 2012
- *iGuzzini Lighting Iberian España Headquarters,* Miàs, Josep, Barcelona, 2011

2007-2011 project_029 iGuzzini Lighting Iberian Headquarters, Sant Cugat del Vallès, Spain
2.00x1.00m line drawing on glass exhibited at 'MIAS The *Making* of Making (Architecture)' at DHUB Barcelona Design Museum in 2021-2022

Concern for the structural behaviour of buildings, research into construction methods, technological innovation, etc. are aspects that I believe I have contributed to developing in these projects, even though I've shared many other areas of research. And above all, the rigour in drawing and geometry, as a mechanism for checking.

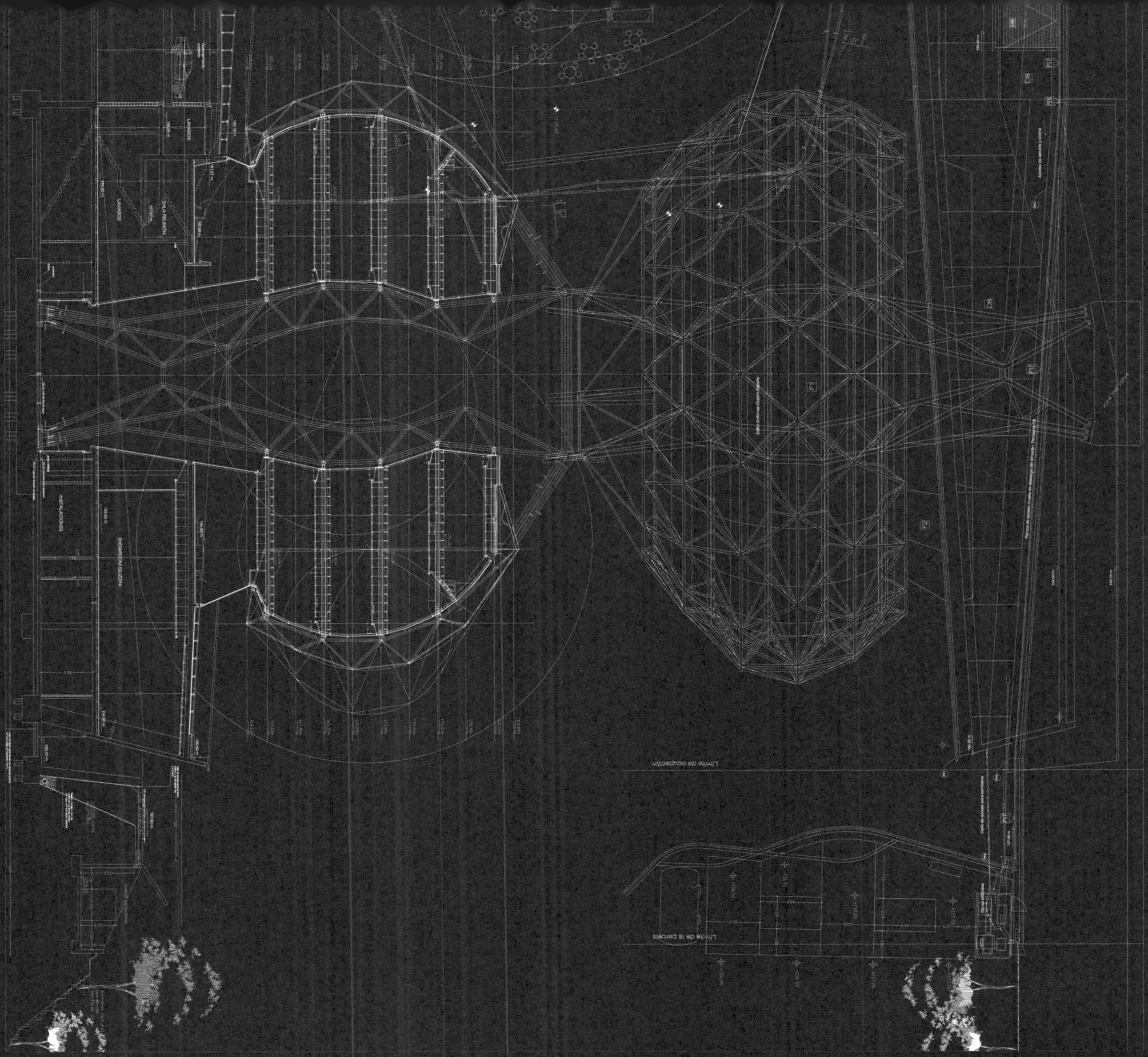

2007-2011 project_029 iGuzzini Lighting Iberian Headquarters, Sant Cugat del Vallès, Spain
2.00x1.00m line drawing on glass exhibited at 'MIAS The *Making* of Making (Architecture)' at DHUB Barcelona Design Museum in 2021-2022

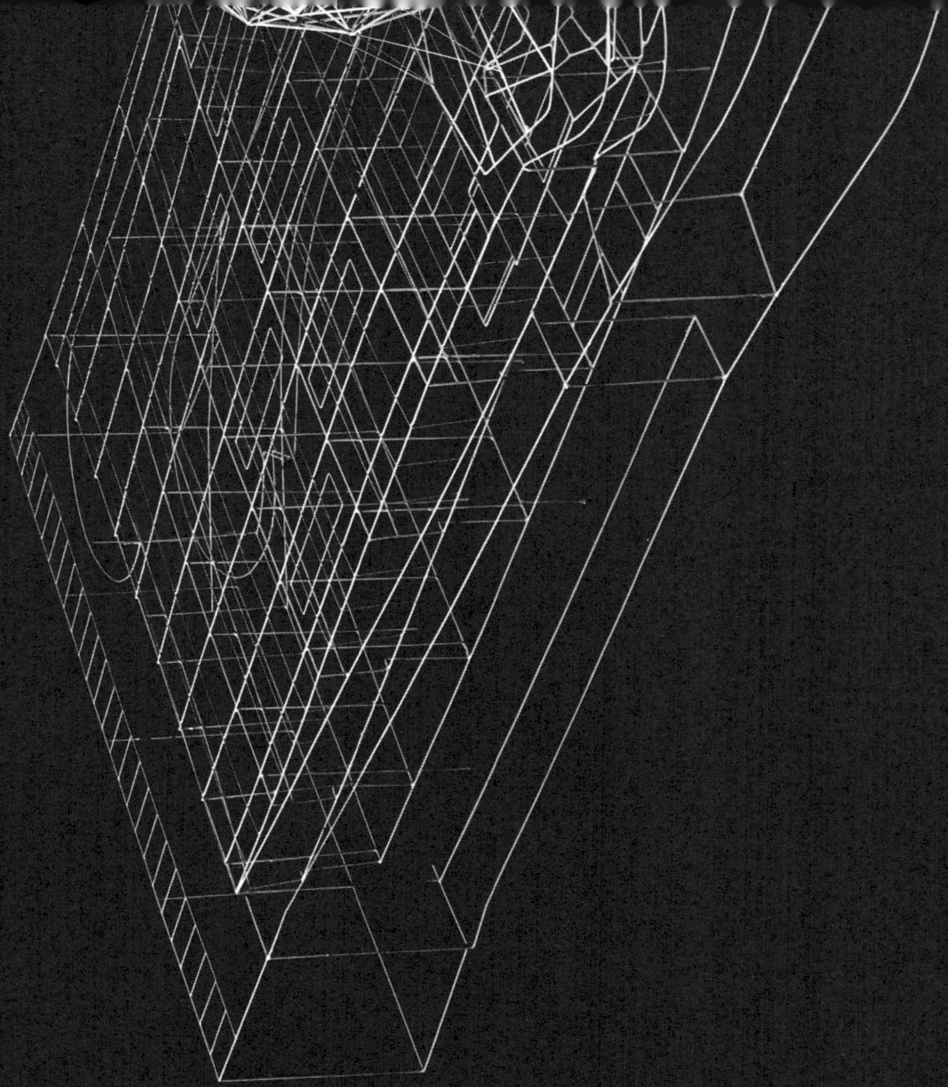

2007-2011 project_029 iGuzzini Lighting Iberian Headquarters, Sant Cugat del Vallès, Spain
model_69 39x120x56cm 1:200 welded wire EC2020-2-AR80 Centre Pompidou Permanent Collection

We feel it is necessary to reconsider the conventional use that has been given to a product or construction system, and we rethink it to discover new possibilities and opportunities.

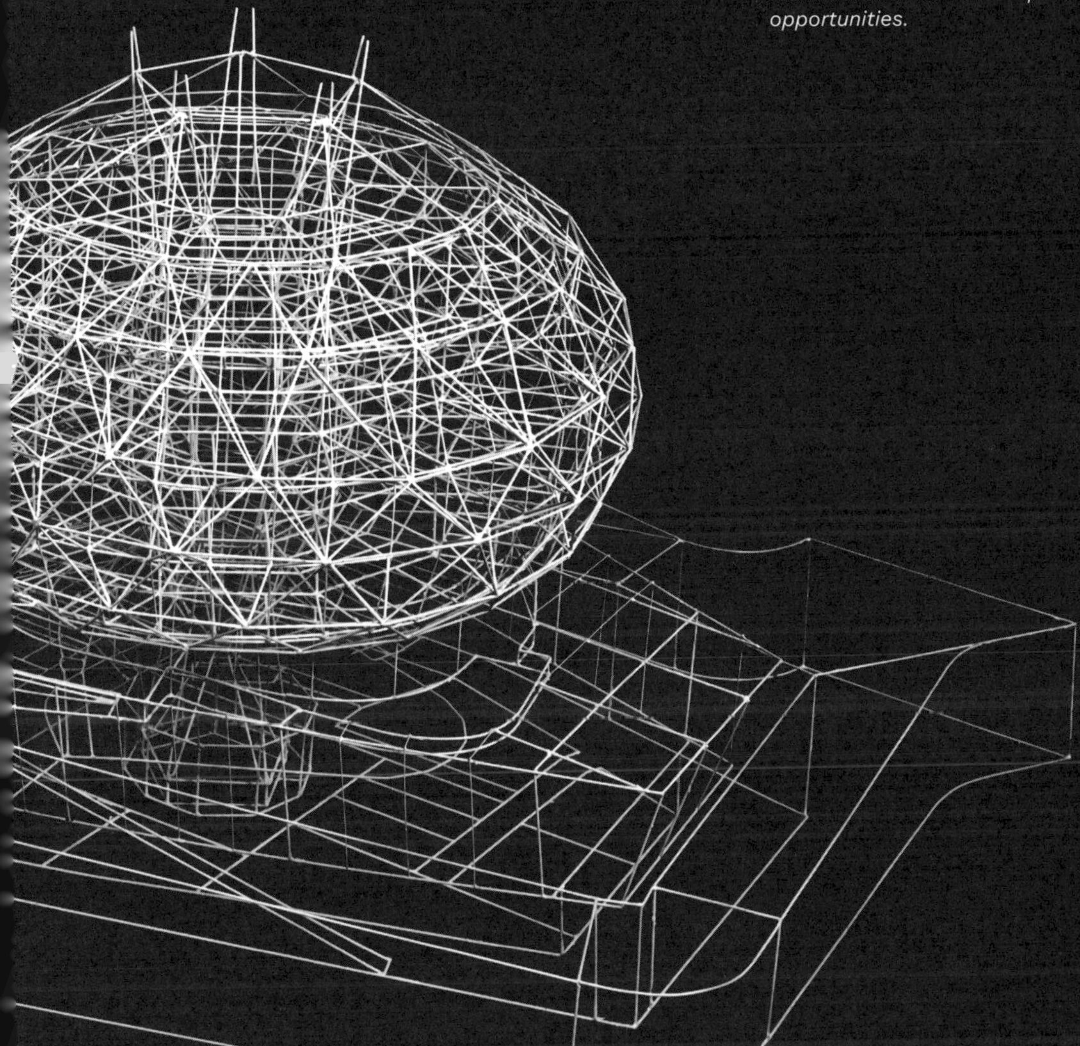

2007-2011 project_029 iGuzzini Lighting Iberian Headquarters, Sant Cugat del Vallès, Spain
model_69 39x120x56cm 1:200 welded wire EC2020-2-AR80 Centre Pompidou Permanent Collection

iGuzzini Lighting Iberian Headquarters

Restricted Competition, Winner
year: 2007-2011
location: Sant Cugat del Vallès, Spain 41°29'28"N 02°03'27" "E
surface: 9000 m²
client: iGuzzini Lighting Iberian

2007-2011 project_029 iGuzzini Lighting Iberian Headquarters, Sant Cugat del Vallès, Spain

2007-2011 project_029 iGuzzini Lighting Iberian Headquarters, Sant Cugat del Vallès, Spain
2.00x1.00m line drawing on glass exhibited at 'MIAS The *Making* of Making (Architecture)' at DHUB Barcelona Design Museum in 2021-2022

2007-2011 project_029 iGuzzini Lighting Iberian Headquarters, Sant Cugat del Vallès, Spain
2.00x1.00m line drawing on glass exhibited at 'MIAS The *Making* of Making (Architecture)' at DHUB Barcelona Design Museum in 2021-2022

2007-2011 project_029 iGuzzini Lighting Iberian Headquarters, Sant Cugat del Vallès, Spain

'MIAS The *Making* of Making (Architecture)'

=25mm
=50mm
=20mm
Soldadures a top
Sede iGuzzini Illuminazione Iberica, Sant Cugat, 2011
iGuzzini Illuminazione Iberica HQ. Sant Cugat,

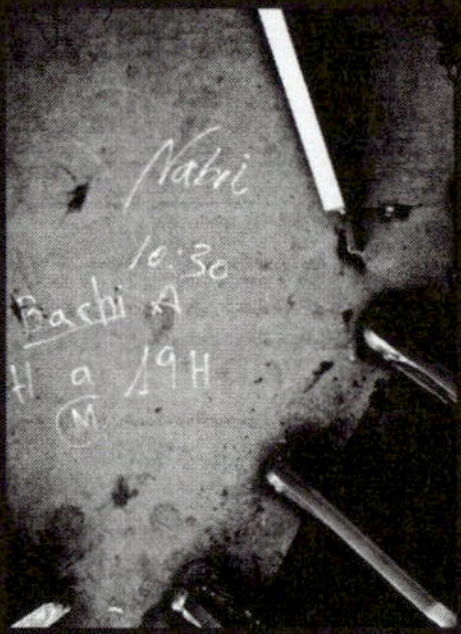

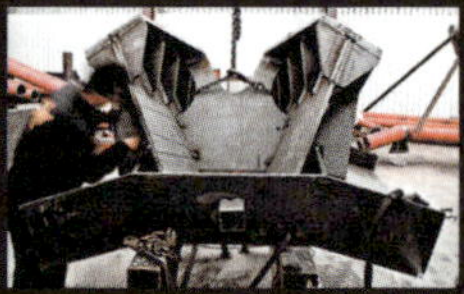

Behind every project there is so much information, so many considerations, so many secrets! Only those who make a great effort, get something back in return. We're only interested in things which require effort and which allow you to learn something every time you come back to them.

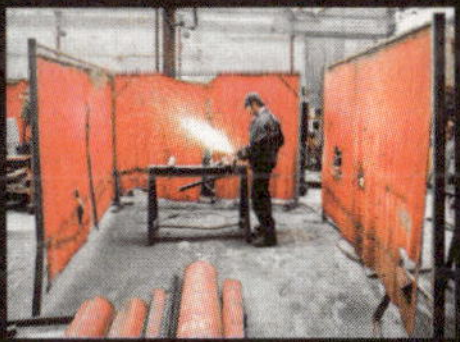

2007-2011 project_029 iGuzzini Lighting Iberian Headquarters, Sant Cugat del Vallès, Spain
model_63 90x180x180cm balsa wood 1:20 exhibited at 'MIAS The *Making* of Making (Architecture)' at DHUB Barcelona Design Museum in 2021-2022

2007-2011 project_029 iGuzzini Lighting Iberian Headquarters, Sant Cugat del Vallès, Spain
model_63 90x180x180cm balsa wood 1:20 exhibited at 'MIAS The *Making* of Making (Architecture)' at DHUB Barcelona Design Museum in 2021-2022

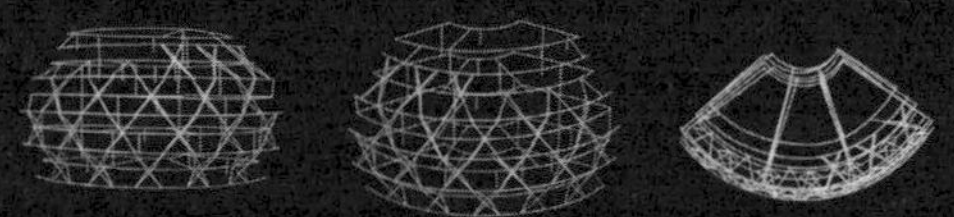

project_029
model_74
EC2020-2-AR16 Pompidou Collection

project_029
model_24

project_029
model_24

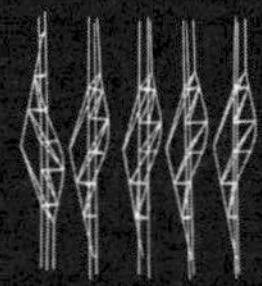

project_029
model_19

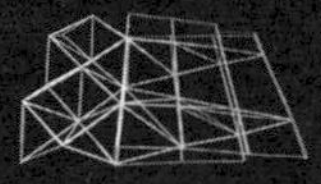

project_029
model_26

project_029
model_75
EC2020-2-AR17 Pompidou Collection

project_029
model_24

project_029
model_24

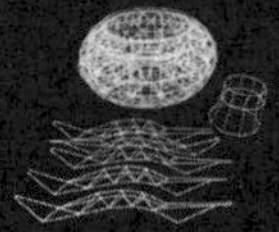

project_029
model_56

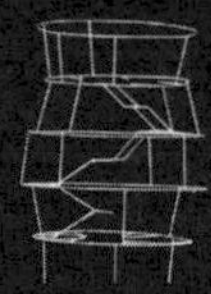

project_029
model_24

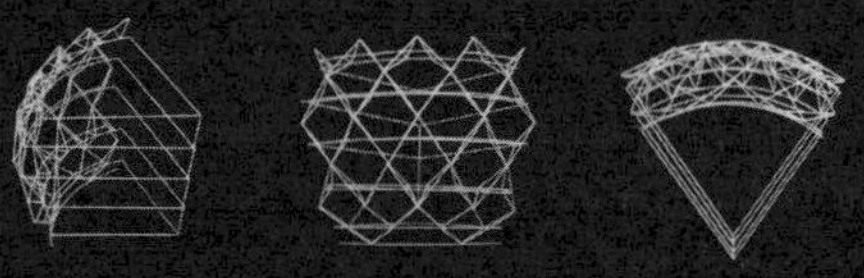

project_029
model_76
EC2020-2-AR18 Pompidou Collection

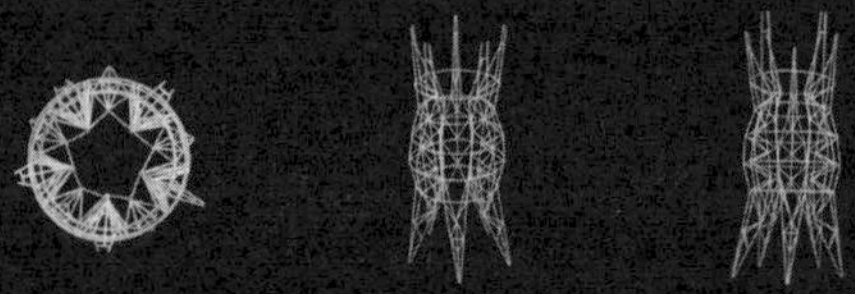

project_029
model_77
EC2020-2-AR20 Pompidou Collection

project_029
model_24

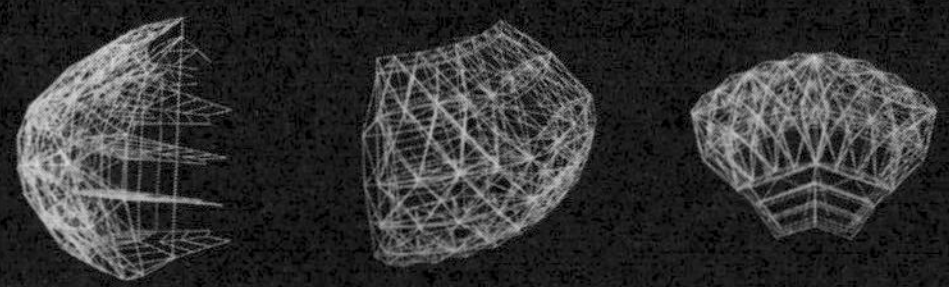

project_029
model_83
EC2020-2-AR79 Pompidou Collection

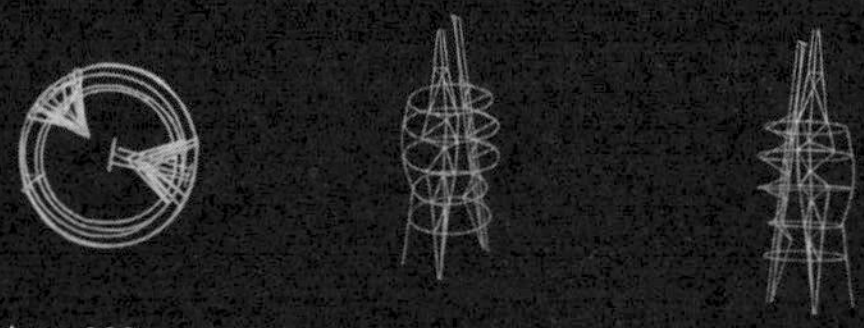

project_029
model_78
EC2020-2-AR21 Pompidou Collection

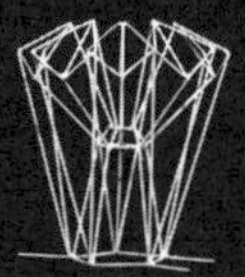

project_029
model_48

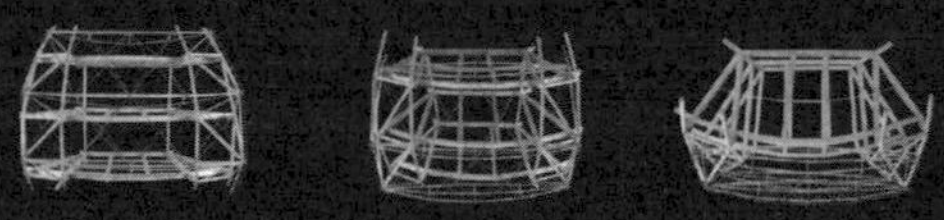

project_029
model_86
EC2020-2-AR25 Pompidou Collection

project_029
model_79
EC2020-2-AR22 Pompidou Collection

project_029
model_48

project_029
model_14

project_029
model_14

project_029
model_14

project_029
model_48

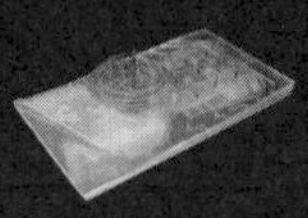

project_029
model_14

project_029
model_14

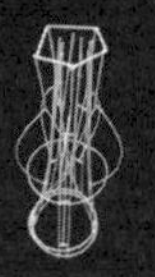

project_029
model_48

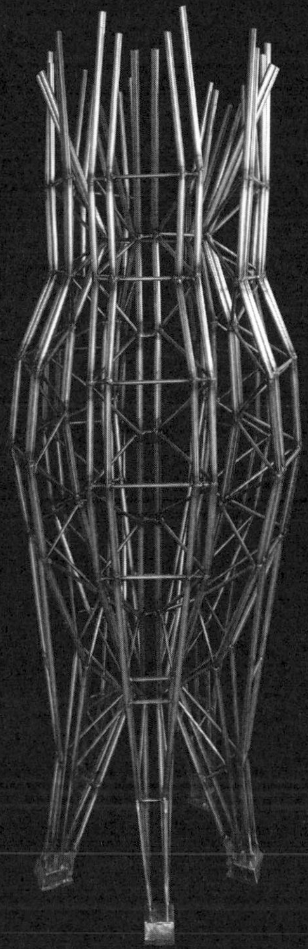

project_029
model_84
EC2020-2-AR26 Pompidou Collection

project_029
model_03

project_029
model_09

project_029
model_09

project_029
model_63_DHUB

project_029
model_03

project_029
model_07

project_029
model_07

project_029
model_50

project_029
model_65
EC2020-2-AR24 Pompidou Collection

project_029
model_63

project_029
model_50

project_029
model_50

project_029
model_41

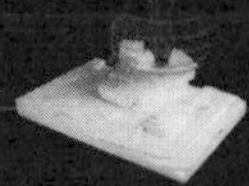

project_029
model_41

project_029
model_41

project_029
model_34

project_029
model_34

project_029
model_34

project_029
model_34

project_029
model_34

project_029
model_64

project_029
model_11

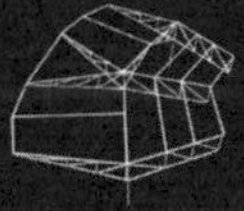

project_029
model_22

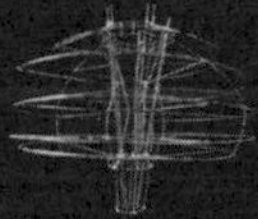

project_029
model_45

project_029
model_45

project_029
model_45

project_029
model_45

project_029
model_33

project_029
model_33

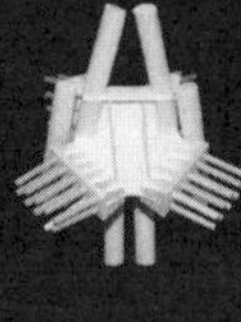

project_029
model_12

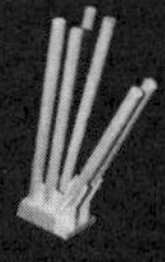

project_029
model_68

project_029
model_12

project_029
model_84
EC2020-2-AR26 Pompidou Collection

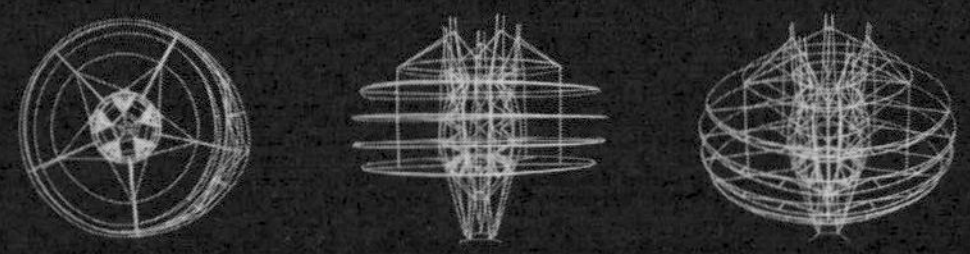

project_029
model_70
EC2020-2-AR12 Pompidou Collection

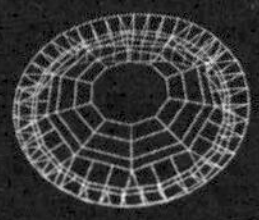

project_029
model_04

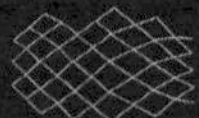

project_029
model_32

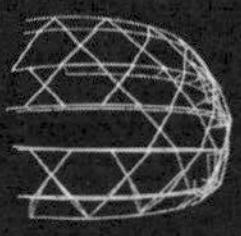

project_029
model_21

project_029
model_46

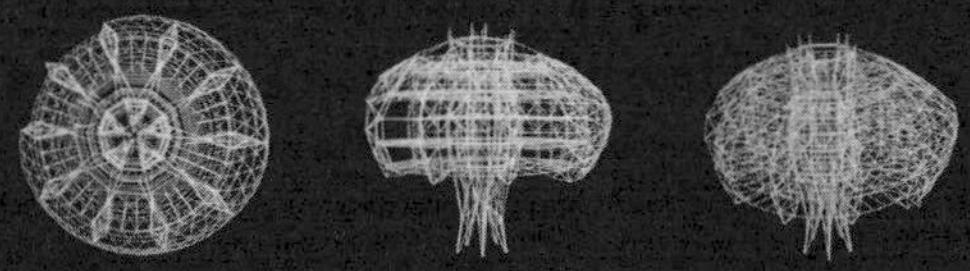

project_029
model_72
EC2020-2-AR14 Pompidou Collection

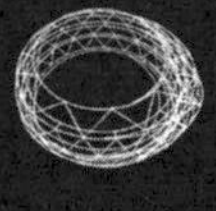

project_029
model_17

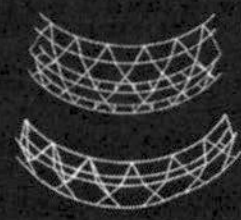

project_029
model_21

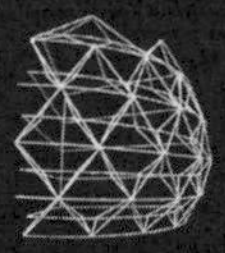

project_029
model_21

project_029
model_46

project_029
model_73
EC2020-2-AR15 Pompidou Collection

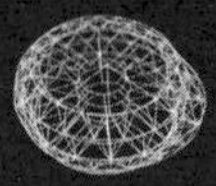

project_029
model_18

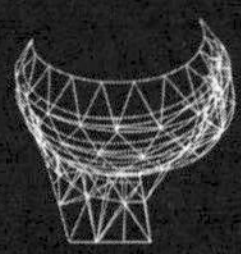

project_029
model_05

project_029
model_21

project_029
model_27

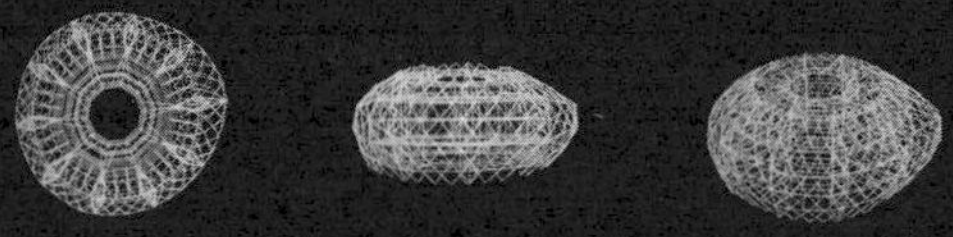

project_029
model_80
EC2020-2-AR45 Pompidou Collection

project_029
model_67

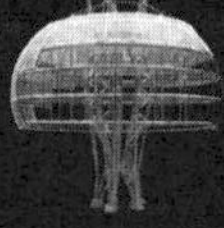

project_029
model_09

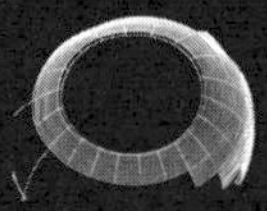

project_029
model_06

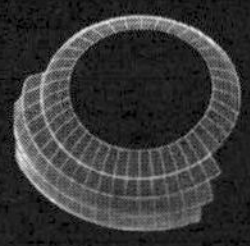

project_029
model_60

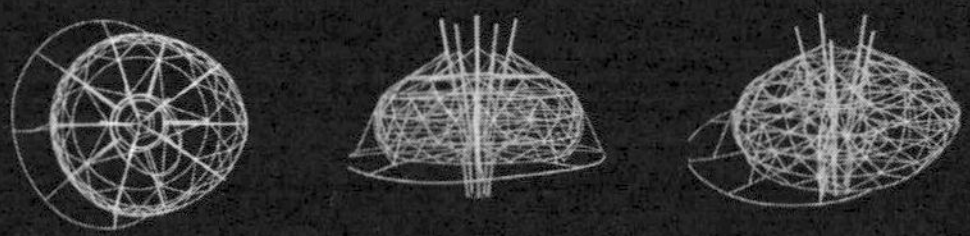

project_029
model_81
EC2020-2-AR27 Pompidou Collection

project_029
model_13

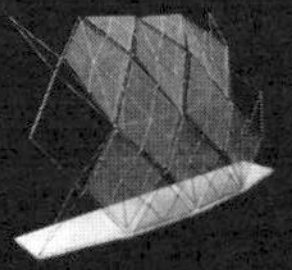

project_029
model_13

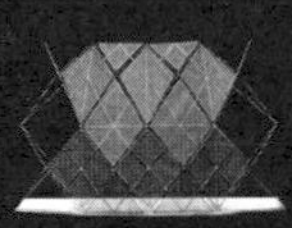

project_029
model_13

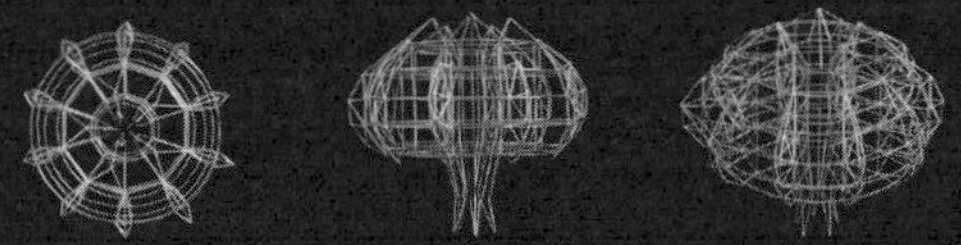

project_029
model_82
EC2020-2-AR23 Pompidou Collection

project_029
model_87_DHUB

project_029
model_87_DHUB

project_029
model_87_DHUB

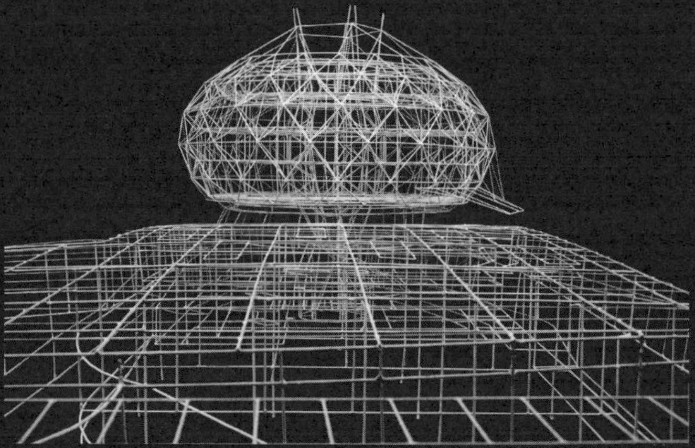

project_029
model_69
EC2020-2-AR80 Pompidou Collection

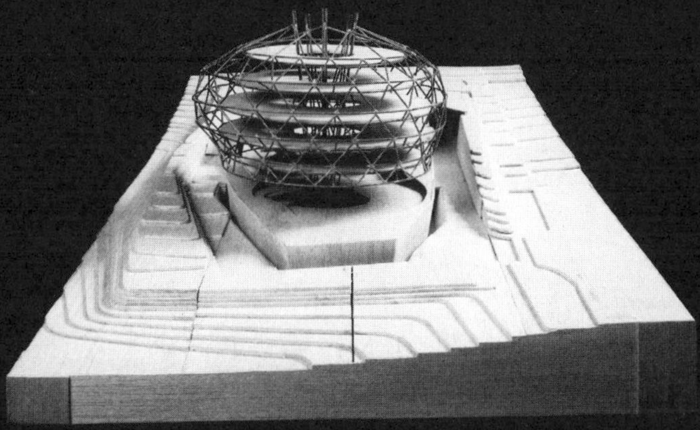
project_029
model_51

project_029
model_08

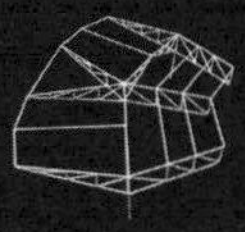
project_029
model_22

project_029
model_15

project_029
model_08

project_029
model_10

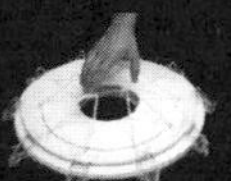
project_029
model_15

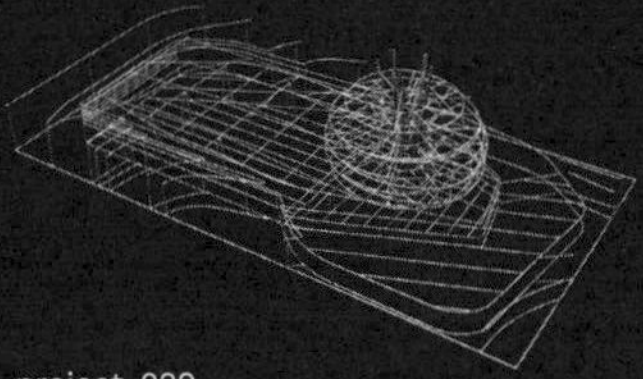
project_029
model_25

project_029
model_51

project_029
model_51

project_029
model_51

project_029
model_13

project_029
model_15

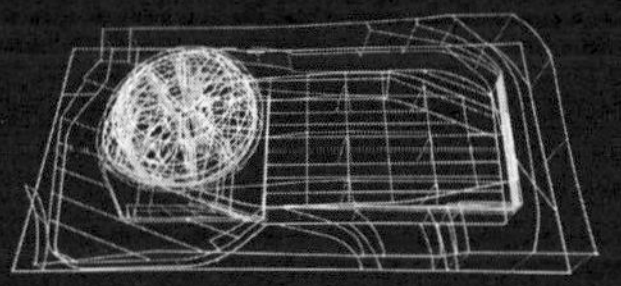
project_029
model_25

project_029
model_51

project_029
model_51

project_029
model_51

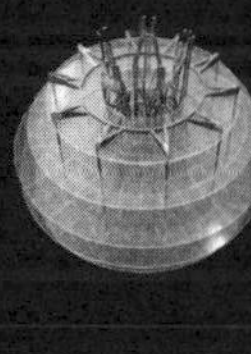
project_029
model_09

project_029
model_15

project_029
model_71
EC2020-2-AR13 Pompidou Collection

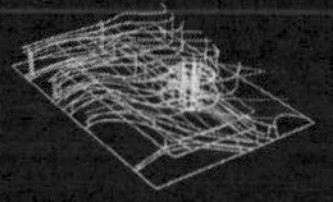

project_029
model_71
EC2020-2-AR13
Pompidou Collection

project_029
model_31

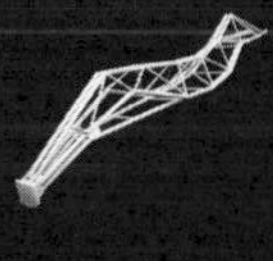
project_029
model_31

project_029
model_15

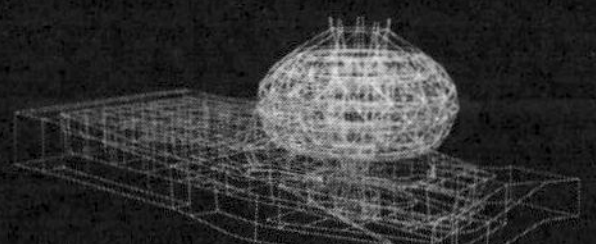
project_029
model_69
EC2020-2-AR80 Pompidou Collection

project_029
model_15

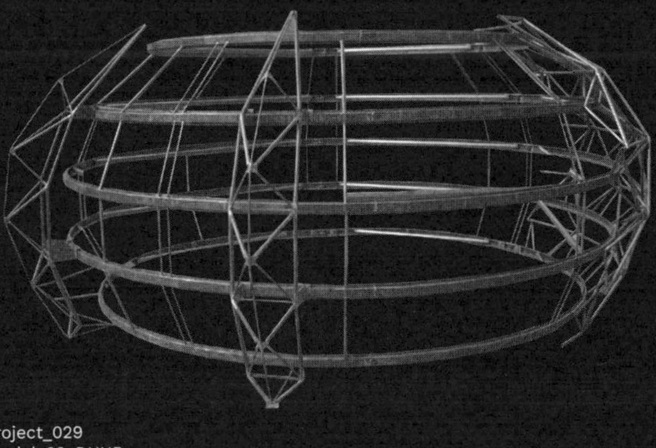
project_029
model_68_DHUB

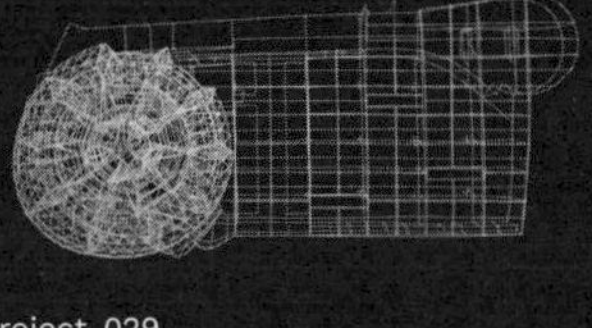
project_029
model_69
EC2020-2-AR80 Pompidou Collection

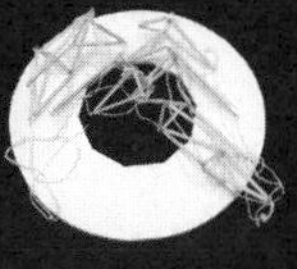
project_029
model_15

I'm interested in projects that can be regarded as urban infrastructure, as artefacts that can transform the city and change the meaning of things. I'm interested in spaces of conflict, especially discomfort, even chaos.
I think these are places of great opportunity. Architecture that doesn't introduce a certain tension in a place doesn't interest me.
I even associate the term "integration" with this tension that architecture is capable of introducing in a place or space, whether it be urban or natural.

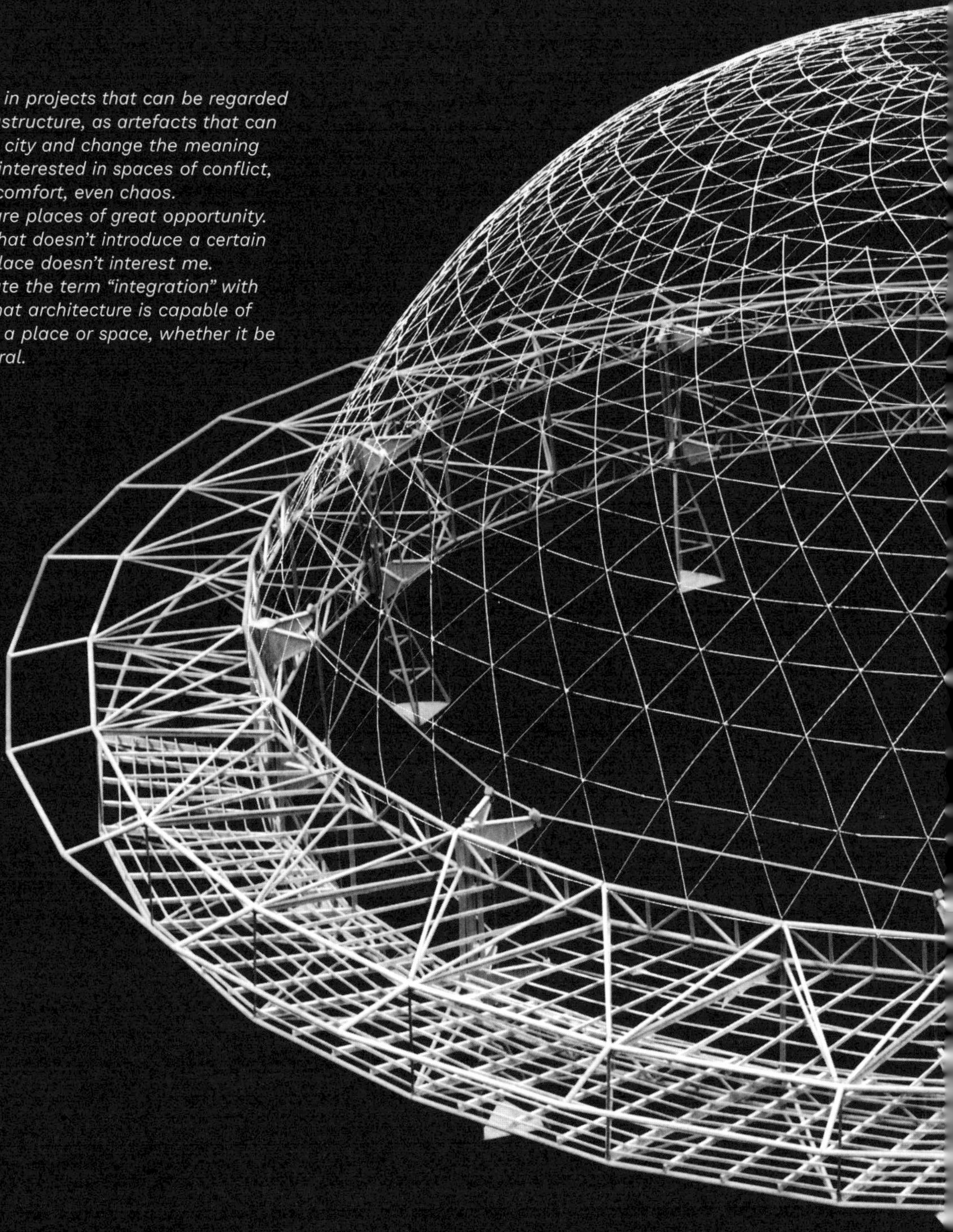

in progress project_110 Vallcarca Industrial Area Transformation, Sitges, Spain
model_01 150x150x90cm 1:50 enamelled welded wire

in progress project_110 Vallcarca Industrial Area Transformation, Sitges, Spain
model_01 150x150x90cm 1:50 enamelled welded wire

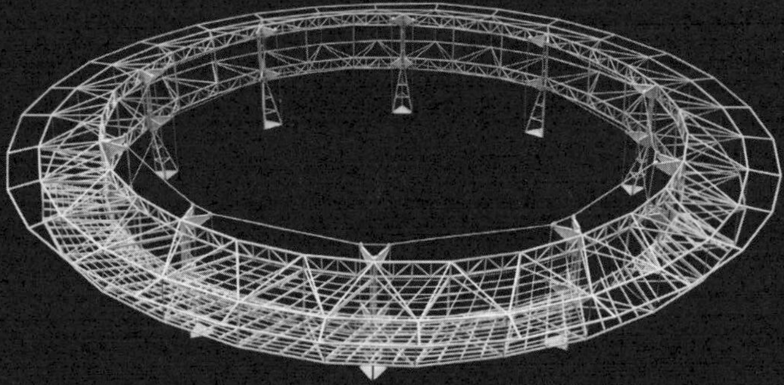

project_110
model_01

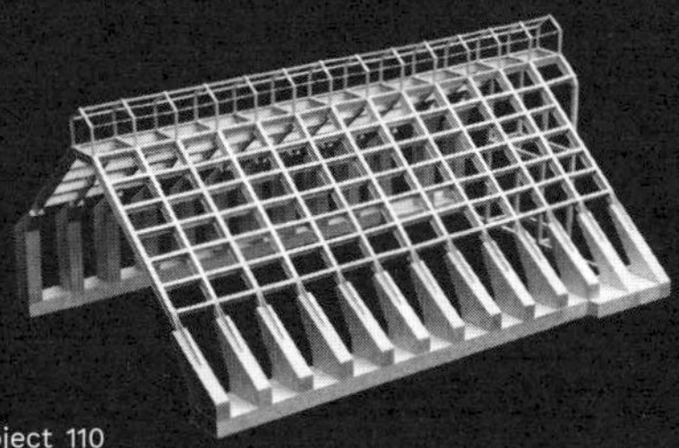

project_110
model_04

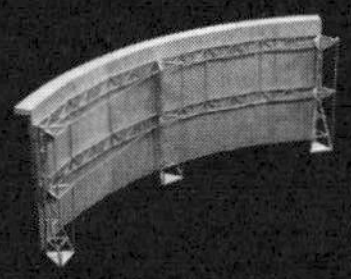

project_110
model_05

project_110
model_06

project_110
model_07

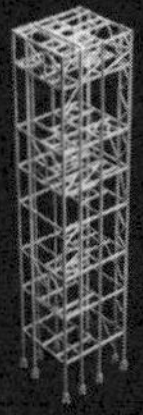

project_110
model_08

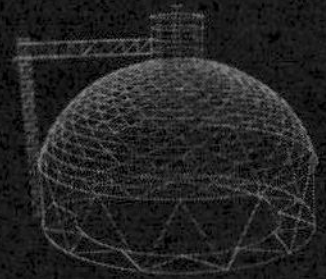

project_110
model_13

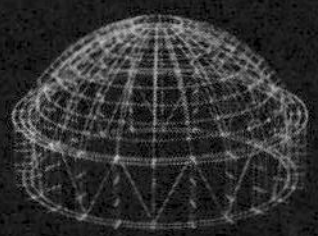

project_110
model_14

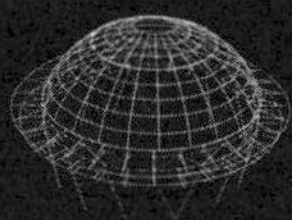

project_110
model_15

project_110
model_17

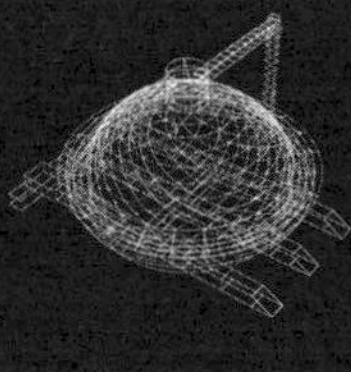

project_110
model_18

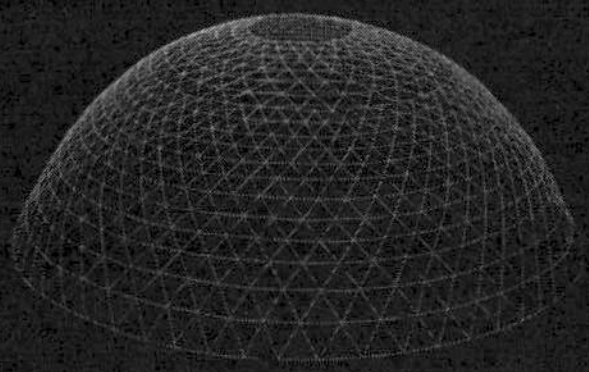

project_110
model_19

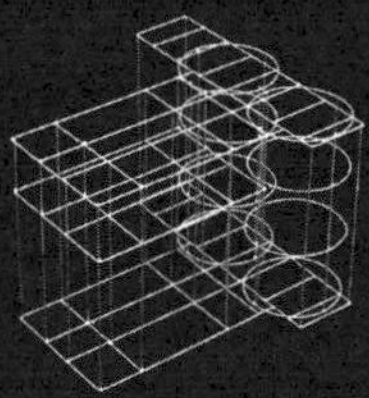

project_110
model_20

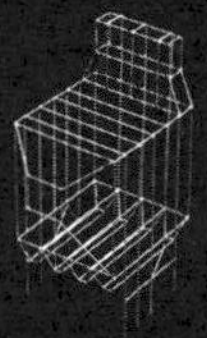

project_110
model_36

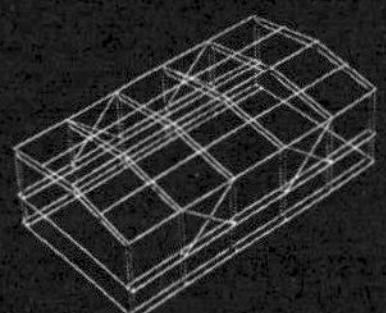

project_110
model_37

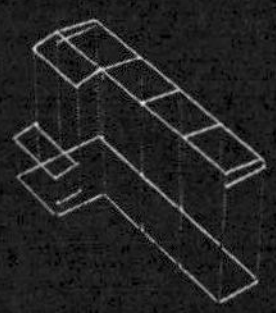

project_110
model_38

project_110
model_39

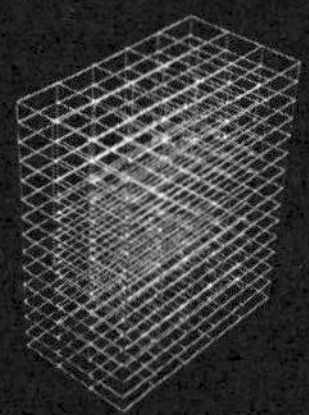

project_110
model_40

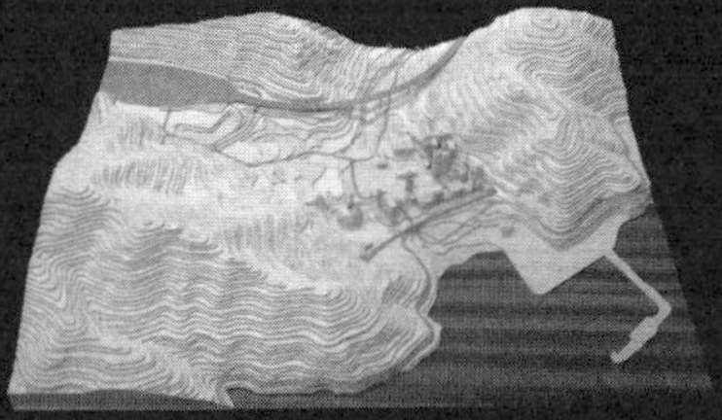
project_110
model_09

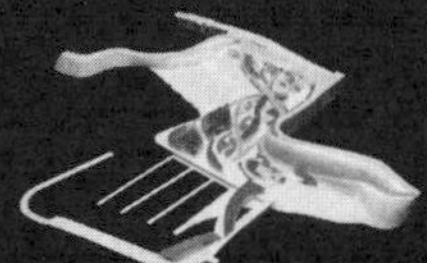
project_110
model_11

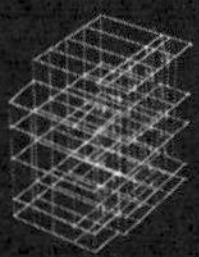
project_110
model_21

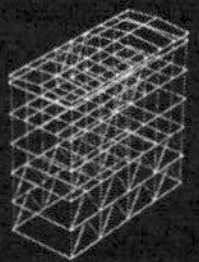
project_110
model_22

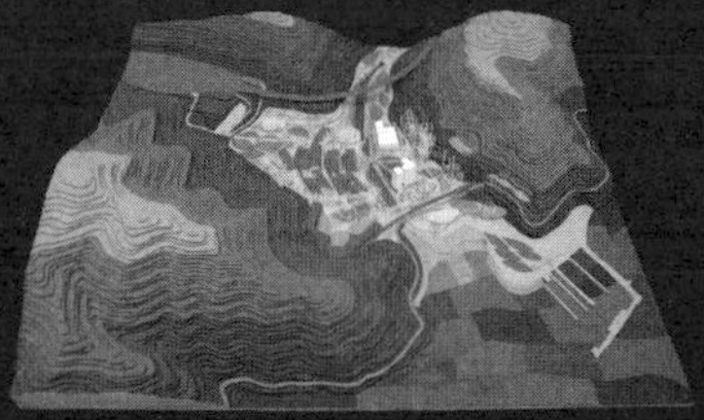
project_110
model_10

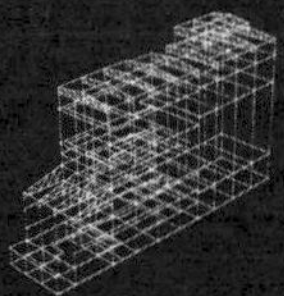
project_110
model_23

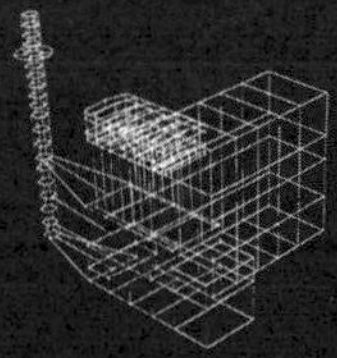
project_110
model_24

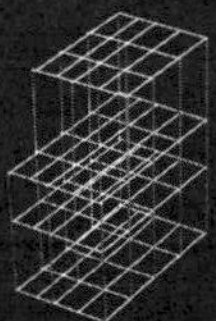
project_110
model_25

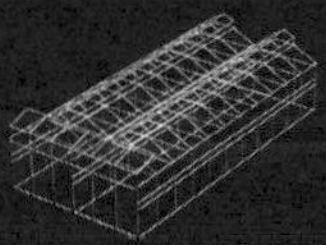
project_110
model_26

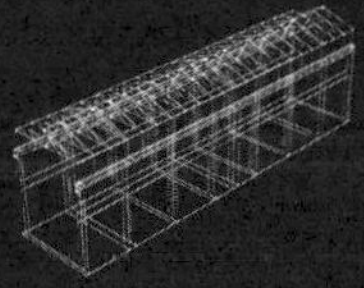
project_110
model_27

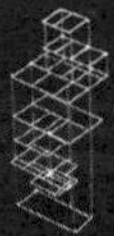
project_110
model_28

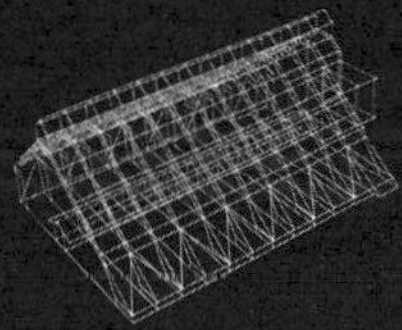
project_110
model_29

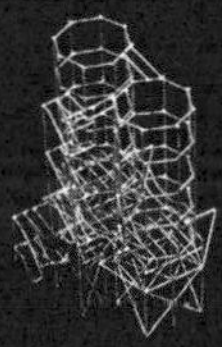
project_110
model_30

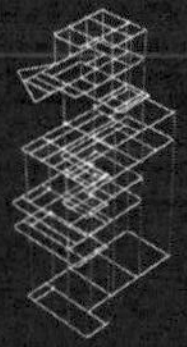
project_110
model_31

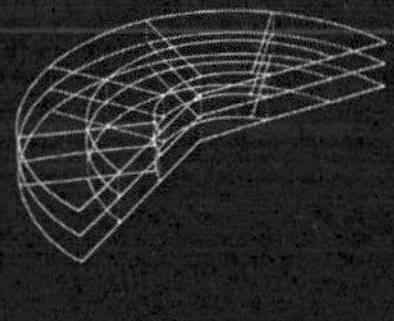
project_110
model_32

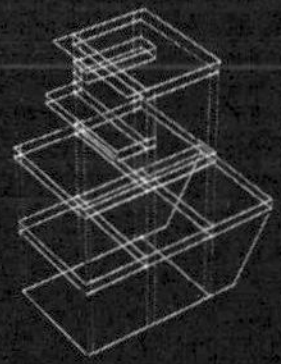
project_110
model_33

project_110
model_34

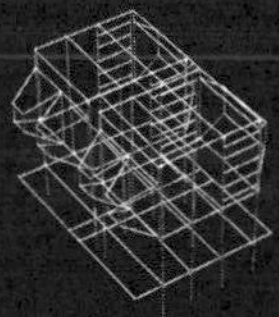
project_110
model_35

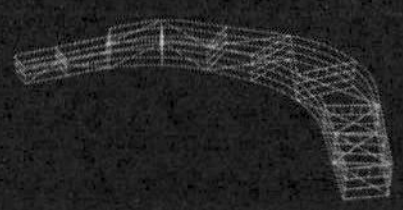
project_110
model_41

project_110
model_42

project_110
model_53

project_110
model_54

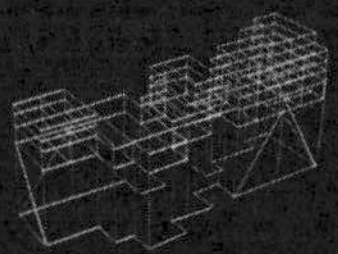
project_110
model_45

Line drawing on glass exhibited at 'MIAS The *Making* of Making (Architecture)' at DHUB Barcelona Design Museum in 2021-2022

project_001 / project_003 / project_005 / project_006 / project_007 / project_008 / project_009 / project_013 / project_027 / project_028 / project_029 / project_030 / project_034 / project_037 / project_039 / project_073 / project_107 / project_112

I can't think of anything better to get through this world than drawing. The truth is that the place of the project is still the drawing. I don't want to talk too much about Enric Miralles, but it's unavoidable. Drawing is already a construction in itself.

For me, drawing is very similar to writing, in that it tries to make sense of things. You try to make your drawing capable of recording what is happening in a place, I'm not just referring to physical records, but also time records. You try to make sure that these drawings don't leave out anything that might be important for asking questions.

Line drawing on glass exhibited at 'MIAS The *Making* of Making (Architecture)' at DHUB Barcelona Design Museum in 2021-2022
project_001 / project_003 / project_005 / project_006 / project_007 / project_008 / project_009 / project_013 / project_027 / project_028 / project_029 / project_030 / project_034 / project_037 / project_039 / project_073 / project_107 / project_112

You ultimately want the questions to contain as much information as possible, so that the answers follow naturally. Building is another way of drawing. The first drawings of a project try to contain as much information as possible, as well as the first constructions in the spaces of these lines. This is why many of the models are made of wire. The 1:1 scale construction is just another phase in the natural development of this initial drawing, with new conditions.

I think my projects acquire the reality that they themselves define.

Tribute to Enric Miralles

Josep Miàs & Mauro Soro

215x123x21cm enamelled welded wire model exhibited at 'MIAS The *Making* of Making (Architecture)' at DHUB Barcelona Design Museum in 2021-2022

project_001 / project_003 / project_006 / project_007 / project_008 / project_009 / project_037 / project_039

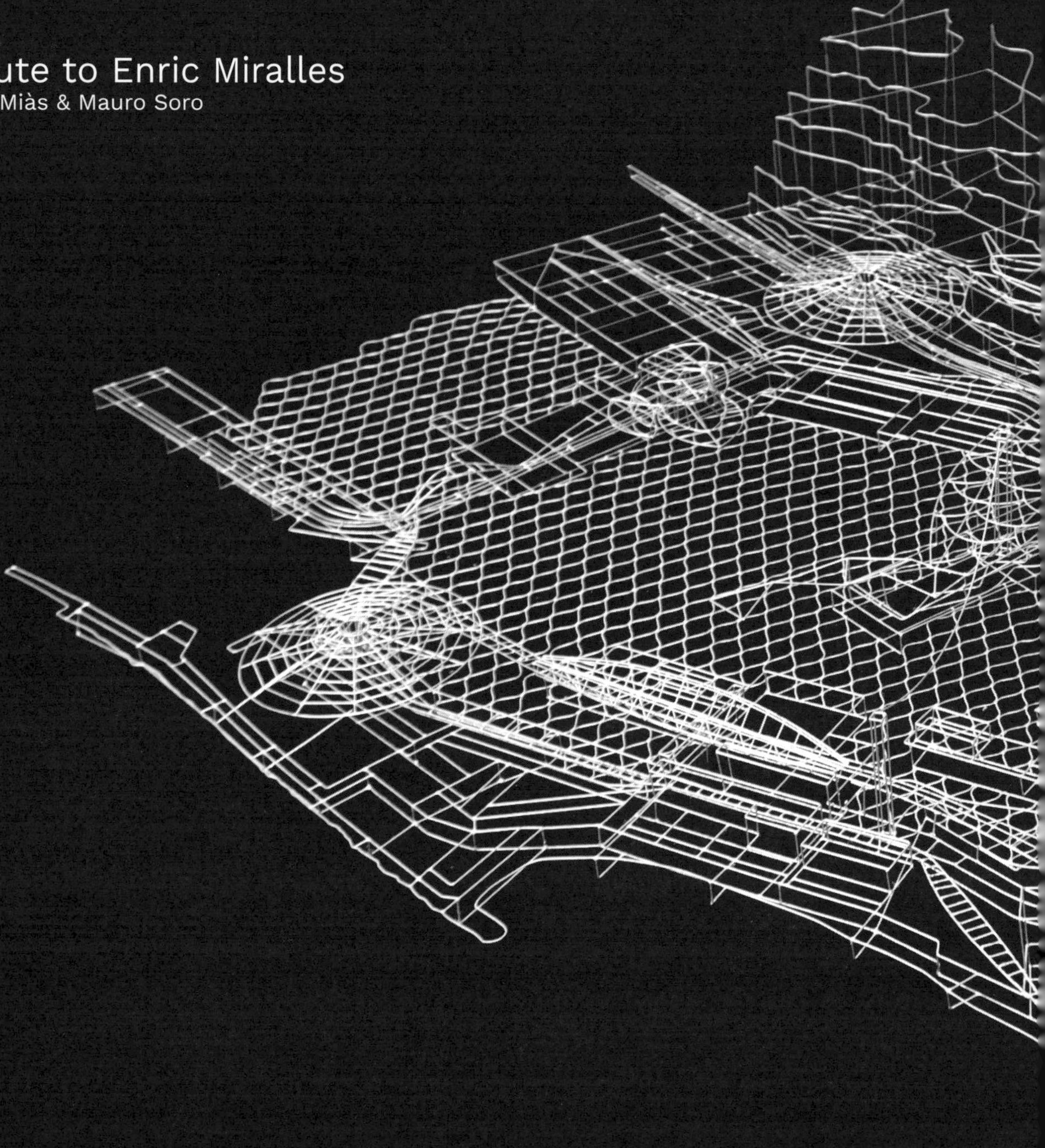

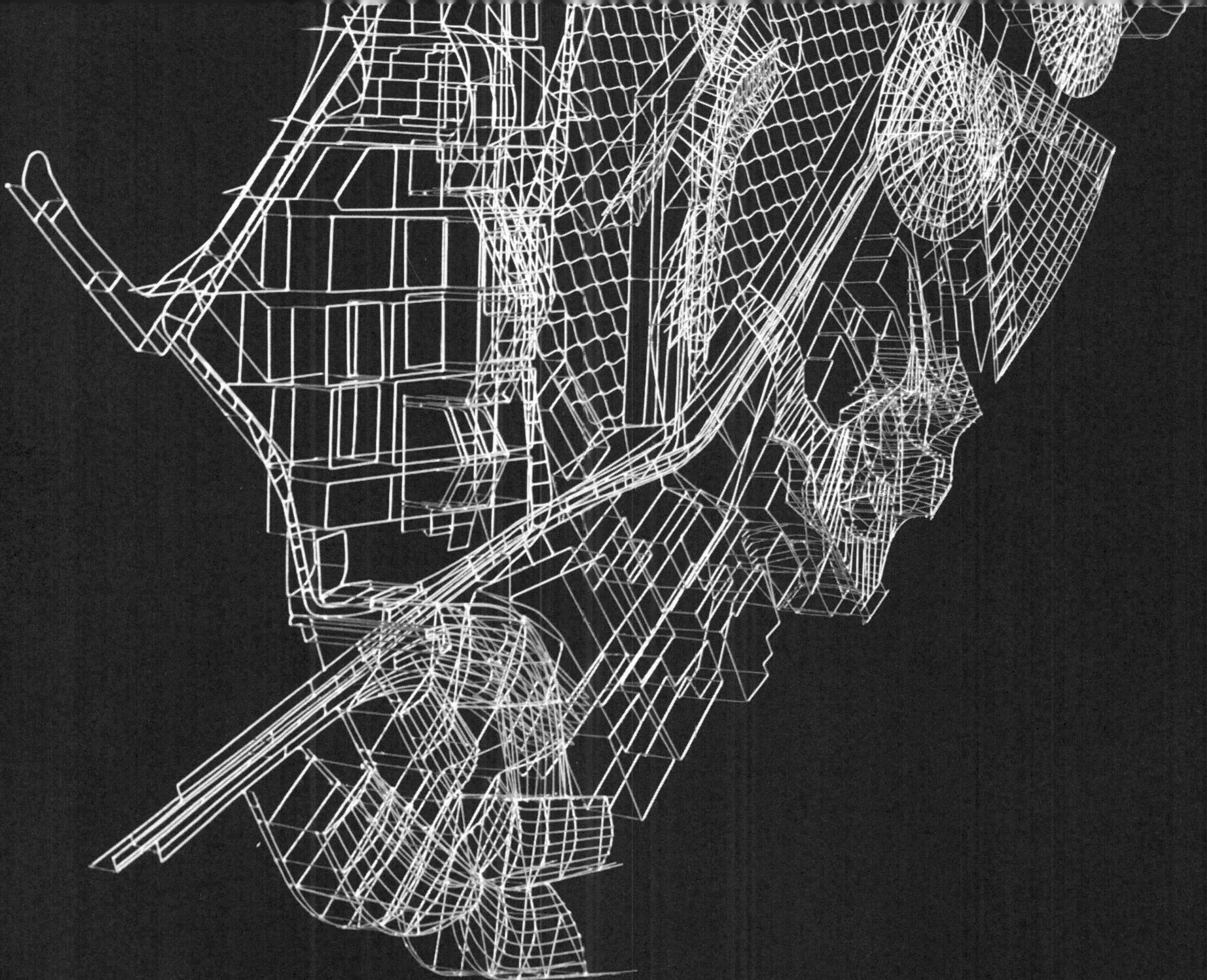

215x123x21cm enamelled welded wire model exhibited at 'MIAS The *Making* of Making (Architecture)' at DHUB Barcelona Design Museum in 2021-2022
project_001 / project_003 / project_006 / project_007 / project_008 / project_009 / project_037 / project_039

Bob Sheil, Speaking Volumes
sketch of project_29 iGuzzini Lighting Iberian Headquarters, Sant Cugat del Vallès, Spain

BOB SHEIL

SPEAKING VOLUMES

Bob Sheil
Professor in Architecture and Design through Production at The Bartlett School of Architecture UCL.
He is an educator, critic, researcher, collaborator and practitioner. Recent projects involve collaboration with the Royal Central School of Speech and Drama, SHUNT, ScanLAB projects, and Thomas Pearce. He has co-designed and built 6 significant artefacts/built works, and been internationally exhibited on 11 occasions. He has edited six books. Co-Founder of the highly acclaimed international triennial conference 'FABRICATE'.

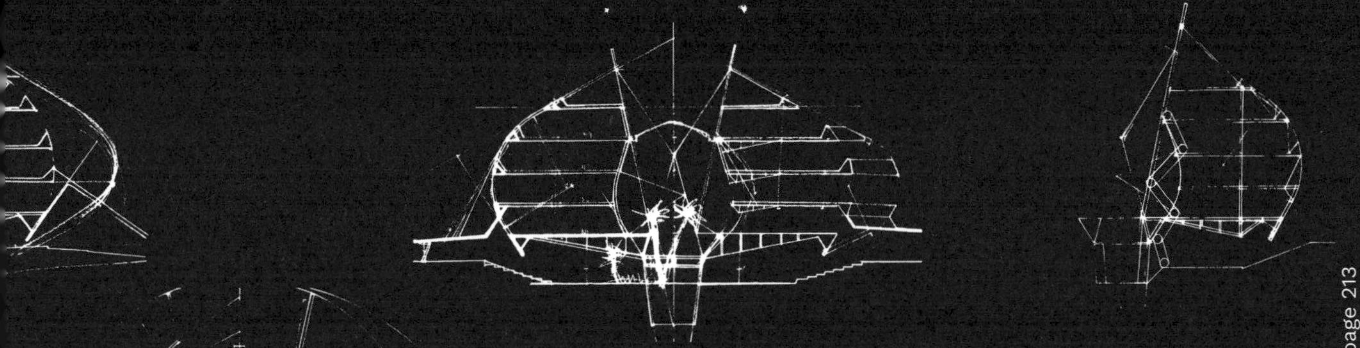

sketch of project_29 iGuzzini Lighting Iberian Headquarters, Sant Cugat del Vallès, Spain

Making architecture, that is, to make buildings, spaces, structures, walls, skins, environments, places and the like, as fragments of the city or landscape, is to navigate a diverse, fraught and meandering journey with no absolute beginning, middle, or end. Making architecture is a perpetual convergence of the ephemeral and the grounded, the illusive and the tactile, the known and the unknown, the controlled and the accidental. All architecture is thus to some degree part prototype, part work in progress, part process and part complete, and thus all architecture is to some degree part previous project, and part genesis of a future project.

What makes the work of MIAS Architects so inspiringly particular is its inherent transparency on all these fronts in simultaneous resonance. Not only is this evidenced through its portfolio of award winning and publicly recognised built works, but also, as this exhibition vividly celebrates, through its prolific and raucous outpouring of models and drawings, in multiple exuberance. Deeply honed and exquisitely crafted, this prolific demonstration is a study in the making of making architecture, through its earliest and slightest emergence as marks on a plane, to its flight in space as a drawing without paper, to its rigorous rehearsal as an investigation of assembly and composition. It is a way of making architecture that layers free speculation upon tacit knowledge and expertise, acquired through unwavering scrutiny of construction methods, engineering principles, material performance, cultural context, and lived experience.
The office from where this work emerges is dispersed across the tightly knit district of Gràcia in Barcelona, where Josep Miàs has lived and practiced throughout his career. Tucked into nooks and crannies, its studio, workshop, library, archive, and meeting rooms are each held apart by short zigzag walks between bars, grocery stores, bakeries, cafes, launderettes, restaurants, and schools. Hence, the place of production and inspiration for Miàs and his collaborators is the sentient world within and between these concentrated nodes, from the cacophony of daily city life to its muted tones in the very early hours. So, though rightfully honoured in their distinguished Parisian setting, remember the bustling visual and sonic environment where these works were born, and contemplate the proximity of Barcelona's seminal and omnipresent architectural heritage, and its food markets with their exotic display of crustaceans.

Architecture that is made this way relies on few words to speak volumes.

X-Rays Room at 'MIAS The *Making* of Making (Architecture)'

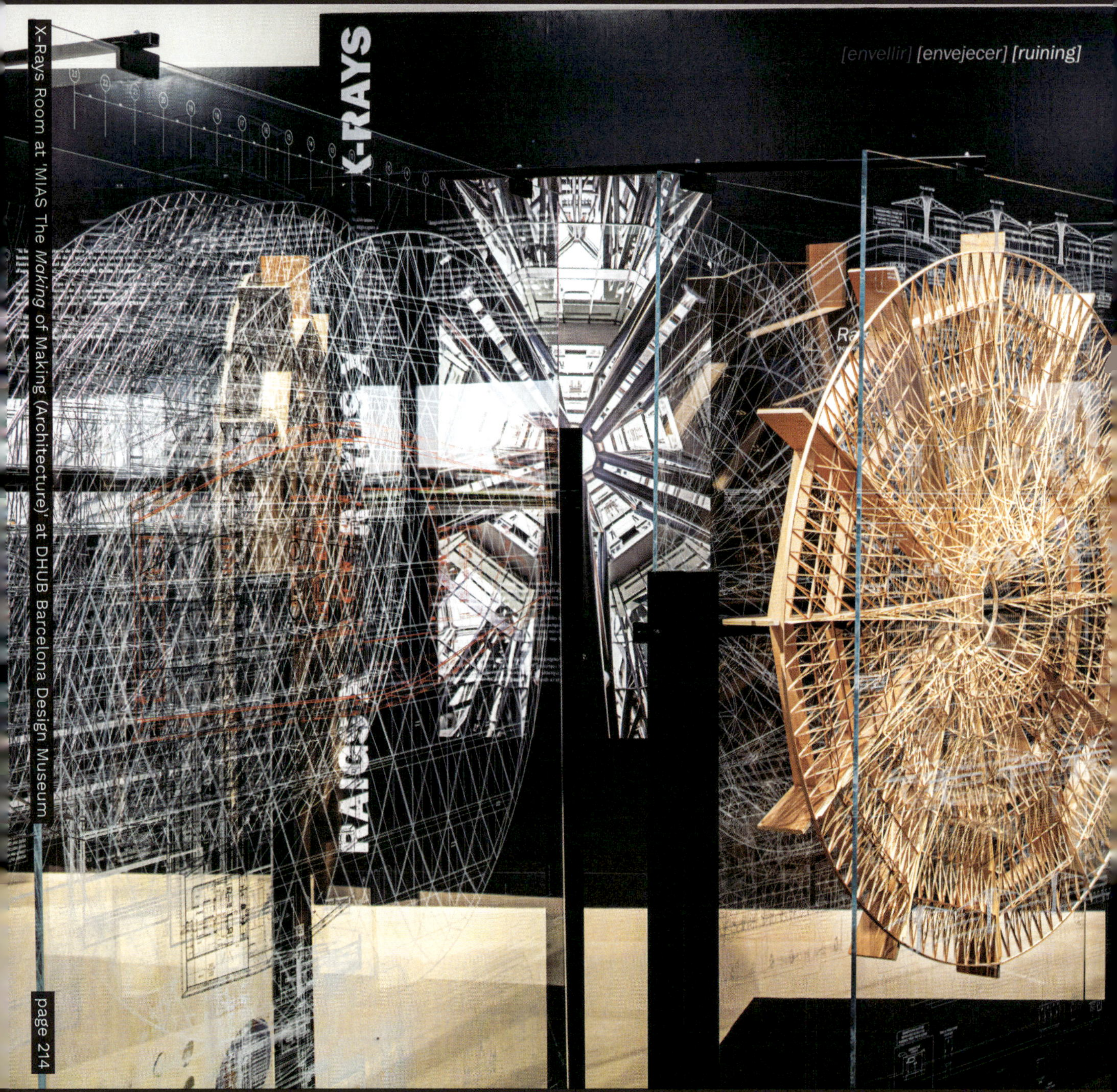

I always end up, quite naturally, stripping the buildings down and trying to understand their structural behaviour, or their constructive approach. That's why I'm so interested in buildings under construction, both my own and those of others, ruins... even the way in which a building has been turned into ruins, how it has fallen to the ground. There is a certain logic to this. The X-Rays photographs of different buildings of ours taken from the same point of view, during construction, and once the building is finished. By overlapping these photos, the photographer Adrià Goula makes some parts visible.
It's about thinking about how our buildings will age, how they will be ruined, and being able to incorporate this moment into the actual design process.

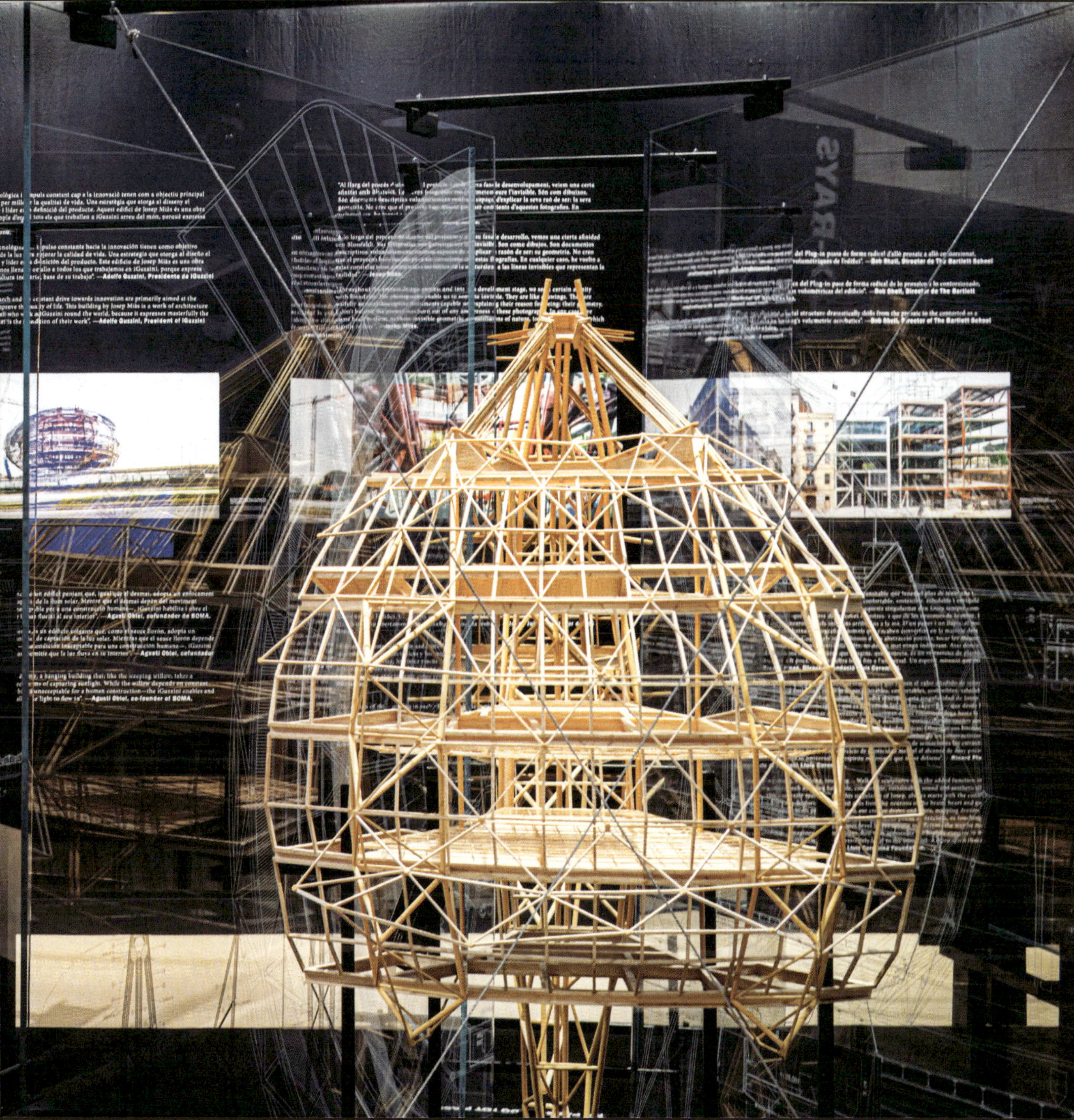

X-Rays Room at 'MIAS The *Making* of Making (Architecture)' at DHUB Barcelona Design Museum

iGuzzini Lighting Iberian Headquarters

2007-2011 project_029 iGuzzini Lighting Iberian Headquarters, Sant Cugat del Vallès, Spain

1.00x0.50m photography printed on metal exhibited at 'MIAS The *Making* of Making (Architecture)' at DHUB Barcelona Design Museum in 2021-2022

page 216

2007-2011 project_029 iGuzzini Lighting Iberian Headquarters, Sant Cugat del Vallès, Spain

1.00x0.50m photography printed on metal exhibited at 'MIAS The *Making* of Making (Architecture)' at DHUB Barcelona Design Museum in 2021-2022

2007-2011 project_029 iGuzzini Lighting Iberian Headquarters, Sant Cugat del Vallès, Spain

2007–2011 project_029 iGuzzini Lighting Iberian Headquarters, Sant Cugat del Vallès, Spain

iGuzzini Lighting Iberian Headquarters

2007-2011 project_029 iGuzzini Lighting Iberian Headquarters, Sant Cugat del Vallès, Spain

1.00x0.50m photography printed on metal exhibited at 'MIAS The *Making* of Making (Architecture)' at DHUB Barcelona Design Museum in 2021-2022

2007-2011 project_029 iGuzzini Lighting Iberian Headquarters, Sant Cugat del Vallès, Spain

1.00x0.50m photography printed on metal exhibited at 'MIAS The *Making* of Making (Architecture)' at DHUB Barcelona Design Museum in 2021-2022

2004-2010 project_004 Municipal Market and Public Space, Rubí, Spain
1.00x0.50m photos printed on metal exhibited at 'MIAS The *Making* of Making (Architecture)' at DHUB Barcelona Design Museum in 2021-2022

2006-2011 project_025 Plug-in Building at 22@, Barcelona, Spain

1.00x0.50m photos printed on metal exhibited at 'MAS The Making of Making (Architecture)' at DHUB Barcelona Design Museum in 2021-2022

2006-2011 project_025 Plug-in Building at 22@, Barcelona, Spain

1.00x0.50m photos printed on metal exhibited at 'MIAS The *Making* of Making (Architecture)' at DHUB Barcelona Design Museum in 2021-2022

page 224

2006–2011 project_025 Plug-in Building at 22@, Barcelona, Spain

1.00x0.50m photos printed on metal exhibited at 'MIAS The *Making* of Making (Architecture)' at DHUB Barcelona Design Museum in 2021-2022

2011-2012 project_005 Topographic House, Llavaneres, Spain

2011–2012 project_005 Topographic House, Llavaneres, Spain
1.00x0.50m photos printed on metal exhibited at 'MIAS The *Making* of Making (Architecture)' at DHUB Barcelona Design Museum in 2021-2022

2001-2007 project_003 Barceloneta Market and Public Space, Barcelona, Spain
100x0.50m photos printed on metal exhibited at 'MIAS The *Making* of Making (Architecture)' at DHUB Barcelona Design Museum in 2021-2022

2001-2007 project_003 Barceloneta Market and Public Space, Barcelona, Spain
1.00x0.50m photos printed on metal exhibited at 'MIAS The Making of Making (Architecture)' at DHUB Barcelona Design Museum in 2021-2022

2001-2007 project_003 Barceloneta Market and Public Space, Barcelona, Spain

1.00x0.50m photos printed on metal exhibited at 'MIAS The *Making of Making (Architecture)*' at DHUB Barcelona Design Museum in 2021-2022

2001-2007 project_003 Barceloneta Market and Public Space, Barcelona, Spain

1.00x0.50m photos printed on metal exhibited at 'MIAS The *Making* of Making (Architecture)' at DHUB Barcelona Design Museum in 2021-2022

Can Vidalet Market

2017-2022 project_038 Can Vidalet Market, Esplugues de Llobregat, Spain

1.00x0.50m photos printed on metal exhibited at MIAS The *Making* of Making (Architecture)' at DHUB Barcelona Design Museum in 2021-2022

2017-2022 project_038 Can Vidalet Market, Esplugues de Llobregat, Spain

1.00x0.50m photos printed on metal exhibited at 'MIAS The *Making* of Making (Architecture)' at DHUB Barcelona Design Museum in 2021-2022

sketch of project_003 Barceloneta Market and Public Space, Barcelona, Spain
sketch of project_007 Pedestrian Bridge, Palafolls, Spain

JOSEP MARIA MONTANER

STRUCTURAL EVOLUTION

Josep Maria Montaner

Doctor of Architecture, Professor at ETSAB Barcelona School of Architecture. Councillor for Housing of the Barcelona City Council 2015-2019, as well as Councillor of the Sant Martí district. Co-director of the Master Laboratorio de la Vivienda del Siglo XXI of the Polytechnic University of Catalonia, with Zaida Muxí. He has been a visiting professor at the Architectural Association School of Architecture in London (1986-1987) and a fellow at the Spanish Academy in Rome (1987). He has received the National Urbanism Award (2005). He has given courses and lectures at various universities and institutions in Europe, the Americas and Asia. He is the author of numerous books.

As Gottfried Semper (1803-1879) wrote in the mid-19th century, architecture is space and this space is constructed and delimited by technique, assembled through the logic of stereotomy.
Throughout the structural evolution of Josep Miàs's work this technical essence beats with an intense and tireless sense of the search, in different directions, for materiality and lightness.

Linking up with his experience of working with Enric Miralles (1955-2000) and, especially, devoting himself to carrying out the works in the thick of the industry, Miàs has been able to evolve towards the formal, spatial and combinatory possibilities of light structures. From the surrealist metaphor of the cloud or the object of desire of the volatile balloon, he has evolved towards an architecture that is light and transparent, and at the same time possible, effective and deeply rooted. In fact, from the dancing pillars in Enric Miralles's imagination, he has moved on to the precision of tubular structure systems. That is, the very logic of technology and materials has been the safe conduit to nature and organic, growth and protein forms and, at the same time, to forms based on symmetry and repetition, rigour and precision.

The fragile and unstable architecture from Enric Miralles and Carme Pinós's beginnings are still perhaps lurking in his models made of welded iron rods; models made of rods that have evolved from the first ones, made of balsa wood. And an evolution that has moved towards the essence of architecture, tending towards the skeleton, towards synthesis.

The way in which the skins are placed between the façades and the roofs is also very "Semperian", like fabrics that adapt to the body of the building and that grow and bulge to accommodate the uses, as if they were an appendage, as he did in the skylights in the Girona railway station car park (1997-2000) and the Barceloneta market (2001-2007).

There is no doubt that two works have been key moments representing a watershed and transition in this metamorphosis. The in-depth study of how to transform and consolidate the structure of the aforementioned Barceloneta market provided him with the secrets of the stereotomic logic for these types of 19th century buildings. And the new headquarters of the company iGuzzini in Sant Cugat (2006-2011) has allowed him to make the leap towards a new repertoire of forms and a new structural network, insufflated by fluidity and continuity, as in Paul Klee's navel drawings: a flattened sphere on a large prismatic base. The cloud has landed and become a luminous object, a great lighthouse.

Other works mark this evolution: the organic and telluric reminiscences in the Fontanals Golf Club (2004), the interweaving in the Palafolls bridge (2012) and the modular combination in the Plug-in office building in the 22@ district of Barcelona (2012), going as far as to recover and reinterpret the stereotomic tradition of warehouses and roofs in the two markets planned in Esplugues de Llobregat (2020).

These architectural meshes remind us of experiments such as those by the German-born engineer Konrad Wachsmann (1901-1980), exiled in the United States, and the driving force behind lightweight tubular structures. And like those by the Chinese-born American architect Anne Tyng (1920-2011), a pioneer of habitable mesh and lightweight roofs who trained at Harvard and worked with Louis Kahn from 1945 to 1964, first when the latter was a partner of Oscar Stonorov and then as the great structural expert who was so indispensable to Kahn for years. And this connection with Anne Tyng is demonstrated by the fact that Miàs invited her to give a lecture at the Vallés School of Architecture (ETSAV) around 2001.

In this evolution, the as yet uncompleted project of the Telecom headquarters in Andorra la Vella (2016) signifies the materialisation of the cloud, where he wants to achieve the surrealist desire and turn it into a metaphor for the digital world: the space that floats in the air, lightly touching the ground. Frederick Kiesler's (1890-1965) dream of living bubbles returns, from the Endless Theatre to the Bucephalus.

There are also exceptions in this evolution that confirm the versatility of the method, such as the project to remodel houses between party walls in the calle Hospital de Barcelona (2018), to reconvert an overcrowded and unsanitary everyday setting into a dignified and habitable place, with air and natural light. Imagination is disciplined and adapted, with rigorous study, recording and diagnosis, to the harsh, varied and picturesque reality of dwellings that seem more like they are in Hanoi than in Barcelona.

The mechanism here consists of the sensible system of emptying volumes: space to further oxygenate the existing courtyards.
And complementing all the work is the extensive collection of models, which recreate, on different scales and from various perspectives, each of the projects, continually probing the key ideas of each structure and assembly. And each project creates a beautiful and lengthy collection of drawings, which follow the path of the creative and artistic impulse that was at the beginning of each of the projects.

Josep Maria Montaner, Structural Evolution
sketch of project_003 Barceloneta Market and Public Space, Barcelona, Spain
sketch of project_007 Pedestrian Bridge, Palafolls, Spain

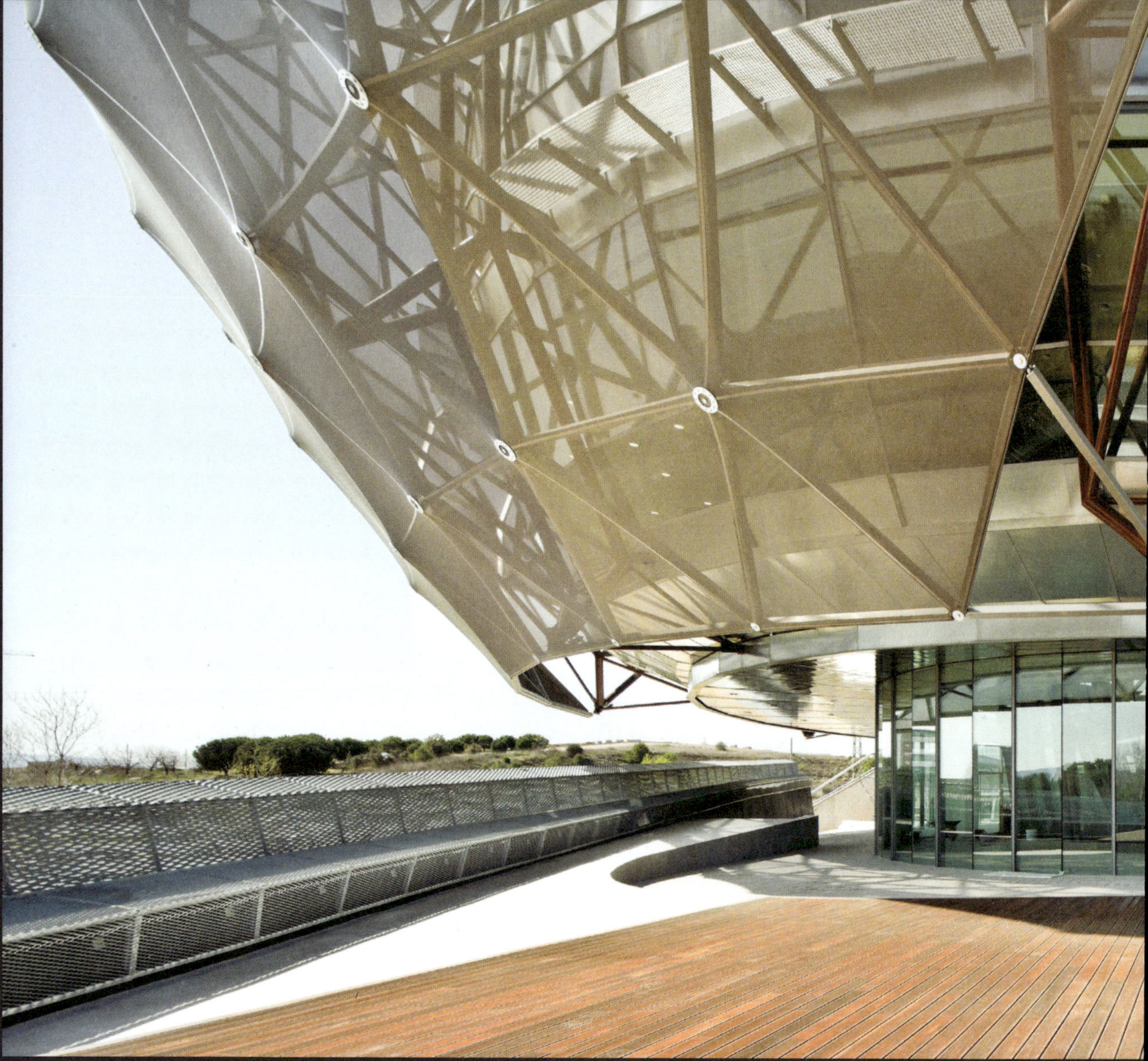

DHUB Barcelona Design Museum

'MIAS The *Making* of Making (Architecture)'

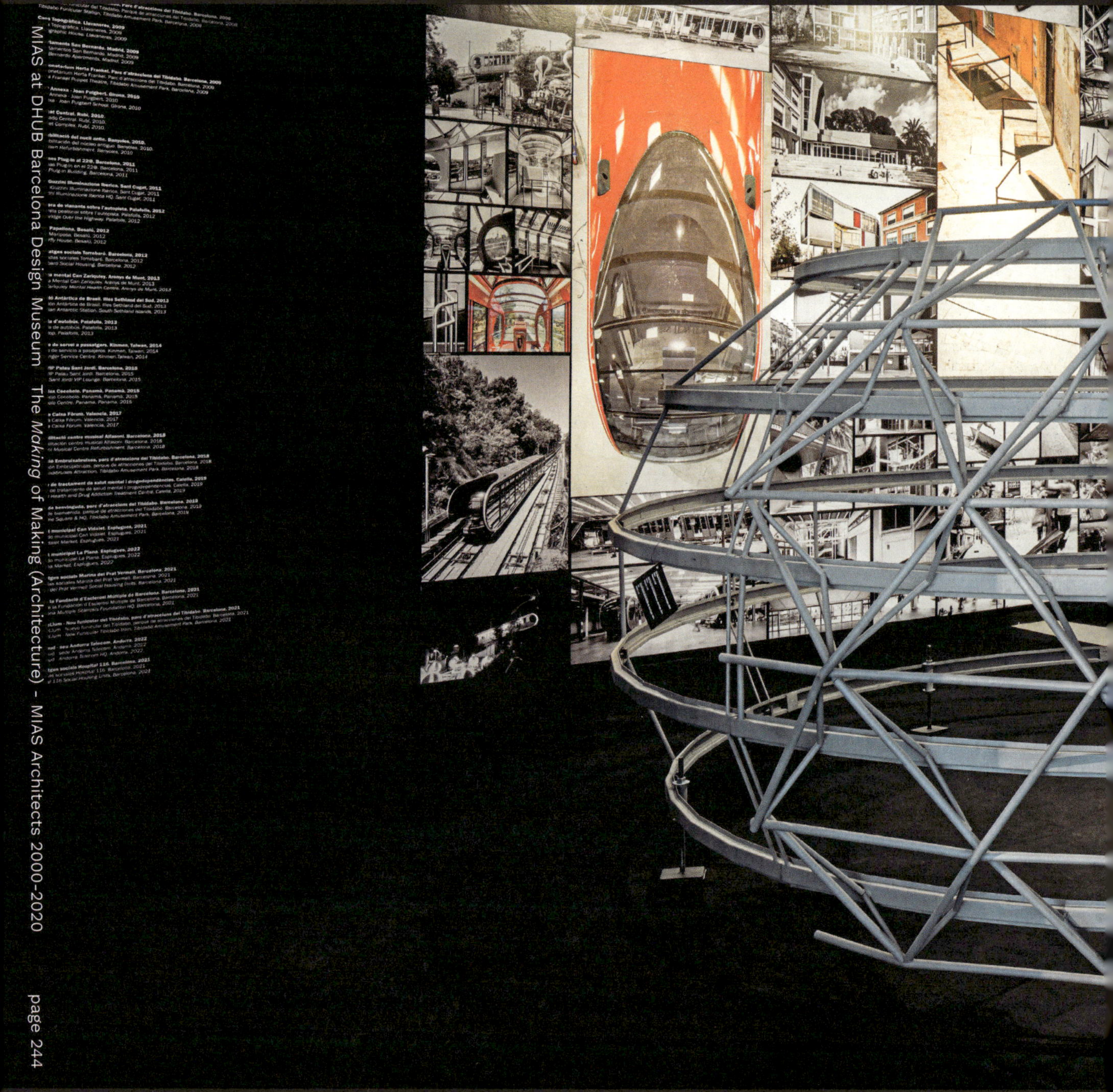

X-RAYS
RAYOS X

Municipal Market and Public Space

Open Competition, Winner
year: 2004-2010
location: Rubí, Spain 41°29'21"N 02°02'06"E"E
surface: 8700 m^2
client: Rubí City Council

Awards
- 2011 Archdaily Building of the Year, Selected
- 2011 Plataforma Arquitectura Work of the Year, Selected

2004–2010 project_004 Municipal Market and Public Space, Rubí, Spain

AL
ME

RUBÍ
MUNICIPAL

RUBÍ
MUNICIPAL
MERCAT

MUNICIPAL

UBI
MUNIC

MERC

2019 project_122 Nuvol Bench, Andorra La Vella, Andorra

page 252

page 256

Excepte serveis
i Pàrquing

'MIAS The *Making* of Making (Architecture)'

ANYTHING COULD HAPPEN
TOT PODRIA OCÓRRER
TODO PODRÍA SUCEDER
acciona

LIDL
MERCAT MUNICIPAL
CAN VIDALET

MERCAT MUNICIPAL
CAN VIDALET

CAN VIDALET

Alfasoni

Plug-in Building at 22@

Restricted Competition, Winner
year: 2006-2011
location: Barcelona, Spain 41°23'44"N 02°11'**31"E**
surface: 7000 m^2
client: 22@ Poblenou

Awards
- 2014 COAC Architects' Association Catalonia, Catalan Architecture Awards, Winner
- 2014 Enor Architectural Awards, Selected
- 2012 Barcelona City Prize for Architecture and Urbanism, Selected
- 2011 Archdaily Building of the Year, Selected
- 2011 Plataforma Arquitectura Work of the Year, Selected

COMARCAS CATALANAS, S. A.

2006-2011 project_025 Plug-in Building at 22@, Barcelona, Spain

44

Annexa Joan Puigbert School

Open Competition, Winner
year: 2007-2010
location: Girona, Spain 41°58'42"N 02°49'38"E
surface: 2300 m^2
client: GISA, Education Department of the Government of Catalonia

Awards
- 2013 Mies van der Rohe Awards, European Union Prize for Contemporary Architecture, Nominated
- 2011 A+ Architectural Awards, Best Spanish Educational Building, Winner
- 2011 COAC Architects' Association Catalonia, Girona Area Architectural Awards, Finalist

2007–2010 project_024 Annexa Joan Puigbert School, Girona, Spain

Curiosity is still my main attitude. I'm interested in architecture if it is able to give an opinion on a problem or subject, whatever it may be. As architects, we are obviously supposed to be competent in building, urban planning, design, etc., but I am increasingly interested in problems and projects that do not fall within the classic disciplines attributed to architects. And this is basically a matter of curiosity and surprising yourself. We invaded areas of competence that were unthinkable until now. And we have discovered that we can create both competent and imaginative contributions. I would like to carry on like this.

ARCHIVO
ESPACIOS ONÍRICOS
Habitatges socials Marina del Prat Vermell. Barcelona, 2021
Viviendas sociales Marina del Prat Vermell. Barcelona, 2021
Marina del Prat Vermell Social Housing Units. Barcelona, 2021

2007-2012 project_007 Pedestrian Bridge, Palafolls, Spain

DRAUL

Topographic House

project_008

Butterfly House

year: 2011-2012
location: Besalú, Spain 42°12'00"N 02°41'43"E
surface: 220 m^2
client: Private

2005-2006 project_008 Butterfly House, Besalú, Spain

'MIAS The *Making* of Making (Architecture)'

I believe I have found a sense and coherence in the work I head in the studio, focused on very personal research, but very attentive to incorporating any kind of external knowledge. Curiosity and constantly surprising yourself is essential.

Golf Clubhouse and Sports Centre

Open Competition, Winner
year: 2000-2004
location: Fontanals de Cerdanya, Spain 42°23'48"N 01°52'37"E
surface: 2500 m^2
client: Fontanals Esportiva SL

Awards
- 2011 Archdaily Building of the Year, Selected
- 2011 Plataforma Arquitectura Work of the Year, Selected
- 2004 AJAC Young Architects Prize to Best Young Architect under 40 for Built Work, Winner
- 2003 COAC Girona, Girona Area Architectural Awards, Finalist

Barcelona Market and Public Space

Open Competition, Winner
year: 2001-2007
location: Barcelona, Spain 41°22'49"N 02°11'21"E
surface: 5200 m^2
client: Barcelona City Council, IMMB Institut Municipal de Mercats de Barcelona

Awards
- 2011 Archdaily Building of the Year, Selected
- 2011 Plataforma Aquitectura Work of the Year, Finalist
- 2008 Catalonia Construction Awards, Winner
- 2007 Barcelona City Prize for Architecture and Urbanism, Winner

Publications
- *Barceloneta Market*, Miàs, Josep, Barcelona, Actar Publishers, 2009
- *Barceloneta Market and Square*, Miàs, Josep, Barcelona, 2011

Open Competition, Winner
year: 2001-2007
location: Barcelona, Spain 41°22'49"N 02°11'21"E
surface: 5200 m^2
client: Barcelona City Council, IMMB Institut Municipal de Mercats de Barcelona

2001-2007 project_003 Barceloneta Market and Public Space, Barcelona, Spain

CARNISSE
especialitat en

MARTINEZ
MARTINEZ
MARTINEZ

I VERDURES SANZ
Cansaladeria
ESPECIALITAT EN PERNILS I EMBOTITS IBÈRICS

POLLERIA
CARNISSE
especialitat en xai, cabrit

Embotits
POLLERIA

project_009

Lower Funicular Station at Tibidabo Amusement Park

page 330

year: 2007-2008
location: Barcelona, Spain 41°24'59"N 02°07'51"E
surface: 400 m²
client: Barcelona City Council + Tibidabo Amusement Park

BAR MERBEYE - BAR

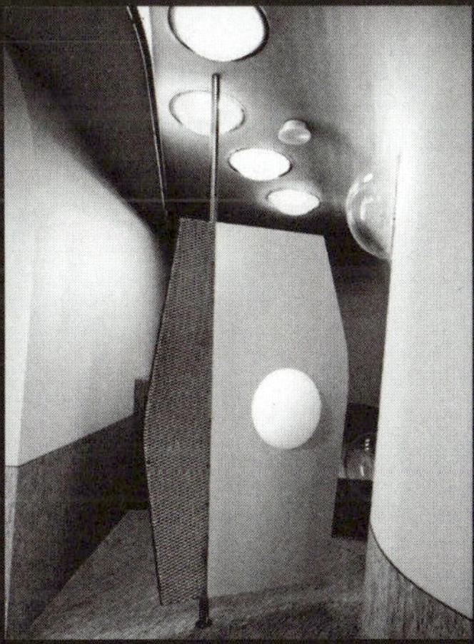

2008-2009 project_012 Historical Building at Tibidabo Amusement Park, Barcelona, Spain

fem
FUNDACIÓ
ESCLEROSI
MÚLTIPLE

RUTA
61

project_015

Can Zariquiey Therapeutic Centre

year: 2007-2013
location: Arenys de Munt, Spain 41°35'57"N 02°32'38"E
surface: 1800 m^2
client: Maresme Therapeutic Community

Awards
- 2015 Mies van der Rohe Awards, Nominated
- 2014 Venice Biennale of Architecture

2007-2013 project_015 Can Zariquiey Therapeutic Centre, Arenys de Munt, Spain

Exhibitions

- "Grafting Architecture" Catalonia at Venice, Venice Biennale 2014

Publications

- *Orquídeas pasra la salud,* Miàs, Josep - Agustí, Valentí, Barcelona, Argra Trading S.L., 2013

Banyoles Old Town Public Space

Open Competition, Winner
year: 1999-2006
location: Banyoles, Spain 42°07'05"N 02°45'53"E
surface: 18.000 m²
client: Banyoles City Council

Awards
- 2015 AADIPA Architects Association for Defence and Intervention in Architectural Heritage Awards, Finalist
- 2015 Taipei City Government, International Design Awards, Finalist
- 2014 Piranesi Prix de Rome, Finalist
- 2013 International Stone Architecture Awards, Winner
- 2013 Taipei City Government, International Design Awards, Finalist
- 2010 FAD Awards, Public Space, Finalist
- 2009 Catalonia Construction Awards, Winner

- 2008 CCCB Urban, European Prize for Public Space, Finalist
- 2008 Barcelona International Biennal of Landscape Architecture, Rosa Barba Prize, Finalist
- 2008 Urban Public Spaces European Prize, Finalist
- 2007 COAC Girona, Girona Area Architectural Awards for Public Space, Winner

Publications

- *Banyoles,* Miàs, Josep, Barcelona, Argra Trading S.L., 2013
- *Banyoles Old City Center*, Miàs, Josep, Barcelona, 2011

Between Lines Room at 'MIAS The *Making* of Making (Architecture)' at DHUB Barcelona Design Museum

page 356

In the old town of Banyoles, the tender brief was to give the old town back to pedestrians. We felt that we had to recover the canals dug into the soil that were formerly used in industry and to irrigate the vegetable gardens at the back of the houses. Recovering the canals was the way to make the presence of the lake feel present in the city, not only visually but also with its music. The formal result of the cuts in the Banyoles travertine paving is the result of a technical analysis of the flow and speed of the water. The sections and geometries of the canal itself have been built to absorb a possible rise in the water level of the lake, so that the excess water moves

Between Lines Room at 'MIAS The *Making* of Making (Architecture)' at DHUB Barcelona Design Museum

freely over the actual paved surface. Furthermore, the zigzagging of the canals corresponds to maintaining the flow, which increases in speed when the area is reduced and can cause a plug or whirlpool effect that prevents the water from flowing. It's as if the water was drawing the project. Something that allows you to avoid certain responsibility in the final result. By this I mean that the project is apparently a formal exercise, when it is actually a very technical exercise or, at least, the result of the interaction between the two.

project_117

El Xampany Commercial and Cultural Centre

year: in progress
location: Cervelló, Spain 41°24'08"N 1°59'23"E

in progress project_117 El Xampany Commercial and Cultural Centre, Cervelló, Spain

in progress project_117 El Xampany Commercial and Cultural Centre, Cervelló, Spain
model_01 180x82x18cm 1:250 balsa wood

in progress project_117 El Xampany Commercial and Cultural Centre, Cervelló, Spain
model_01 180x82x18cm 1:250 balsa wood

Anis del Mono Factory Refurbishment

year: in progress
location: Badalona, Spain 41°26'33''N 02°14'47"E

NIS DEL MONO

in progress project_106 Anis del Mono Factory Refurbishment, Badalona, Spain
model_01 77x63x29cm 1:100 balsa wood

in progress project_106 Anis del Mono Factory Refurbishment, Badalona, Spain
model_01 77x63x29cm 1:100 balsa wood

Vallcarca Industrial Area Transformation

year: in progress
location: Sitges, Spain 41°14'30"N 01°51'35"E

'MIAS The *Making* of Making (Architecture)'

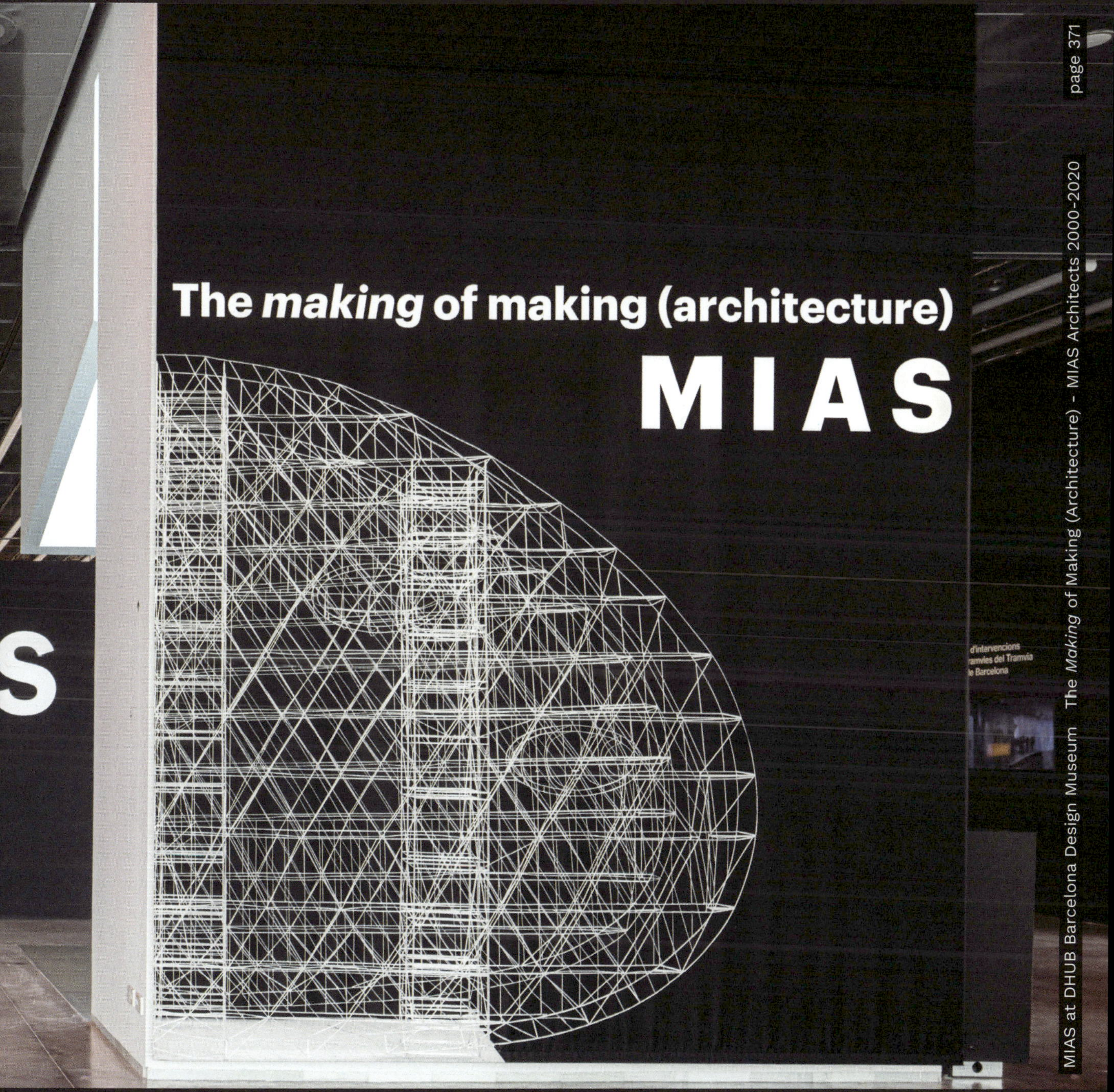
The *making* of making (architecture)
MIAS

MIAS
The making of making
(architecture)
DISSENY HUB BARCELONA
EXPOSICIÓ 12.11.2021 > 09.01.2022
RIGOLETTO
VERDI
28 NOV
19 DES
LA VANGUARDIA

MIAS
The making of making
(architecture)
DISSENY HUB BARCELONA
EXPOSICIÓ 12.11.2021 > 09.01.2022
MIAS

SIR PETER COOK

Architect Sir Peter Cook was a founder of ARCHIGRAM in the late 1960s, teacher at the Architectural Association from 1964 to 1990, Professor at the Staedelschule Frankfurt 1984 to 2009, Bartlett Professor and Chair 1990 to 2006. RIBA Royal Gold Medallist (with Archigram) 2007. Authored 9 books, drawings in MOMA, Centre Pompidou, Deutsches Architekturmuseum, FRAC,etc. Built : Kunsthaus Graz : with Colin Fournier; Law School Vienna/Architecture School Bond University/Drawing Studio AUB Bournemouth : with Gavin Robotham.

As a kid who wanted to be an architect you could either make clay shapes, drag pieces of driftwood into vague boxes - or put together Meccano cages. I followed the last option and surely so did Josep Miàs.

Tracing through the pieces being exhibited, you sense that he is essentially a man who takes strips and edges and develops them into meshes, and then maybe combs, and then maybe honeycombs with a conspicuously boyish delight in making the sketch, the linear diagram, the scale model and the built building.

I write this having enjoyed Josep's company in reviews and enthusiastic conversations about *stuff* – a constituent – and therefore an aspect of architecture that is readily dismissed in intellectual circles.

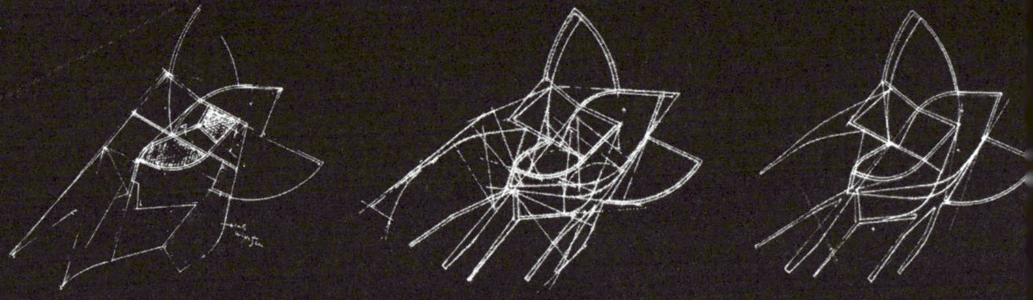

I first met him when he was already a key player in Enric Miralles' office and clearly playing a role in the realisation of Enric's extraordinary output which surely – of anybody's – was the embodiment of 'stuff' harnessed to fearlessness. Yet underlying the apparently fearless is a sense of what can fly, swing, lurch, lean or rest: in other words the composite that makes something possible to be as it is in space.

The activities of these two men are the fruit of instinct harnessed to enthusiasm.

The instinctive rather than the well informed is an interesting distinction in the current architectural scene. It leads perhaps to a certain delightful obsessiveness: so that with the sketches in particular, you see Josep's fascination with the skeletal and with that which can be created out of the skeletal. If, in observing architectural trends and fashion, we notice that such a preoccupation has been given less prominence in recent years than the parametric or other variations of the manipulated digital, this should not blind us to the importance of a territory of inspiration having an essential connectivity to that which can be made simply and efficiently.

In other words: steel comes readily in straight strips. If we can make magic out of these straight strips, why look further? Why get involved in complex cutting and endless deviations – even if it can be done?

Strange coming from Spain, where I suspect the common instinct is to build walls, whereas Josep's instinct is to create swathes? Unless we consider that other tradition that originates in the Spain of the seafarer. This leads to a dependency upon the mast, the sail, the surf-breaker, all of which are taut and stressed.

Most fascinating is Josep's own definition of 'unpredictable traces' – and we have to take such a term on trust, for I believe that there is a nanosecond's gap between the instinctive move and the unpredictable. Or the condition that we would wish to predict – but we move into it with creative trepidation. In this connection, one notes that the 'Sketches' section suggests that there are *primary* thrust lines that are then supported by secondary lines. Whereas the linear sketches notate most of the lines as of equal weight. Of course, this is deceptive and Josep surely knows and feels the relative roles of the various lines.

Surely this is both a fascinating and a meaningful territory of architecture and Josep Miàs explores it for our delight and instruction.

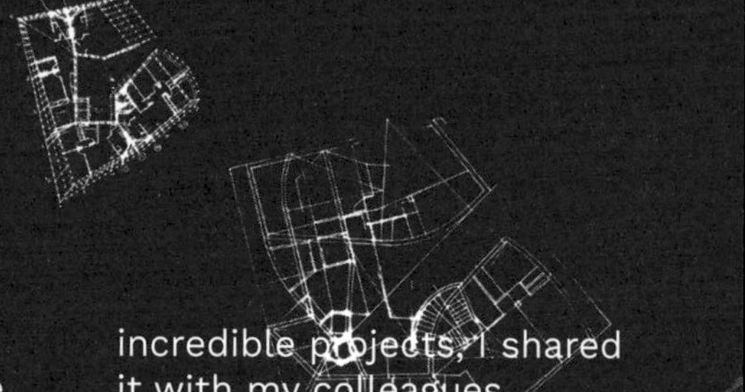

MARCOS CRUZ

DESIGN DISOBEDIENCE: THE UNCOMPROMISING FORCE OF JOSEP MIÀS'S ARCHITECTURE

Marcos Cruz
Architect and Professor of Innovative Environments at the UCL. Co-Director of the MArch, MSc in Bio-Integrated Design (Bio-ID). Director of the Bartlett 2010 to 2014. Teaching activity at IAAC where he runs the C-Biom.A group, (UCLA) and UCL. RIBA Gold Medallist for the thesis 2008. Co-founder the atelier mam/ marcosandmarjan. Built : Kunsthaus Graz with Sir Peter Cook, Colin Fournier.
Author and editor.

Have you ever walked under the canopies of the Barceloneta market, and seen the protruding corner twist of the plug-in offices in Poblenou, or experienced the outward projected structure of the Llavaneres Topographic House? Did you ever touch the running water in the zig-zagging pavement-voids of the Banyoles old town public space, or simply driven passed the suspended dome of the iGuzzini Headquarters in Sant Cugat del Valles? All of these architectural moments have something in common: they have a tectonic force that is mystifying due to the unconditional expression of its physical form. They are invigorating and surely do not leave any user or visitor indifferent. Design in this work is taken to an extreme as it has the power to exert a defining influence on us and our surrounding.

I got to know Josep Mias for the first time around 2011 when I was the Director of the Bartlett School of Architecture at UCL. I had just received an email from him where we started looking at some possible teaching involvement in our school. After checking out his incredible projects, I shared it with my colleagues Frederic Migayrou, Christine Hawley and Jonathan Hill, all of whom were amazed to discover his prolific yet still relatively unknow work in the English context. We invited him over and immediately felt a sense of affinity with him; not only was he this friendly and jolly chap, but we found a common ambition in what concerns the exploration of buildings with unique and iconographic features, which in turn result from a great spatial complexity, structural expression as well as a distinctive linguistic mannerism. Without really knowing it, Josep had reached out to an architectural 'family' in London that was welcoming him with open arms as many of us were pursuing parallel agendas. In those years the Bartlett was enriched with a buzz of new commuters from the European continent who were flying in regularly for tutorials, including Kristina Schinegger and Stefan Rutzinger from Vienna, Izaskun Chinchilla from Madrid, David Garcia from Copenhagen, later Johan Berglund from Stockholm, amongst others. But few had Josep's building repertoire, which made his presence in the school of great importance. We ended up creating the opportunity for him to run Diploma Unit 16 which he led with some younger colleagues to become one of the key units of the Bartlett in those years.

Along with his teaching, we organised a solo exhibition at the Bartlett and invited him for lectures. From all the contact with him, I got to realise that Josep belongs to a vanishing stripe of architects who always push the boundaries of the impossible regardless of any programmatic, financial or time constraints. Josep's work is imbued with a rough authenticity and strength that is very unusual, but it also has a formal eccentricity that those with a more minimalist pedigree find overtly complicated and rather arrogant. However, the truth is that buildings like the Mollet Landscape House, Fontanals Golf Clubhouse, Tibidabo Funicular Station, and Can Zariquiey Health Centre allow us to be immersed in an extraordinary experiential field. The projects are designed to be all-embracing, inhabitable manifolds that are multi-dimensional, while allowing people to indulge with a theatrical dimension that offers inspiration and surprise.

Josep's buildings incite us to think of one of architecture's great powers: to move us out of the daily norm into a something we have never experienced before. Something memorable! Deep down, with every building he is also overtly counteracting against pervasive conceptual conservativism, unappealing commercialism and tectonic flatness in much of our contemporary built environment. I see Josep's oeuvre within a much more avant-garde lineage that is risk-taking and highly erudite. I see parallels with some of the most experimental architects who always created a vital counterpoint to the mainstream: Bruce Goff, Reima and Raili Pietilä, Lina Bobardi, Pancho Guedes, Hans Scharoun, Ralph Erskine, Sir Peter Cook, Masaharu Takasaki, Günther Domenig, and of course, Enric Miralles with whom Josep collaborated and taught with for many years. What associates these architects is an irreverence against the establishment and an impossibility to be categorised when every project is unique and an experiment in its own right. For Josep every commission or competition offers the opportunity to transgress and contradict preconceived mindsets. It allows to pull off from traditional protocols in an incessant pursuit for new structural and spatial dimensions. In this context, we should not forget that to be daring and provocative in architecture is so much more difficult to pursue than what we see in the majority of simplistic buildings around us. Ultimately, Josep's design expresses an uncompromising force that is inherently defiant and disobedient against the mundanity and repetition of our lives.

I can't wait for his next design steps and the opportunity to break with new rules.

sketches of project_027 Torrebaró Social Housing, Barcelona, Spain

MIAS at Centre Pompidou

Unpredictable Traces - Monographic Exhibition

MIAS at Centre Pompidou *Unpredictable Traces* - Monographic Exhibition

In 2020 the Centre Pompidou has acquired 42 models, 14 drawings and 18 engravings for the Permanent Collection.

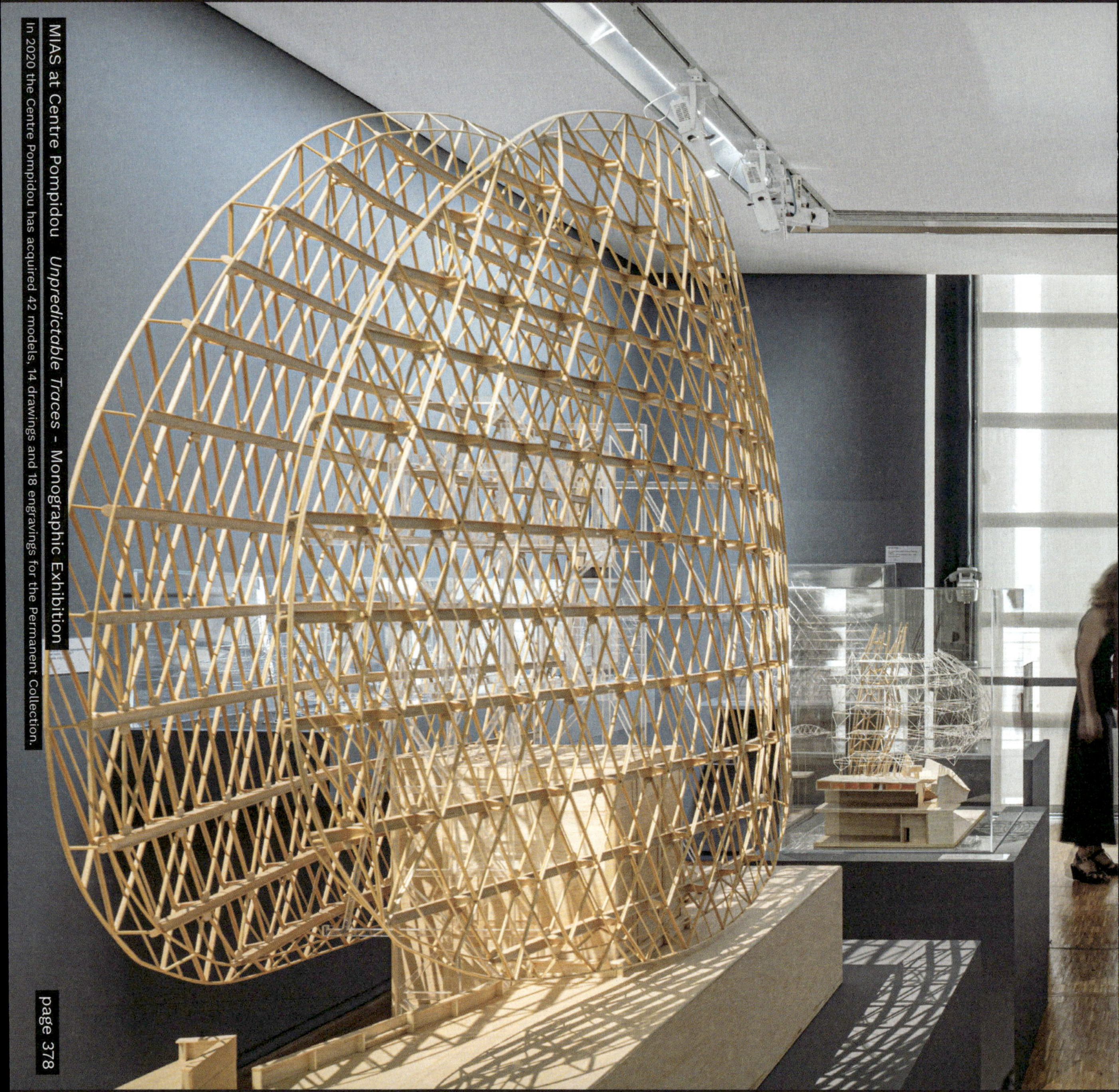

year: September 2020 — September 2021
location: Paris, France 48°51'38.5"N 2°21'07.1"E

Centre Pompidou · Generalitat de Catalunya · institut ramon llull

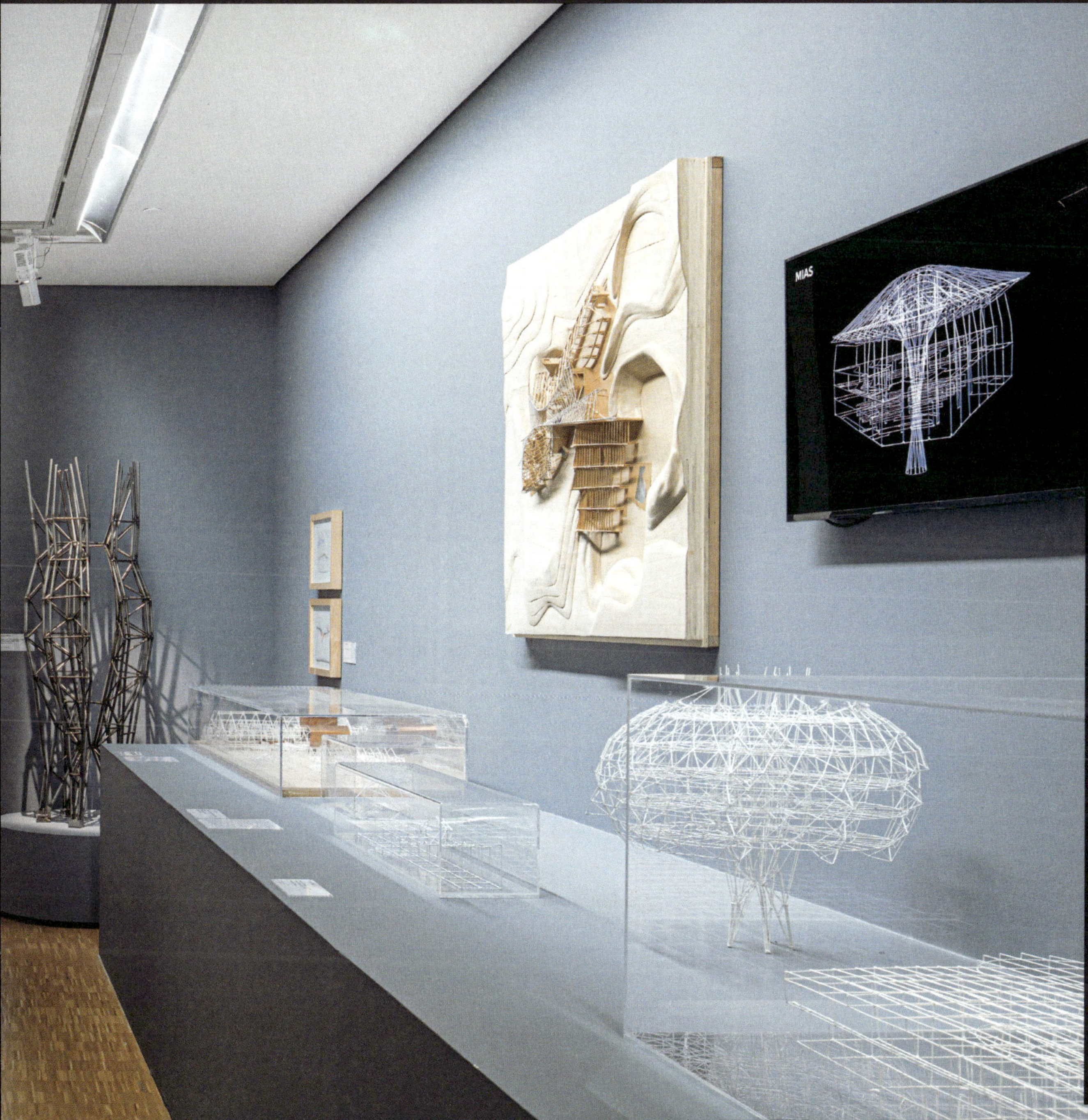

MIAS at Centre Pompidou *Unpredictable Traces* - Monographic Exhibition

In 2020 the Centre Pompidou has acquired 42 models, 14 drawings and 18 engravings for the Permanent Collection.

The Centre Pom
recognized the t
MIAS Architects
international rel
monographic ro

In 2020, the mu
42 models, 14 d
18 engravings fo
Permanent Coll

idou in Paris
ajectory of
or its
vance with a
m.
eum acquired
wings and
their
ction.

Centre Pompidou P

MIAS at Centre Pompidou *Unpredictable Traces* - Monographic Exhibition
In 2020 the Centre Pompidou has acquired 42 models, 14 drawings and 18 engravings for the Permanent Collection.
project_003 / project_005 / project_006 / project_007 / project_029 / project_030 / project_040

project_029
model_84
EC2020-2-AR26

project_030
model_27
EC2020-2-AR56

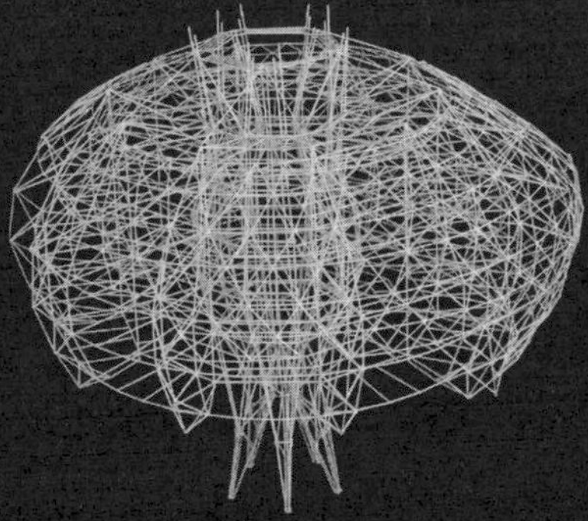
project_029
model_72
EC2020-2-AR14

project_029
model_74
EC2020-2-AR16

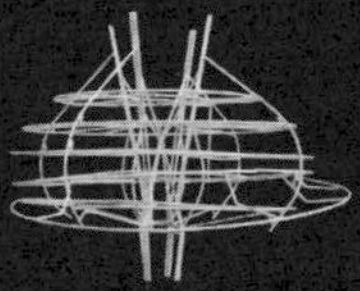
project_029
model_73
EC2020-2-AR15

project_029
model_75
EC2020-2-AR17

project_029
model_70
EC2020-2-AR12

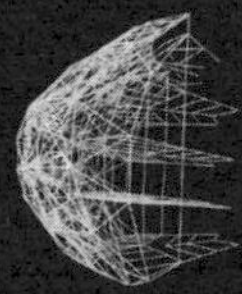
project_029
model_83
EC2020-2-AR79

project_029
model_76
EC2020-2-AR18

project_029
model_78
EC2020-2-AR21

project_029
model_80
EC2020-2-AR45

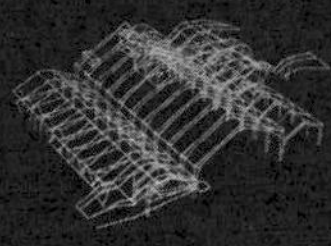
project_003
model_41
EC2020-2-AR85

project_006
model_15
EC2020-2-AR50

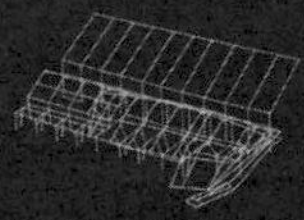
project_003
model_42
EC2020-2-AR84

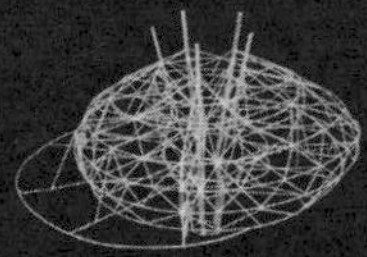
project_029
model_48
EC2020-2-AR27

project_030
model_25
EC2020-2-AR53

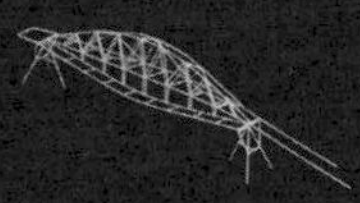
project_007
model_17
EC2020-2-AR40

project_029
model_79
EC2020-2-AR22

project_005
model_58
EC2020-2-AR58

project_030
model_24
EC2020-2-AR52

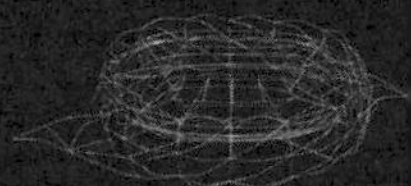
project_040
model_05
EC2020-2-AR51

rmanent Collection

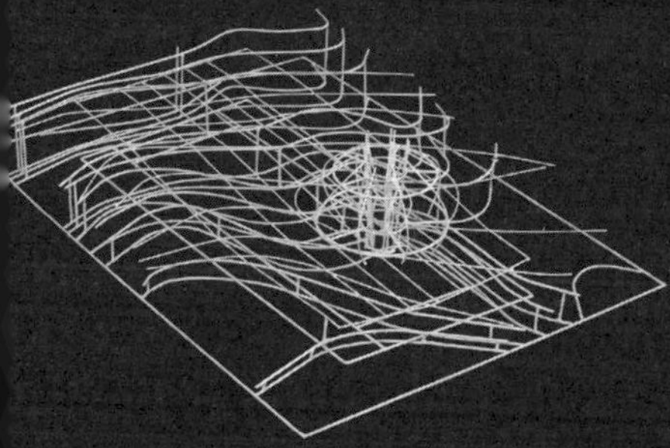

project_029
model_71
EC2020-2-AR13

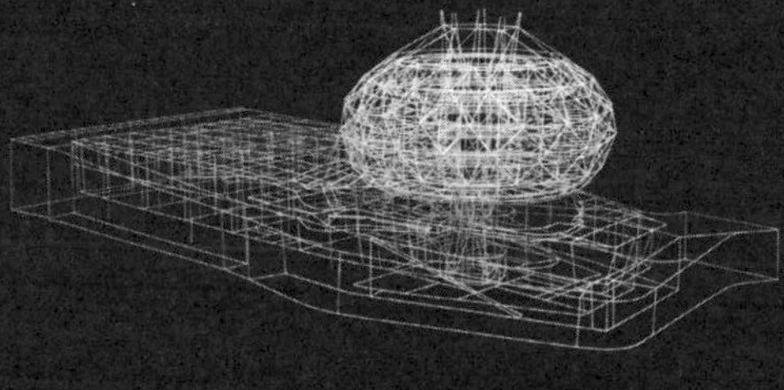

project_029
model_69
EC2020-2-AR80

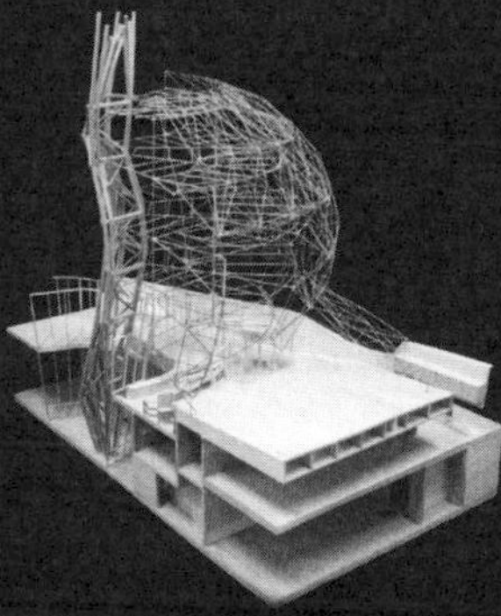

project_029
model_65
EC2020-2-AR24

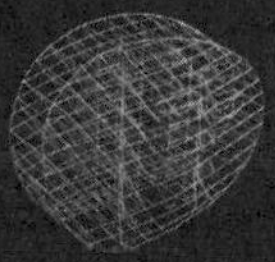

project_030
model_26
EC2020-2-AR52

project_037
model_08
EC2020-2-AR78

project_029
model_77
EC2020-2-AR20

project_030
model_29
EC2020-2-AR54

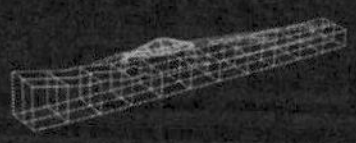

project_007
model_18
EC2020-2-AR41

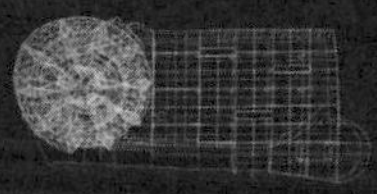

project_029
model_69
EC2020-2-AR80

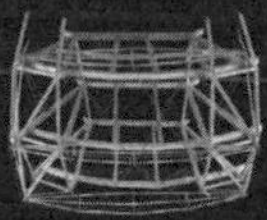

project_029
model_86
EC2020-2-AR25

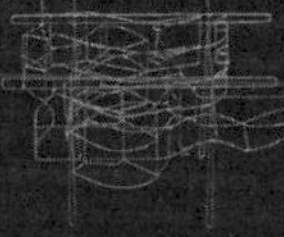

project_009
model_18
EC2020-2-AR49

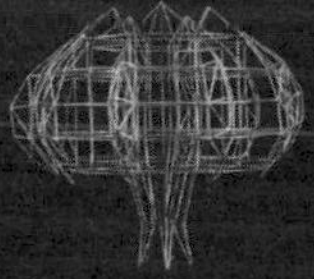

project_029
model_82
EC2020-2-AR23

project_038
model_11
EC2020-2-AR57

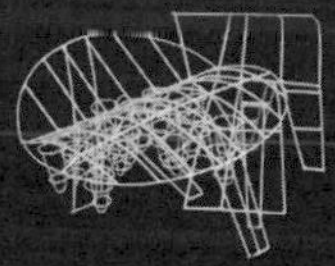

project_003
model_43
EC2020-2-AR46

project_029
model_72
EC2020-2-AR14

project_003
model_45
EC2020-2-AR47

project_008
model_18
EC2020-2-AR60

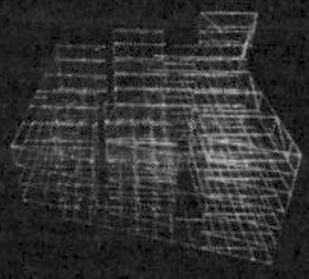

project_025
model_16
EC2020-2-AR83

project_039
model_02
EC2020-2-AR64

project_003
model_44
EC2020-2-AR48

project_029
model_84
EC2020-2-AR26

MIAS at Centre Pompidou *Unpredictable Traces* - Monographic Exhibition

In 2020 the Centre Pompidou has acquired 42 models, 14 drawings and 18 engravings for the Permanent Collection.

project_003 / project_007 / project_008 / project_009 / project_025 / project_029 / project_030 / project_037 / project_038 / project_039

MIAS at Centre Pompidou *Unpredictable Traces* - Monographic Exhibition

MIAS at Centre Pompidou *Unpredictable Traces* - Monographic Exhibition
In 2020 the Centre Pompidou has acquired 42 models, 11 drawings and 18 engravings for the Permanent Collection

MIAS at Centre Pompidou *Unpredictable Traces* - Monographic Exhibition
In 2020 the Centre Pompidou has acquired 42 models, 14 drawings and 18 engravings for the Permanent Collection.

MIAS at Centre Pompidou *Unpredictable Traces* - Monographic Exhibition

In 2020 the Centre Pompidou has acquired 42 models, 14 drawings and 18 engravings for the Permanent Collection.

MIAS at Centre Pompidou *Unpredictable Traces* - Monographic Exhibition

In 2020 the Centre Pompidou has acquired 42 models, 14 drawings and 18 engravings for the Permanent Collection.

page 388

MIAS at Centre Pompidou *Unpredictable Traces* - Monographic Exhibition
In 2020 the Centre Pompidou has acquired 42 models, 14 drawings and 18 engravings for the Permanent Collection.

MIAS at Centre Pompidou *Unpredictable Traces* - Monographic Exhibition

In 2020 the Centre Pompidou has acquired 42 models, 14 drawings and 18 engravings for the Permanent Collection.

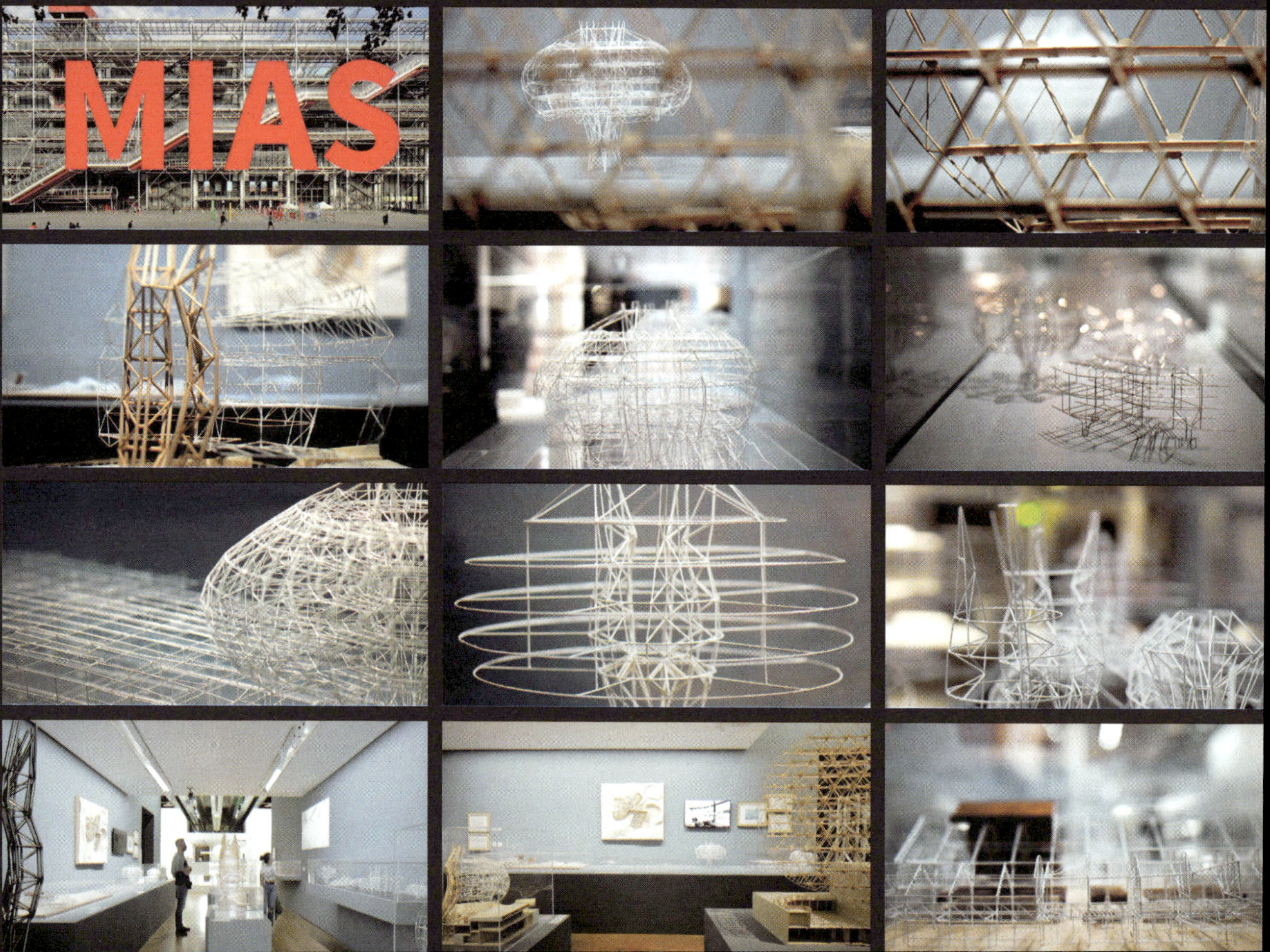

MIAS at Centre Pompidou *Unpredictable Traces* - Monographic Exhibition

In 2020 the Centre Pompidou has acquired 42 models, 14 drawings and 18 engravings for the Permanent Collection.

MIAS at Centre Pompidou *Unpredictable Traces* – Monographic Exhibition
In 2020 the Centre Pompidou has acquired 42 models, 14 drawings and 18 engravings for the Permanent Collection.

MIAS at Centre Pompidou *Unpredictable Traces* - Monographic Exhibition
In 2020 the Centre Pompidou has acquired 42 models, 14 drawings and 18 engravings for the Permanent Collection.

MIAS at Centre Pompidou *Unpredictable Traces* - Monographic Exhibition
Iñaqui Carnicero, Angels Ponsa, Maria Rosa Pons, Bernard Blistène, Frederic Migayrou, Assumpció Puig, Josep Miàs, Carme Pigem, Ramon Vilalta, Olga Anglada, Marc Subirana, Arnau Miàs, Pablo Klatz

MIAS at Centre Pompidou
Actar Publishers, 2021

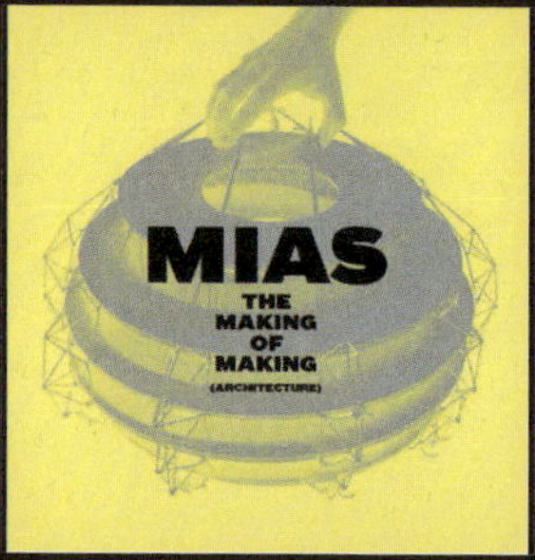

MIAS The Making of Making (Architecture)
Actar Publishers, 2021

Barceloneta Market
Actar Publishers, 2009

The Glow-Worm - Cucadellum Funicular Tibidabo Barcelona
Actar Publishers, 2023

iGuzzini Barcelona Corporate Building
Actar Publishers, 2012

Plug-in Barcelona
2013

Orquídeas para la salud
Argra Trading S.L., 2013

El edificio que nació de una ventana
2021

Banyoles
2013

Pujades 22@
Plug-in Building

Torrebaró
Housing Building

Barceloneta
Market and
Square

Fontanals
Pyrenees
Golf Centre

Llavaneres
Topographic House

Banyoles
Old City Center

San Bernardo
Apartments

Caselles Single
House

Joan Puigbert
School

Herta Frankel
Puppet Theatre

iGuzzini Lighting
Iberian España
Headquarters

Tibidabo Funicular
Lower Station

Miàs Architects - The Cloud
The Bartlett Edition

Miàs Architects - Funicular
del Tibidabo
The Bartlett Edition

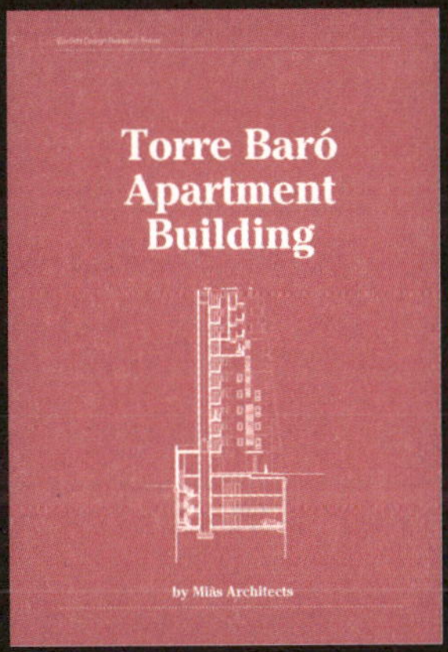

Miàs Architects - Torre Baró
Apartment Building
The Bartlett Edition

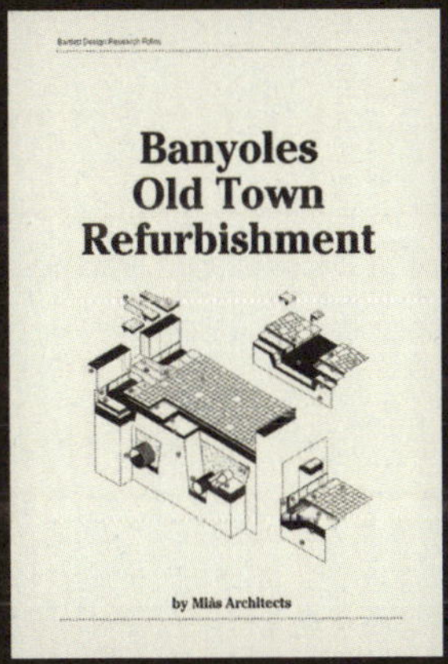

Miàs Architects - Banyoles
Old Town Refurbishment
The Bartlett Edition

Miàs Architects - Markets
Barcelona
The Bartlett Edition

JOSEP MIÀS

MIAS Architects is an internationally recognized Architecture and Urbanism Studio, founded by Josep Miàs in 2000, known for both its experimental projects and its practice combining sustainable technology, innovative manufacturing and cutting-edge construction practices.

Before founding MIAS, Josep Miàs was an Associate Architect at Enric Miralles' studio from 1990 to 2000. Since then, MIAS Architects has gained international recognition for projects such as the Fontanals Golf Club, the Urbanization of the Historic Center of Banyoles, the Barceloneta Market, the 22@Plug-in Building, the iGuzzini Lighting Iberian Headquarters, the Torre Baró Apartment Tower, the Cloud Andorra Telecom Headquarters, their ongoing collaboration with Tibidabo Amusement Park and with their shortlisted proposal for the New Camp Nou, F.C. Barcelona Stadium.

MIAS has received numerous international awards such as the COAC Barcelona Catalonia Architecture Award for the Best Building between 2008 – 2013, the International Stone Architecture Award (2013), the Architizer Building of the World Award (2013), the Archdaily Building of the Year Award (2011), A + Architecture Award for the Best Educational Building in Spain (2011), the Catalonia Construction Award (2009), the City of Barcelona Architecture and Urbanism Award (2007), the Girona Architecture Award (2007), and AJAC Best Young Catalan Architect Award (2004).

Selected projects have been published in international journals, books and magazines and have been exhibited in over 40 exhibitions, the most notable being two Monographic Exhibitions, MIAS - Unpredictable Traces at the Centre Pompidou in Paris (2020) and MIAS - The Making of Making (Architecture) at the DHUB in Barcelona (2021). Other exhibitions have been displayed at COAC (Barcelona), Cité de l'Architecture (Paris), Nuevos Ministerios (Madrid), Satdelschule (Frankfurt), Architektur Forum (Zurich), TU University (Berlin), House of the Architect (Kiev), The Bartlett School of Architecture (London), Anhembi Morumbi (Sao Paulo), WAF (Singapore), University of Belgrade (Belgrade), and in 2012 and 2014 at the Biennale di Venezia (Venice).

Due to his influence and recognition, Josep Miàs is frequently invited to give lectures, workshops, and participate in juries at numerous universities, conferences and festivals all over the world. He has also been engaged in academic activities since 1990 at numerous institutions across the globe including many universities in Barcelona (ETSAB, ETSAV), Staedelschule (Frankfurt), ESALA - Edinburgh School of Architecture and Landscape Architecture (Edinburgh), and Harvard GSD (Cambridge). Josep Miàs is currently a Professor of Architectural Practice at the Bartlett School of Architecture, UCL (London) and is an Associate Professor at UNISS Università degli studi di Sassari, Dipartimento di Architettura, design e Urbanistica (Alghero).

In 2020, the Centre Pompidou acquired 42 models, 14 drawings and 18 engravings for the Permanent Collection. In 2021, the Catalan Government and the Barcelona City Council recognized the international career of MIAS Architects with the first monographic exhibition at the Museum of Design and Architecture of Barcelona, dedicated to a currently working firm.

FIRST PRIZES IN COMPETITIONS

2018 project_035 Cucadellum Funicular to Tibidabo Amusement Park, Barcelona, Spain
project_026 Marina del Prat Vermell Social Housing, Barcelona, Spain
project_031 Nebula Caixa Forum, Valencia, Spain, FINALIST
project_018 Raval Housing, Barcelona, Spain
project_069 Cal Xerta Paper Centre, Sant Pere de Riudebitlles, Spain
project_67 El Forn Museum, Sant Cugat de Sesgarrigues, Spain
project_101 Passeig de la Industria Public Space, Banyoles, Spain
project_075 Zizkov Housing, FINALIST
project_120 Gran Casino Resort
2017 project_038 Can Vidalet Market, Esplugues de Llobregat, Spain
project_039 La Plana Market, Esplugues de Llobregat, Spain
project_036 Welcome Square and Headquarters at Tibidabo Amusement Park, Barcelona, Spain
2016 project_030 The Cloud, Andorra Telecom Headquarters, Andorra la Vella, Andorra
project_040 New Camp Nou FC Barcelona Stadium, Barcelona, Spain, FINALIST
project_033 Embruixabruixes Attraction at Tibidabo Amusement Park, Barcelona, Spain
project_076 Skylight Sport Centre, Port d'Envalira, Andorra
project_100 Prčanj Resort, Kotor, Montenegro, 1ST PRIZE
2015 project_028 Cocobolo Centre, Panama City, Panama
2014 project_037 Passenger Terminal and Service Centre, FINALIST
2012 project_080 Miño Still Water Confederation Headquarters, Ourense, Spain
2011 project_111 Collserola Natural Park Phytoduct
2008 project_027 Torrebaró Social Housing, Barcelona, Spain
2007 project_024 Annexa Joan Puigbert School, Girona, Spain
project_012 Historical Building at Tibidabo Amusement Park
2006 project_029 iGuzzini Lighting Iberian Headquarters, Sant Cugat del Vallés, Spain
project_025 Plug-in Building at 22@, Barcelona, Spain
2004 project_004 Municipal Market and Public Space, Rubí, Spain
2001 project_003 Barceloneta Market and Public Space, Barcelona, Spain
2000 project_006 Golf Clubhouse and Sports Centre, Fontanals de Cerdanya, Spain
project_002 Central Train Station Public Space and Parking, Girona, Spain
1998 project_023 Old Town Public Space, Banyoles, Spain
1997 project_001 Banys Vells Swimming Club and Bar, Banyoles, Spain

AWARDS

2023 German Design Awards, Urban Space and Infrastructure category, Nominated, project_035 Cucadellum Funicular to Tibidabo Amusement Park, Barcelona, Spain

LOOP Design Awards, Landscape Urban Design category, Winner, project_035 Cucadellum Funicular to Tibidabo Amusement Park, Barcelona, Spain

LOOP Design Awards, Multi Unit category, Nominated, project_026 Marina del Prat Vermell Social Housing, Barcelona, Spain

LOOP Design Awards, Public Space category, Citation Winner, project_036 Welcome Square and Headquarters at Tibidabo Amusement Park, Barcelona, Spain

LOOP Design Awards, Healthcare Architecture category, Winner, project_014 Therapeutic Community Centre, Calella, Spain

LOOP Design Awards, Exhibition & Museums category, Winner, project_069 Cal Xerta Paper Centre, Sant Pere de Riudebitlles, Spain

DNA Paris Design Awards, Infrastructures & Transportation category, Winner, project_035 Cucadellum Funicular to Tibidabo Amusement Park, Barcelona, Spain

Architizer A+ Popular Choice Awards, Sustainable Transportation category, Winner, project_035 Cucadellum Funicular to Tibidabo Amusement Park, Barcelona, Spain

2022 COAC Architects' Association Catalonia, Garraf, Alt Penedès Museum Awards, Winner, project_069 Cal Xerta Paper Centre, Sant Pere de Riudebitlles, Spain

Dux Award to Sustainability for Tibidabo Amusement Park

2021 Yuanye Awards, Environmental Art and Design Category, Award of Honor, project_014 Therapeutic Community Centre, Calella, Spain

Yuanye Awards for Public Building, Award of Merit, project_036 Welcome Square and Headquarters at Tibidabo Amusement Park, Barcelona, Spain

2020 Rebuild Awards, Sustainability Decarbonisation and Self-Generation of Energy, Finalist, project_036 Welcome Square and Headquarters at Tibidabo Amusement Park, Barcelona, Spain

2019 Eco Tech Green Awards, Special Mention, project_036 Welcome Square and Headquarters at Tibidabo Amusement Park, Barcelona, Spain

2015 AADIPA Architects Association for Defence and Intervention in Architectural Heritage Awards, Finalist, project_023 Old Town Public Space, Banyoles, Spain

Taipei City Government, International Design Awards, Finalist, project_023 Old Town Public Space, Banyoles, Spain

Mies van der Rohe Awards, Nominated, project_015 Can Zariquiey Therapeutic Centre, Arenys de Munt, Spain

2014 Piranesi Prix de Rome, Finalist, project_023 Old Town Public Space, Banyoles, Spain

Venice Biennale of Architecture, project_015 Can Zariquiey Therapeutic Centre, Arenys de Munt, Spain

COAC Architects' Association Catalonia, Catalan Architecture Awards, Winner, project_025 Plug-in Building at 22@, Barcelona, Spain

Enor Architectural Awards, Selected, project_025 Plug-in Building at 22@, Barcelona, Spain

2013 International Stone Architecture Awards, Winner, project_023 Old Town Public Space, Banyoles, Spain

Architizer A+ Awards, Winner, project_029 iGuzzini Lighting Iberian Headquarters, Sant Cugat del Vallés, Spain

Mies van der Rohe Awards, European Union Prize for Contemporary Architecture, Nominated, project_024 Annexa Joan Puigbert School, Girona, Spain

Taipei City Government, International Design Awards, Finalist, project_023 Old Town Public Space, Banyoles, Spain

WAN Awards to Façades, Finalist, project_029 iGuzzini Lighting Iberian Headquarters, Sant Cugat del Vallés, Spain

2012 Barcelona City Prize for Architecture and Urbanism, Selected, project_025 Plug-in Building at 22@, Barcelona, Spain

Barcelona City Prize for Architecture and Urbanism, Selected, project_027 Torrebaró Social Housing, Barcelona, Spain

Catalonia Construction Awards, Selected, project_029 iGuzzini Lighting Iberian Headquarters, Sant Cugat del Vallés, Spain

WAF World Architecture Festival of Singapore Awards, Shortlisted, project_029 iGuzzini Lighting Iberian Headquarters, Sant Cugat del Vallés, Spain

2011 Archdaily Building of the Year, Winner, project_029 iGuzzini Lighting Iberian Headquarters, Sant Cugat del Vallés, Spain

Plataforma Arquitectura Work of the Year, Finalist, project_029 iGuzzini Lighting Iberian Headquarters, Sant Cugat del Vallés, Spain

A+ Architectural Awards, Best Spanish Educational Building, Winner, project_024 Annexa Joan Puigbert School, Girona, Spain

Archdaily Building of the Year, Selected, project_003 Barceloneta Market and Public Space, Barcelona, Spain

Archdaily Building of the Year, Selected, project_004 Municipal Market and Public Space, Rubí, Spain

Archdaily Building of the Year, Selected, project_005 Topographic House, Llavaneres, Spain

Archdaily Building of the Year, Selected, project_006 Golf Clubhouse and Sports Centre, Fontanals de Cerdanya, Spain

Archdaily Building of the Year, Selected, project_025 Plug-in Building at 22@, Barcelona, Spain

Plataforma Aqrquitectura Work of the Year, Finalist, project_003 Barceloneta Market and Public Space, Barcelona, Spain

Plataforma Arquitectura Work of the Year, Selected, project_004 Municipal Market and Public Space, Rubí, Spain

Plataforma Arquitectura Work of the Year, Selected, project_005 Topographic House, Llavaneres, Spain

Plataforma Arquitectura Work of the Year, Selected, project_006 Golf Clubhouse and Sports Centre, Fontanals de Cerdanya, Spain

Plataforma Arquitectura Work of the Year, Selected, project_025 Plug-in Building at 22@, Barcelona, Spain

COAC Architects' Association Catalonia, Girona Area Architectural Awards, Finalist, project_024 Annexa Joan Puigbert School, Girona, Spain

2010 FAD Awards, Public Space, Finalist, project_023 Old Town Public Space, Banyoles, Spain

2009 Catalonia Construction Awards, Winner, project_023 Old Town Public Space, Banyoles, Spain

2008 Catalonia Construction Awards, Finalist, project_003 Barceloneta Market and Public Space, Barcelona, Spain

CCCB Urban, European Prize for Public Space,, Finalist, project_023 Old Town Public Space, Banyoles, Spain

Barcelona International Biennal of Landscape Architecture, Rosa Barba Prize, Finalist, project_023 Old Town Public Space, Banyoles, Spain

Urban Public Spaces European Prize, Finalist, project_023 Old Town Public Space, Banyoles, Spain

2007 Barcelona City Prize for Architecture and Urbanism, Winner, project_003 Barceloneta Market and Public Space, Barcelona, Spain

COAC Girona, Girona Area Architectural Awards for Public Space, Winner, project_023 Old Town Public Space, Banyoles, Spain

2006 COAC Girona, Girona Architectural Awards, Selected, project_021 Promenade House, Caselles d'Avall, Spain

2005 COAC Girona, Girona Architectural Awards, Special Mention, project_022 Landscape House, Mollet de Peralada, Spain

2004 AJAC Young Architects Prize to Best Young Architect under 40 for Built Work, Winner, project_006 Golf Clubhouse and Sports Centre, Fontanals de Cerdanya, Spain

COAC Girona, Girona Area Architectural Awards. Finalist, project_087 Iberia Social Housing, Girona, Spain

FAD Awards, Selected, project_006 Golf Clubhouse and Sports Centre, Fontanals de Cerdanya, Spain

2003 COAC Girona, Girona Area Architectural Awards, Finalist, project_006 Golf Clubhouse and Sports Centre, Fontanals de Cerdanya, Spain

2001 COAC Girona, Girona Area Architectural Awards for Public Space, Selected, project_002 Central Train Station Public Space and Parking, Girona, Spain

2000 O. Tusquets Foundation, Década Prize, Selected, project_121 Tubo Bar, Barcelona, Spain

1997 COAC Girona, Girona Area Architectural Awards, Finalist, project_001 Banys Vells Swimming Club and Bar, Banyoles, Spain

Index of topics

INDEX OF PROJECTS

project_001 Banys Vells Swimming Club and Bar
Year 1995
Open Competition Winner
Location Banyoles, Spain
Surface 200 m^2
Architect Josep Miàs
Project Team Oliver Bals, Sophie Lambert, Thomas Westerholm
Awards - 1997 COAC Girona, Girona Area Architectural Awards, Finalist
Pages 8, 12, 40, 92, 208-211, 320-321

project_002 Central Train Station Public Space and Parking
Year 2000
Open Competition Winner
Location Girona, Spain
Surface 6000 m^2
Architect Josep Miàs
Project Team Marta Cases, Sophie Lambert, Julie Nicaise, Xavi Rodríguez, Judit Segura
Awards - 2001 COAC Girona, Girona Area Architectural Awards for Public Space
Pages 8

project_003 Barceloneta Market and Public Space
Year 2001-2007
Open Competition Winner
Location Barcelona, Spain
Surface 5200 m^2
Client Barcelona City Council, IMMB Institut Municipal de Mercats de Barcelona
Architect Josep Miàs
Project Leader Bárbara Fachada
Project Team Emiliano Armani, Lluís Carballeda, Orlando Melo, Marta Cases, Carlota Martínez, Raúl Castaño, Lara Lupi, Xavier Ribera, Horacio Arias
Awards - 2011 Archdaily Building of the Year, Selected
- 2011 Plataforma Aqrquitectura Work of the Year, Finalist
- 2008 Catalonia Construction Awards, Winner
- 2007 Barcelona City Prize for Architecture and Urbanism, Winner
Publications - *Barceloneta Market*, Miàs, Josep, Barcelona, Actar Publishers, 2009
- *Barceloneta Market and Square*, Miàs, Josep, Barcelona, 2011
Pages 8-9, 12-13, 39, 40, 68-81, 208-211, 228-231, 234-235, 322-329, 382-383

project_004 Municipal Market and Public Space
Year 2004-2010
Open Competition Winner
Location Rubí, Spain
Surface 8700 m^2
Client Rubí City Council
Architect Josep Miàs
Project Leader Silvia Brandi
Project Team Adriana Porta, Maria Chiara Ziliani, Pablo Varesi, Fausto Raposo, Mafalda Batista, Barbara Fachada, Baptiste Marconnet, Xavier Bas
Awards - 2011 Archdaily Building of the Year, Selected
- 2011 Plataforma Arquitectura Work of the Year, Selected
Pages 9, 13-14, 222, 246-249

project_005 Topographic House
Year 2006-2009
Location Llavaneres, Spain
Surface 700 m^2
Architect Josep Miàs
Project Team Silvia Brandi, Adriana Porta, Mario Blanco, Josep Puigdemont, Fausto Raposo, Daniel Montes, Francesca Giovaninni, Benedetta Slucca, Blanca Tai, Victoria Ayesta
Awards - 2011 Archdaily Building of the Year, Selected
- 2011 Plataforma Arquitectura Work of the Year, Selected
Publications - *Llavaneres Topographic House*, Miàs, Josep, Barcelona, 2011
Pages 9, 14, 40-41, 95, 101-103, 105, 208, 226-227, 298-303, 382, 407

project_006 Golf Clubhouse and Sports Centre
Year 2000-2004
Open Competition, Winner
Location Fontanals de Cerdanya, Spain
Surface 2500 m^2
Client Fontanals Esportiva SL
Architect Josep Miàs
Project Team Marta Cases, Joan Poca, Orlando Melo, Horacio Arias, Marco Chirdel, Alejandra Vázquez, Thomas Stellmach, Inés Moreira, José Ulloa, Solange Delanais, Julie Nicaise, Josep Masachs
Awards - 2011 Archdaily Building of the Year, Selected
- 2011 Plataforma Arquitectura Work of the Year, Selected
- 2004 AJAC Young Architects Prize to Best Young Architect under 40 for Built Work, Winner
- 2003 COAC Girona, Girona Area Architectural Awards, Finalist
Publications - *Fontanals Pyrenees Golf Centre*, Miàs, Josep, Barcelona, 2011
Pages 8, 9, 14-15, 82-93, 208-211, 312-319, 382

project_007 Pedestrian Bridge
Year 2007-2012
Location Palafolls, Spain
Surface 1300 m^2
Client Municipality of Palafolls
Architect Josep Miàs
Project Team Adriana Porta, Silvia Brandi, Mafalda Batista, Pablo Varesi, Horacio Arias, Mario Blanco, Blanca Rieder, Nina Dorici, Andreu Canut, José Pedro Abé, Daniel Pastor Arellano, Sebastián de Iruarrizaga
Pages 1, 8, 15-16, 41, 106-111, 208-211, 234-235, 294-297, 382-383

project_008 Butterfly House
Year 2011-2012
Location Besalú, Spain
Surface 220 m^2
Architect Josep Miàs
Project Team Adriana Porta, Silvia Brandi, Josep Puigdemont, Horacio Arias, Neus Caylà, Pablo Varesi, Mario Blanco, Hélène Barbot, Luciano Rotoli, Elena Alfaro Alvarez, Dafna Servadio, Nadejda Avramova, François de Montgolfier, Patrick Hitzberger, Blanca Rieder, Nina Dorici
Pages 9, 16, 40, 94, 98-100, 104, 208-211, 306-309, 374, 383

project_009 Lower Funicular Station at Tibidabo Amusement Park
Year 2007-2008
Location Barcelona, Spain
Surface 400 m^2
Client Barcelona City Council + Tibidabo Amusement Park
Architect Josep Miàs
Project Leader Silvia Brandi
Project Team Horacio Arias, Mario Blanco, Anna Mañosa, Neus Caylà
Pages 8, 16-17, 67, 208-211, 330-332, 383

project_010 Kindergarden
Year 1997
Location Porqueres, Spain
Architect Josep Miàs

project_011 Can Sisó House
Year 2008
Location Banyoles, Spain
Architect Josep Miàs
Pages 17

project_012 Historical Building at Tibidabo Amusement Park
Year 2008-2009
Open Competition, Winner
Location Barcelona, Spain
Surface 1000 m^2
Client Barcelona City Council + Tibidabo Amusement Park
Architect Josep Miàs
Project Leader Silvia Brandi
Project Team Pablo Martínez, Lighting Pablo Varesi, Mario Blanco, Mariana Antia
Exhibitions - "Los monstruos marinos del Tibidabo" Herta Frankel Puppet Theatre, Tibidabo Amusement Park, 2010
Pages 9, 17-18, 66, 333-334

project_013 Bus Stop
Year 2013
Location Palafolls, Spain
Surface 13 m^2
Client Municipality of Palafolls
Architect Josep Miàs
Project Leader Marc Subirana
Project Team Marta Cases, Maria Chiara Ziliani
Pages 8, 18, 64-66, 208, 336

project_014 Therapeutic Community Centre
Year 2017-2019
Location Calella, Spain
Surface 884 m^2
Client Maresme Therapeutic Community
Architect Josep Miàs
Project Team Marta Cases, Maria Chiara Ziliani, Marc Subirana
Awards - 2023 LOOP Design Awards, Healthcare Architecture, Winner
- 2021 Yuanye Awards, Environmental Art and Design Category, Finalist
Publications - *El edificio que nació de una ventana*, Miàs, Josep, Agustí Valentí, Barcelona, 2021
Pages 9, 18, 62-63, 342-343

project_015 Can Zariquiey Therapeutic Centre
Year 2007-2013
Location Arenys de Munt, Spain
Surface 1800 m^2
Client Maresme Therapeutic Community
Architect Josep Miàs
Project Leader Silvia Brandi, Adriana Porta
Project Team Fausto Raposo, Daniel Montes, Nuno Marques, Sebastián de Iruarrizaga, Alfonso Abé, Christian Giovanetti, Giovanni Galdieri, Gabriele Mura, Laura Pomesano, Federico Licini, Marc Subirana, Xavier Bas
Awards - 2015 Mies van der Rohe Awards, Nominated
- 2014 Venice Biennale of Architecture
Publications - *Orquídeas para la salud*, Miàs, Josep - Agustí, Valentí, Barcelona, Argra Trading S.L., 2013
Exhibitions - "Grafting Architecture" Catalonia at Venice, Venice Biennale 2014
Pages 9, 18-19, 54-61, 344-347, 408

project_016 San Bernardo Apartments
Year 2005-2009
Location Madrid, Spain
Surface 2200 m^2
Architect Josep Miàs, Rafael Fernández del Amo
Project Team Adriana Porta, Silvia Brandi, Daniel Montes, Barbara Fachada, Mario Blanco, Diogo Herniques
Pages 8, 19, 338-339

project_017 Font Honrada Apartments
Year 2019
Location Barcelona, Spain
Surface 1400 m^2
Client OnBcn
Architect Josep Miàs
Project Team Maria Chiara Ziliani, Marc Subirana, Marta Cases
Pages 8, 50-51, 340-341

project_018 Raval Housing
Year in progress
Open Competition, Winner
Location Barcelona, Spain
Client Barcelona City Council
Architect Josep Miàs
Project Team Marta Cases, Maria Chiara Ziliani, Marc Subirana
Pages 19, 52-53

project_019 Alfasoni Musical Centre
Year 2018-2019
Location Barcelona, Spain
Surface 8500 m^2
Architect Josep Miàs
Project Team Marc Subirana, Marta Cases, Laura Vidal, Maria Ziliani, Adriana Porta, Carla Bach, Paola Idini, Cristina Herrero, Bernardo García, Òscar Berbel
Pages 9, 19, 270-271

project_020 Willow Boat
Year 2017-2021
Location Malaga, Spain
Architect Josep Miàs
Project Team Marta Cases, Maria Chiara Ziliani, Marc Subirana

project_021 Promenade House
Year 2002-2005
Location Caselles D'avall, Spain
Surface 500 m^2
Architect Josep Miàs
Project Team Horacio Arias, Lluís Carballeda, Marta Cases, Bárbara Fachada, Carlota Martínez, Orlando Melo, Marco Miglioli, Carolina Momparler, Alejandra Vázquez
Awards - 2006 COAC Girona, Girona Architectural Awards, Selected
Pages 9, 19, 305

project_022 Landscape House
Year 2000-2004
Location Mollet de Peralada, Spain
Surface 230 m^2
Architect Josep Miàs
Project Team Marta Cases, Solange Delanais, Adela Framis, Carlota Martínez, Inés Moreira, Thomas Stellmach, José Ulloa, Alejandra Vázquez
Awards - 2005 COAC Girona, Girona Architectural Awards, Special Mention
Pages 9, 19-20, 304

project_023 Old Town Public Space
Year 1998-2010
Open Competition, Winner
Location Banyoles, Spain
Surface 18000 m^2
Client Banyoles City Council
Architect Josep Miàs
Project Team Judith Segura, Sophie Lambert, Sven Holzgreve, Thomas Westerholm, Oliver Bals, Marta Cases, Julie Nicaise, Lluís A. Casanovas, Anna Mallén, Bárbara Fachada, Marco Miglioli, Josep Puigdemont, Fausto Raposo, Adriana Porta, Silvia Brandi, Mafalda Batista, Mario Blanco, Emanuela Scano, Stefania Carboni, François de Montgolfier, Dafna Servadio, Nina Dorici, Blanca Rieder, Patrick Hitzberger
Awards - 2015 AADIPA Architects Association for Defence and Intervention in Architectural Heritage Awards, Finalist
- 2015 Taipei City Government, International Design Awards, Finalist
- 2014 Piranesi Prix de Rome, Finalist
- 2013 International Stone Architecture Awards, Winner
- 2013 Taipei City Government, International Design Awards, Finalist
- 2010 FAD Awards, Public Space, Finalist
- 2009 Catalonia Construction Awards, Winner
- 2008 CCCB Urban, European Prize for Public Space,, Finalist
- 2008 Barcelona International Biennal of Landscape Architecture, Rosa Barba Prize, Finalist
- 2008 Urban Public Spaces European Prize, Finalist
- 2007 COAC Girona, Girona Area Architectural Awards for Public Space, Winner
Publications - *Banyoles*, Miàs, Josep, Barcelona, Argra Trading S.L., 2013
- *Banyoles Old City Center*, Miàs, Josep, Barcelona, 2011
Pages 2-3, 8, 20, 40, 42-49, 348-357

project_024 Annexa Joan Puigbert School
Year 2007-2010
Open Competition, Winner
Location Girona, Spain
Surface 2300 m^2
Client GISA Education Department of the Government of Catalonia
Architect Josep Miàs
Project Team Adriana Porta
Silvia Brandi, Josep Puigdemont, Fausto Raposo, Lluis A. Casanovas, Mario Blanco, Cristina Cattina, Piera Doré, Xavier Bas
Awards - 2013 Mies van der Rohe Awards, European Union Prize for Contemporary Architecture, Nominated
- 2011 A+ Architectural Awards, Best Spanish Educational Building, Winner
- 2011 COAC Architects' Association Catalonia, Girona Area Architectural Awards, Finalist
Pages 9, 20, 280-283

project_025 Plug-in Building at 22@
Year 2006-2011
Restricted Competition, Winner
Location Barcelona, Spain
Surface 7000 m^2
Client 22@ Poblenou
Architect Josep Miàs
Project Leader Adriana Porta
Project Team Silvia Brandi, Daniel Montes, Mario Blanco, Diogo Hernique, Xavier Bas
Awards - 2014 COAC Architects' Association Catalonia, Catalan Architecture Awards, Winner
- 2014 Enor Architectural Awards, Selected
- 2012 Barcelona City Prize for Architecture and Urbanism, Selected
- 2011 Archdaily Building of the Year, Selected
- 2011 Plataforma Arquitectura Work of the Year, Selected
Publications - *Plug-in Barcelona*, Miàs, Josep, Barcelona, 2012
- *Pujades 22@ Plug-in Building*, Miàs, Josep, Barcelona, 2011
Pages 8, 21, 41, 122-128, 223-225, 272-279, 383

project_026 Marina del Prat Vermell Social Housing
Year In progress
Open Competition, Winner
Location Barcelona, Spain
Surface 8000 m^2
Client Barcelona City Council, IMHAB Barcelona Municipal Housing Institute
Architect Josep Miàs, CollLeclerc
Project Team Maria Chiara Ziliani, Marc Subirana, Mauro Soro
Awards - 2023 LOOP Design Awards, Multi Unit category, Nominated
Pages 9, 21, 256-259

project_027 Torrebaró Social Housing
Year 2009-2012
Open Competition, Winner
Location Barcelona, Spain
Surface 5000 m^2
Client Barcelona City Council, BAGURSA, REGESA
Architect Josep Miàs
Project Leader Adriana Porta
Project Team Silvia Brandi, Fausto Raposo, Bárbara Fachada, Mafalda Batista, Lluís A. Casanovas, Cristina Feijoo, Francesca Giovaninni, Anna Mallén, Anna Mañosa, Daniel Montes, Josep Puigdemont, Benedetta Slucca, Pablo Varesi, Mario Blanco, Horacio Arias, Stefania Carboni, Margherita Corbetta, Mannick Eigenheer, Isabelle Glenz, Diogo Henriques, Silvia Lai, Pier Francesco Lisci, Roberta Luna, Francisca Marzotto, Ines Reis, Diego Romero, Emanuela Scano, María Tapias, Enric Argemí, Laura Pomesano, Giovanni Galdieri, Christian Giovanetti, Gabriele Mura, Xavier Bas
Awards - 2012 Barcelona City Prize for Architecture and Urbanism, Selected
Publications - *Torrebaró Housing Building*, Miàs, Josep, Barcelona, 2011
Pages 9, 21-22, 40-41, 138-144, 208, 254-255, 377

project_028 Cocobolo Centre
Year In progress
Restricted Competition, Winner
Location Panama City, Panama
Surface 85000 m2
Architect Josep Miàs, SALCEDO, CARBALLEDA
Project Team Marc Subirana, Marta Cases, Laura Vidal, Maria Ziliani, Adriana Porta, Carla Bach, Paola Idini, Cristina Herrero, Bernardo García, Òscar Berbel
Pages 9, 22, 145-149, 160, 208

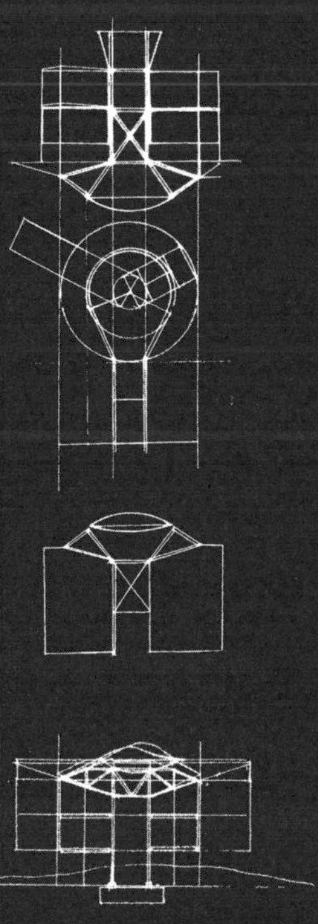

project_029 iGuzzini Illuminazione Iberica Headquarters
Year 2007-2011
Restricted Competition, Winner
Location Sant Cugat Del Vallés, Spain
Surface 9000 m^2
Client iGuzzini Illuminazione
Architect Josep Miàs
Project Leader Silvia Brandi
Project Team Pablo Varesi, Fausto Raposo, Hélène Barbot, Andrés Dejanon, Mario Blanco, Horacio Arias, Anna Mañosa, Adriana Porta, Janine Woitoshek, Elena Alfaro Alvarez, Jordi Capella, Mario Blanco, Horacio Arias, Stefania Carboni, Margherita Corbetta, Mannick Eigenheer, Isabelle Glenz, Diogo Henriques, Silvia Lai, Pier Francesco Lisci, Roberta Luna, Francisca Marzotto, Ines Reis, Diego Romero, Emanuela Scano, María Tapias, François de Montgolfier, Dafna Servadio, Nina Dorici, Blanca Rieder, Patrick Hitzberger, Stefania Carboni, Stefania Ballero, Antonello Ragnedda, Ugo D'Ascanio, Davide Balestrazzi, Marika Leoni, Xavier Bas
Awards - 2013 Architizer A+ Awards, Winner
- 2013 WAN Awards to Façades, Finalist
- 2012 Catalonia Construction Awards, Selected
- 2012 WAF World Architecture Festival of Singapore Awards, Shortlisted
- 2011 Archdaily Building of the Year, Winner
- 2011 Plataforma Arquitectura Work of the Year, Finalist
Publications - *iGuzzini Barcelona Corporate Building*, Miàs, Josep, Barcelona, Actar Publishers, 2012
- *iGuzzini Lighting Iberian España Headquarters*, Miàs, Josep, Barcelona, 2011
Exhibitions - Venice Biennale 2012
- "iGuzzini BCN Corporate Building", The Bartlett School of Architecture, 2012
- "Il Cielo iGuzzini", COAC Barcelona, 2008
Pages 8, 22-25, 41, 178-203, 208, 212-213, 216-221, 236-243, 382-383

project_030 The Cloud Andorra Telecom Headquarters
Year In progress
Open Competition, Winner
Location Andorra La Vella, Andorra
Surface 15.000 m^2
Client Andorra Telecom
Architect Josep Miàs, ARID
Project Team Marc Subirana, Marta Cases, Laura Vidal, Maria Ziliani, Adriana Porta, Carla Bach, Cristina Herrero, Bernardo García, Òscar Berbel, Aina Tapias
Pages 8, 25-26, 162-171, 208, 382-383

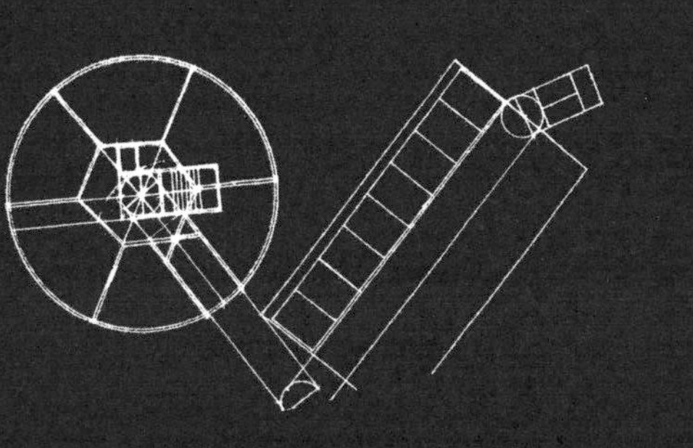

project_031 Nebula Caixa Forum
Year 2017
Restricted Competition, Finalist
Location Valencia, Spain
Surface 2790 m^2
Client La Caixa
Architect Josep Miàs
Project Team Marc Subirana, Marta Cases, Laura Vidal, Maria Ziliani, Adriana Porta, Carla Bach, Cristina Herrero
Pages 9, 26, 41, 159-161

project_032 Palau Sant Jordi VIP Lounge
Year 2015
Location Barcelona, Spain
Surface 700 m^2
Client Barcelona City Council, Palau Sant Jordi
Architect Josep Miàs
Project Team Marc Subirana, Paola Idini, Xavi Bas, Oscar Berbel, Maria Coma, Cristina Herrero, Silvia Marcet, Alex Pineda
Pages 9, 26, 284-285

project_033 Embruixabruixes Attraction at Tibidabo Amusement Park
Year 2017-2019
Open Competition, Winner
Location Barcelona, Spain
Client Barcelona City Council, PATSA Tibidabo Amusement Park
Architect Josep Miàs
Project Leader Marc Subirana
Project Team Laura Vidal, Marta Cases, Bernardo García, Maria Ziliani, Adriana Porta, Carla Bach, Cristina Herrero, Òscar Berbel
Awards - 2022 Best Attraction of the Tibidabo Amusement Park voted by the public
Pages 9, 26, 335

project_034 Brazilian Antarctic Station
Year 2013
Location South Sethland Islands Antarctica
Surface 2000 m^2
Architect Josep Miàs, Francesco Santoro, Johan Berglund
Pages 8, 26, 41, 159, 208, 403

project_035 Cucadellum Funicular to Tibidabo Amusement Park
Year 2017-2020
Open Competition, Winner
Location Barcelona, Spain
Client Barcelona City Council, PATSA Tibidabo Amusement Park
Architect Josep Miàs
Project Team Marc Subirana, LEITNER, SIGMA, Telefericos y Nieve
Awards - 2023 LOOP Design Awards, Landscape, Urban Design category, Winner
- 2023 German Design Awards, Nominated
- 2023 DNA Paris Design Awards, Infrastructures & Transportation category, Winner
- 2023 Architizer A+ Awards, Sustainable Transportation category, Winner
- 2022 Dux Award to Sustainability for the Tibidabo Amusement Park
Publications - *The Glow-Worm, Cucadellum Funicular Tibidabo Barcelona*, Miàs, Josep, LEITNER, Barcelona, Actar Publisher, 2023
Awards - 2023 Winner Architizer A+ Popular Choice Awards, Sustainable Transportation category
Pages 8, 27, 40, 112-121, 286-293

project_063 Folding House
Year 2008
Location Banyoles, Spain
Architect Josep Miàs
Pages 31

project_064 Baltic Sea Park
Year 2013
Location Pärnu, Estonia
Architect Josep Miàs
Pages 31-32, 111

project_065 Can Ricart Centre
Year 2010
Location Barcelona, Spain
Architect Josep Miàs
Pages 32

project_066 Sport Centre
Year 2008
Location Blanes, Spain
Architect Josep Miàs
Pages 32

project_067 El Forn Museum
Year 2019-2022
New Museology Intervention
Open Competition, Winner
Location Sant Cugat De Sesgarrigues, Spain
Surface 126 m^2
Client Sant Cugat De Sesgarrigues City Council
Architect Josep Miàs
Project Team Marina Povedano, Mauro Soro, Guillem Hernández, Caterina Gentini, Mei Anglada, Daniela Salaris, Arnau Miàs, Francesco Sanna, Marco Ghisaberti, Ivan Mavuli, Anna Rosell
Pages 32

project_068 Multiple Sclerosis Foundation Headquarters
Year 2019-2022
Location Barcelona, Spain
Surface 432 m^2
Client Multiple Sclerosis Foundation
Architect Josep Miàs
Project Team Marta Cases, Maria Chiara Ziliani, Marc Subirana
Pages 9, 32 337

project_069 Cal Xerta Paper Centre
Year 2022
New Museology Intervention
Open Competition, Winner
Location Sant Pere De Riudebitlles, Spain
Surface 472 m^2
Client Sant Pere De Riudebitlles City Council
Architect Josep Miàs
Project Team Marc Subirana, Marina Povedano, Mauro Soro, Guillem Hernández, Caterina Gentini, Mei Anglada, Daniela Salaris, Arnau Miàs, Francesco Sanna, Marco Ghisaberti, Ivan Mavuli, Anna Rosell
Awards - 2023 LOOP Design Awards, Exhibition and Museums category, Winner
- 2022 COAC Architects' Association Catalonia, Garraf, Alt Penedès Museums Awards, Winner
Pages 9, 32, 268-269

project_070 Floating House
Year 2008
Location India
Pages 32

project_071 Yablonsky Musical Center
Year 2010
Location Puigcerdà, Spain
Architect Josep Miàs
Pages 32

project_072 Mas Jordà Social Housing
Year 2008
Location Palafolls, Spain
Architect Josep Miàs
Pages 32

project_073 Guggenheim Museum
Year 2014
Location Helsinki, Finland
Surface 7000 m^2
Client Salomon R.Guggenheim Foundation
Architect Josep Miàs
Project Team Marta Cases, Maria Chiara Ziliani, Marc Subirana
Pages 32, 208

project_074 Cultural Centre
Year 1992
Location Banyoles, Spain
Architect Josep Miàs
Pages 32

project_075 Zizkov Housing
Year 2018
Open Competition, Finalist
Location Prague, Czech Republic
Surface 140.000 m^2
Client CCEA MOBA
Architect Josep Miàs, OCA, CMC
Project Team Marc Subirana, Nadia Bakhtafrouz, Javier Lopez-Alascio, Katarzyna Czyzewska, Malgorzata Traczynska, Maria Chiara Ziliani
Pages 33

project_076 Skylight Sport Centre
Year 2015
Open Competition, 1st Prize
Location Port d'Envalira, Andorra
Surface 6000 m^2
Architect Josep Miàs
Project Team Marc Subirana, Marta Cases, Laura Vidal, Maria Ziliani, Adriana Porta, Carla Bach, Cristina Herrero, Bernardo García, Òscar Berbel
Pages 9, 33

project_077 KCP Convention Centre
Year 2017
Location Prague, Czech Republic
Architect Josep Miàs
Pages 33

project_078 Collider Activity Centre
Year 2013
Location Sofia, Bulgaria
Architect Josep Miàs
Project Team Marc Subirana, Xavier Bas, Federica Bufalo, Enric Argemì Carnicer
Pages 33

project_079 Bao'an Culture and Art Centre
Year 2015
Location Shenzhen, China
Surface 10.000 m^2
Architect Josep Miàs
Project Team Marc Subirana, Marta Cases, Josep Domènech Jofre, Josep Masachs, Josep Ramòn
Pages 9, 33, 40, 161

project_080 Miño Still Water Confederation Headquarters
Year 2017
Open Competition, Winner
Location Ourense, Spain
Surface 8.500 m^2
Client Ministry of Agriculture and Environment
Architect Josep Miàs
Project Leader Silvia Brandi
Project Team Adriana Porta, Cristina Güemes, Diego Pastoriza, Xavier Bas, Samuel Drago, Federico Licini
Pages 33

project_081 Spanish Pavilion at Milan Exhibition
Year 2014
Location Milan, Italy
Surface 7000 m^2
Client Spanish Government
Architect Josep Miàs
Project Team Marc Subirana, Marta Cases, Maria Chiara Zillani
Pages 33

porject_082 Architects Association Headquarters
Year 2007
Location Cordoba, Spain
Architect Josep Miàs
Pages 33

project_083 La Salle Library
Year 2002
Location Barcelona, Spain
Architect Josep Miàs
Pages 34

projetc_084 Braus House
Year 2001
Location Olot, Spain
Architect Josep Miàs
Pages 34

project_085 America Square and Public Space
Year 2004-2006
Location L'Hospitalet De Llobregat, Spain
Surface 10.000 m^2
Client L'H2010
Architect Josep Miàs
Project Team Horacio Arias, Bárbara Fachada, Sonia Maia, Cristina Rodríguez
Pages 8, 34

project_086 Castle Attraction at Tibidabo Amusement Park
Year 2016
Location Barcelona, Spain
Architect Josep Miàs
Pages 34

project_087 Iberia Social Housing
Year 2000-2002
Location Girona, Spain
Surface 2300 m^2
Architect Josep Miàs
Project Team Victoria Ayesta, Marta Cases, Solange Delaunais, Adela Framis, Carlota Martinez, Inés Moreira, Thomas Stellmach, José Ulloa, Alejandra Vázquez
Awards - 2004 COAC Girona, Girona Area Architectural Awards. Finalist
Pages 9, 34

project_088 Vilamarí Scout Centre
Year 2008
Location Barcelona, Spain
Architect Josep Miàs
Pages 34

project_089 Raval Barceló Hotel
Year 2006
Location Barcelona, Spain
Architect Josep Miàs
Pages 34

project_090 Guinardó Market
Year 2014
Location Barcelona, Spain
Architect Josep Miàs
Pages 34

project_091 Santa Maria Housing
Year 2006
Location Banyoles, Spain
Architect Josep Miàs
Pages 34

project_092 Eixample Hotel
Year 2010
Location Barcelona, Spain
Architect Josep Miàs
Pages 34

project_093 Auditorium
Year 2008
Location Avila, Spain
Architect Josep Miàs
Pages 34-35

project_094 Elderly People Residence Centre
Year 2007
Location Granollers, Spain
Architect Josep Miàs
Pages 35

project_095 Social Housing
Year 2008
Location Bilbao, Spain
Acrhitect Josep Miàs
Pages 35

project_096 Library
Year 2008
Location Pamplona, Spain
Architect Josep Miàs
Pages 35, 40

project_097 St. Lluís Housing
Year 2008
Location Palafolls, Spain
Architect Josep Miàs
Pages 35

project_098 Catalan Pavilion
Year 2004
Location Guadalajara, Mèxico
Architect Josep Miàs
Pages 35, 40

project_099 Zhengzhou Park
Year 2014
Location China
Architect Josep Miàs
Pages 35

project_100 Prčanj Resort
Year 2014
Open Competition, 1st Prize
Location Kotor, Montenegro
Surface 3500 m^2
Client Kotor City Council
Architect Josep Miàs
Project Team Marc Subirana, Marta Cases, Maria Chiara Ziliani
Pages 35

project_101 Passeig de la Industria Public Space
Year 2018
Open Competition, Winner
Location Banyoles, Spain
Client Banyoles City Council
Architect Josep Miàs
Project Team Marta Cases, Maria Chiara Ziliani, Marc Subirana
Pages 35

project_102 Eixample Housing
Year 2008
Location Barcelona, Spain
Architect Josep Miàs
Pages 35

project_103 Tibidabo Amusement Park Sign Landmark
Year 2022
Location Barcelona, Spain
Architect Josep Miàs
Pages 35

project_104 Gran Via Housing
Year 2022
Location Barcelona, Spain
Architect Josep Miàs
Pages 36

project_105 Multiple Sclerosis Foundation Tamarit
Year 2022
Location Barcelona, Spain
Architect Josep Miàs
Pages 36

project_106 Anis del Mono Factory Refurbishment
Year in progress
Location Badalona, Spain
Architect Josep Miàs, OUA
Project Team Mauro Soro, Marina Povedano, Ivan Mavuli, Manuel Giró, Angelo Desole, Daniela Salaris, Mireia Simò, Anna Rosell, Ilaena Napier, Francesco Sanna
Pages 8, 36, 362-365

project_107 National Ceramic Museum
Year 2016
Location Seoul, South Korea
Surface 12.800 m^2
Project Team Josep Miàs
Marc Subirana, Marta Cases, Maria Chiara Zillani
Pages 9, 36, 40, 160, 208

project_108 Kip Island Auditorium
Year 2016
Location Riga, Latvia
Surface 12.000 m^2
Architect Josep Miàs
Project Team Marc Subirana, Ona Marija Auskelyte, Ilaria Egidi, Bernardo Garcia
Pages 9, 36

project_109 Market and Cultural Centre
Year 2009
Location Cuenca, Spain
Architect Josep Miàs
Pages 36, 40

project_110 Vallcarca Industrial Area Transformation
Year In progress
Location Sitges, Spain
Architect Josep Miàs, OUA
Project Leader Mauro Soro
Project Team Marina Povedano, Ivan Mavuli, Manuel Girò, Angelo Desole, Daniela Salaris, Mireia Simò, Anna Rosell, Ilaena Napier, Francesco Sanna
Pages 8, 36-38, 41, 204-207, 366-369

project_111 Collserola Natural Park Phytoduct
Year 2011
Open Competition, Winner
Location Barcelona, Spain
Surface 840.000 m^2
Architect Josep Miàs, 42 Architects (Johan Berglund)
Pages 8, 38, 137

project_112 M.K. Čiurlionis International Concert Hall
Year 2017
Location Kaunas, Lithuania
Surface 4000 m^2
Client Kaunas City Council
Architect Josep Miàs
Project Team Marta Cases, Maria Chiara Ziliani, Marc Subirana
Pages 38, 208

project_113 Dune Residential
Year In progress
Open Competition, Winner
Location Cubelles, Spain
Surface 14.000 m^2
Architect Josep Miàs, OUA
Project Leader Mauro Soro
Project Team Marta Cases, Marina Povedano, Ivan Mavuli, Manuel Girò, Guillem Hernandez, Angelo Desole, Daniela Salaris, Mireia Simò, Anna Rosell, Ilaena Napier, Francesco Sanna

project_114 S'Agaró Housing
Year In progress
Location Castell-Platja d'Aro, Spain
Surface 2300 m^2
Architect Josep Miàs
Project Team Marta Cases, Marina Povedano, Mauro Soro, Mireia Simò, Ivan Mavuli, Manuel Girò, Angelo Desole, Daniela Salaris, Anna Rosell, Ilaena Napier, Francesco Sanna
Pages 9

project_115 Parc Logistic Entrance at Zona Franca
Year In progress
Location Barcelona, Spain
Architect Josep Miàs
Project Leader Mauro Soro
Project Team Marina Povedano, Angelo Desole, Ivan Mavuli, Manuel Girò, Daniela Salaris, Mireia Simò, Anna Rosell, Ilaena Napier, Francesco Sanna

project_116 Diagonal Penthouse
Year In progress
Location Barcelona, Spain
Surface 650 m^2
Architect Josep Miàs
Project Team Mireia Simò, Mauro Soro, Manuel Girò, Marina Povedano, Ivan Mavuli, Angelo Desole, Daniela Salaris, Anna Rosell, Ilaena Napier, Franesco Sanna

project_117 El Vampany Commercial and Cultural Centre
Year In progress
Location Cervelló, Spain
Surface 45.514 m²
Architect Josep Miàs
Project Leader Mauro Soro
Project Team Marina Povedano, Ivan Mavuli, Manuel Girò, Guillem Hernandez, Angelo Desole, Daniela Salaris, Mireia Simò, Anna Rosell, Ilaena Napier, Francesco Sanna
Pages 8, 358-361

project_118 Passenger Terminal and Service Centre
Year 2016
Location Magallanes, Punta Arenas, Chile
Architect Josep Miàs
Project Team Marc Subirana, Miguel Hernández, Diego Pastoriza, Cristina Guemes
Pages 8

project_119 Playground Headquarters
Year 2017
Location Barcelona, Spain
Surface 4000 m²
Architect Josep Miàs
Project Team Marc Subirana, Marta Cases
Pages 8

project_120 Gran Casino Resort
Year 2018
Open Competition, Winner
Location Andorra La Vella, Andorra
Surface 20.000 m²
Client GENTING
Architect Josep Miàs, ARID
Project Team Marc Subirana, Maria Chiara Zillani, Marta Casas
Pages 9

project_121 Tubo Bar
Year 1992
Location Barcelona, Spain
Architect Josep Miàs, Francesc Pla, Pep Salló
Awards - 2000 O. Tusquets Foundation, Década Prize
Pages 9

project_122 Nuvol Bench
Year 2019
Location Andorra La Vella, Andorra
Architect Josep Miàs
Pages 9, 250-251

project_123 Meritxell Public Space
Year 2016
Location Andorra La Vella, Andorra
Architect Josep Miàs, Mario Blanco, Gerard Arias
Pages 8

IN PROGRESS

project_124 The Blue Museum
Location Red Sea

project_125 Elderly People Resort
Location Sant Pere de Ribes

project_126 Telefonica Museum
Location Spain

project_127 Jiri Myron Theatre
Location Ostrava, Czech Republic

project_128 Auditori del Parc
Location Esplugues de Llobregat, Spain

project_129 Museum of Arts
Location South Korea

project_130 Luxury Resort
Location Red Sea

project_131 Poble Sec Social Housing
Location Barcelona, Spain

project_132 El Corte Ingles Square
Location Spain

project_133 Private Museum
Location Spain

project_134 Public Library
Location Czech Republic

project_135 Conference Centre
Location Spain

project_136 Municipal Market
Location Barcelona, Spain

project_137 Natural Science Museum
Location Rome, Italy

project_138 Primary School Extension
Location 2023

project_139 Revnice, Czech Republic
Location Josep Miàs

project_140 New Primary School
Location 2023

project_141 Stara Boleslav, Czech Republic
Location Josep Miàs

project_142 Golf Clubhouse
Location Red Sea

project_143 Headquarters Building
Year Zaragoza

project_144 Formula 1 and MotoGP Paddock Building Refurbishment
Year Spain

project_145 Elementary School
Location Czech Republic

project_146 Gran Via Park
Location Barcelona, Spain

project_147 Circus Facilities
Location Spain

project_148 Barri de Dalt Residential Complex
Location Sant Pere de Ribes, Spain

project_149 Historical Monastery Rehabilitation
Location Spain

project_150 Winery Building
Location Spain

project_151 Panoramic Hotel
Location Sitges, Spain

project_152 New Urban District
Location Spain

project_153 Futuristic City
Location Spain

project_154 La Liga Sports Club
Location Spain

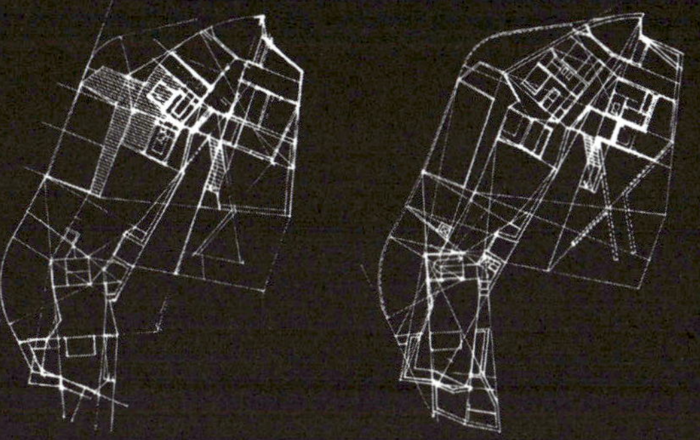

Josep Miàs
MIAS ARCHITECTS
www.miasarchitects.com

THE LOOP PROJECT

EDITED BY
Actar Publishers

MANAGING DIRECTOR
Mauro Soro

GRAPHIC DESIGN
Daniela Salaris

EDITING
Ilaena Napier

TEXTS
Josep Miàs
Sir Peter Cook
Marcos Cruz
Frédéric Migayrou
Josep Maria Montaner
Bob Sheil

PHOTOGRAPHIES
© MIAS Architects
© Adrià Goula
© DelRioBani
© Jordi Bernardo
© Duccio Malagamba
© Jordi Anguera
© Jaume Llorens
© Eugeni Pons
© Toni Cumella
© Eva Serrats
© LEITNER / Sigma Cabins

MIAS at Centre Pompidou

Team: Marc Subirana, Marina Povedano, Mauro Soro, Roberto, Marco Catta, Caterina Gentini, Aditya Mandlik, Chelsey Watthy, Olga Anglada, Arnau Miàs

MIAS at DHUB Barcelona Design Museum

Team: Marina Povedano, Olga Anglada, Mauro Soro, Marta Cases, Marc Subirana, Caterina Gentini, Guillem Hernández, Daniela Salaris, Artur Roig, Arnau Miàs, Mei Anglada, Lucrezia Muscas, Mario Balletta, Andrea Careddu, Lisa Brunello, Karina Iurkova, Kalina Helena Slominska, Francesco Marongiu, Roberto Mura, Clara González, Hadrien Legait, Zeinab Tannir, Zuhair Elhaj, Alicia Mathevon, Nadina Stroia, Anna Fatourou-Sipsi, Dominika Rams, Zuzanna Pawłowicz, Francesco Sanna, Marco Ghisaberti

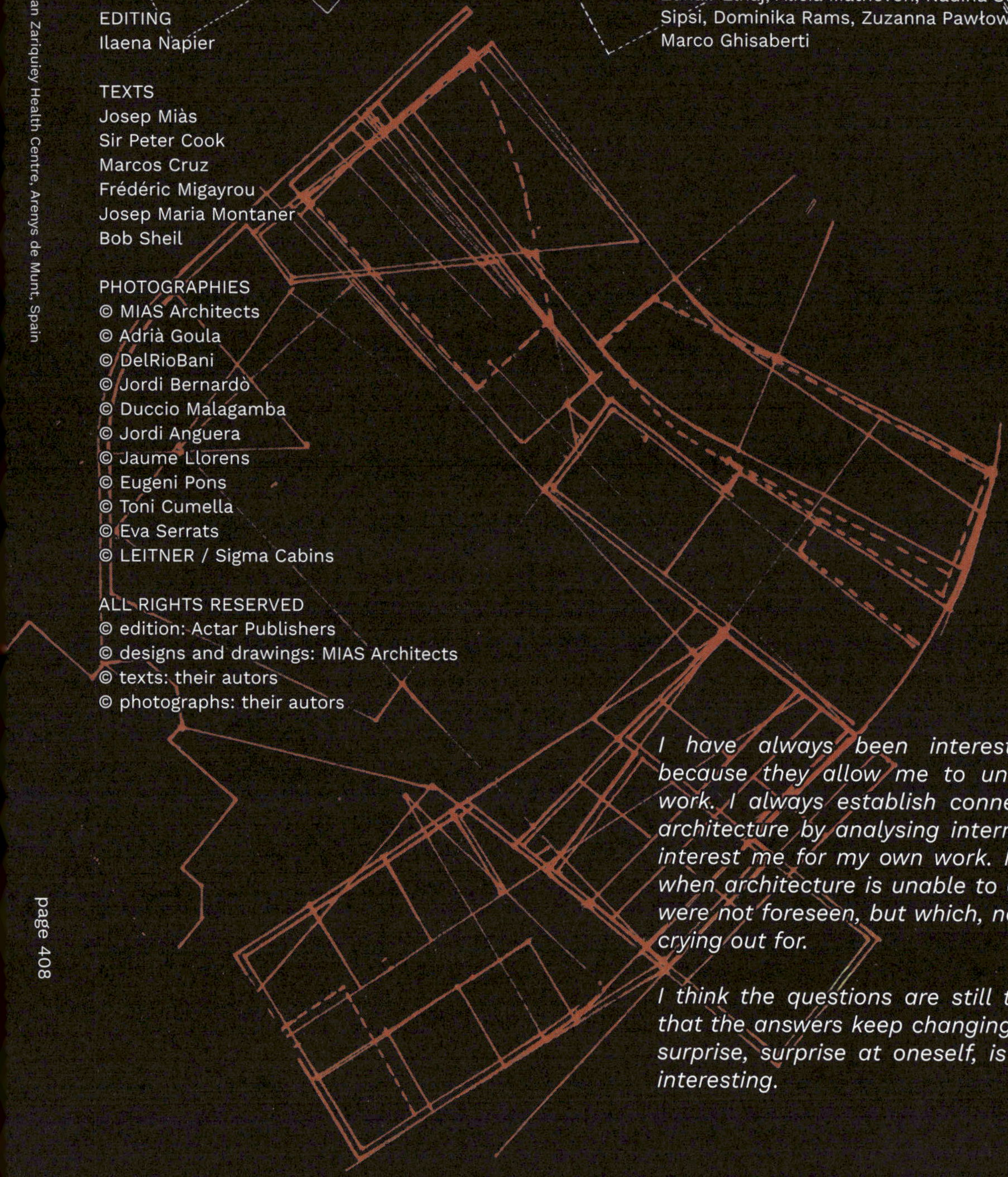

I have always been interested in processes because they allow me to understand my own work. I always establish connections with other architecture by analysing internal processes that interest me for my own work. I don't understand when architecture is unable to accept things that were not foreseen, but which, nevertheless, it was crying out for.

I think the questions are still the same, it's just that the answers keep changing. And this state of surprise, surprise at oneself, is what I find most interesting.